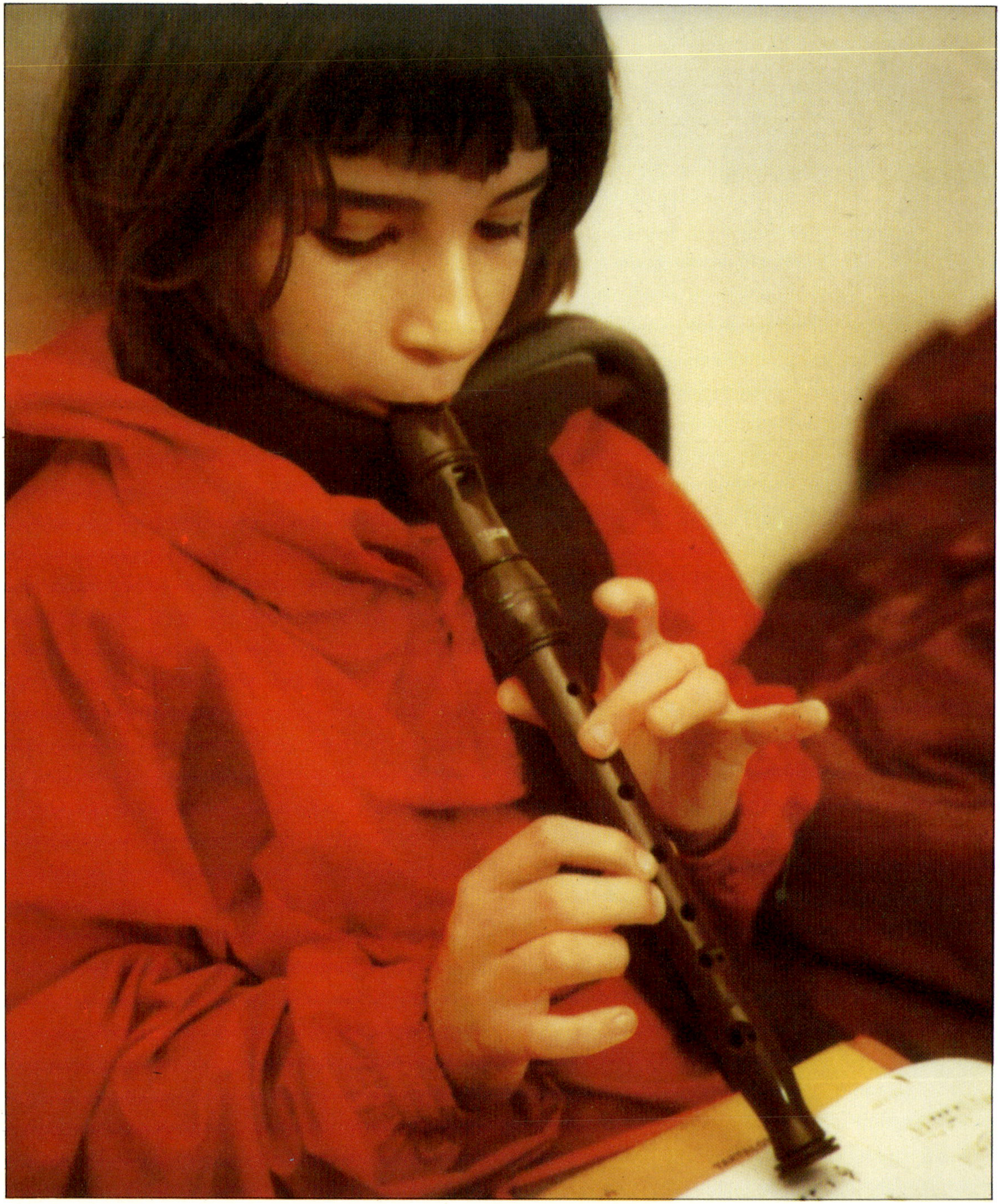

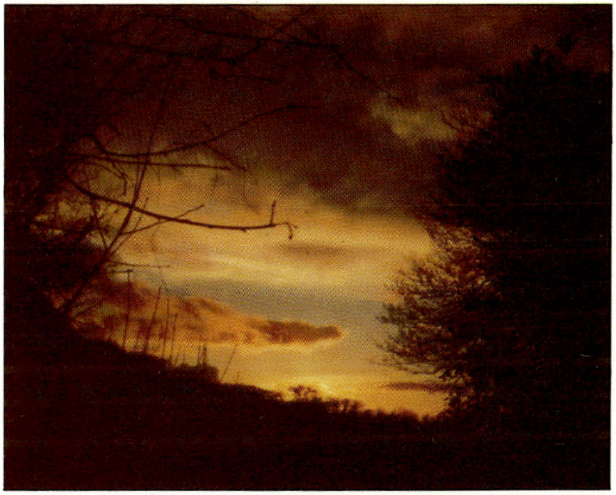

THE INSTANT PICTURE CAMERA HANDBOOK

Series editor
Michael Langford

Alfred A. Knopf New York

The Instant Picture Camera Handbook was conceived,
designed and edited by **Dorling Kindersley Limited,**
9 Henrietta Street, London WC2

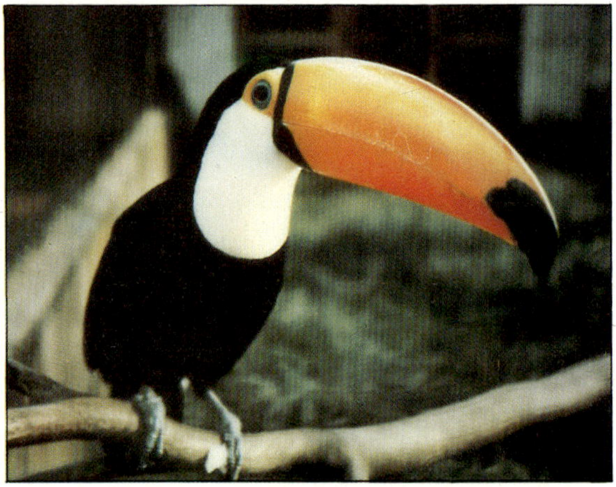

Technical adviser **Adrian Holloway**

Editor **Judith More**
Designer **Debra Lee**
Art editor **David McGrail**
Managing editor **Joss Pearson**
Managing art editor **Stuart Jackman**
Editorial director **Christopher Davis**

All the pictures in the book were shot
on Polaroid or Kodak instant films.

This is a Borzoi Book
published by Alfred A. Knopf, Inc.

Published in the United States by Alfred A. Knopf, Inc., New York and
simultaneously in Canada by Random House of Canada Limited, Toronto
Distributed by Random House Inc., New York

Library of Congress Cataloging in Publication Data
Langford, Michael John, 1933–
The Instant Picture Camera Handbook.
Includes index.
1. Polaroid Land camera. 2. Kodak instant camera.
3. Photography – Handbooks, manuals, etc. I. Title.
TR263.P6L36 1980 770.282 79–3472
ISBN 0–394–51091–7

Printed in the Netherlands by Smeets Offset B.V., Weert

Contents

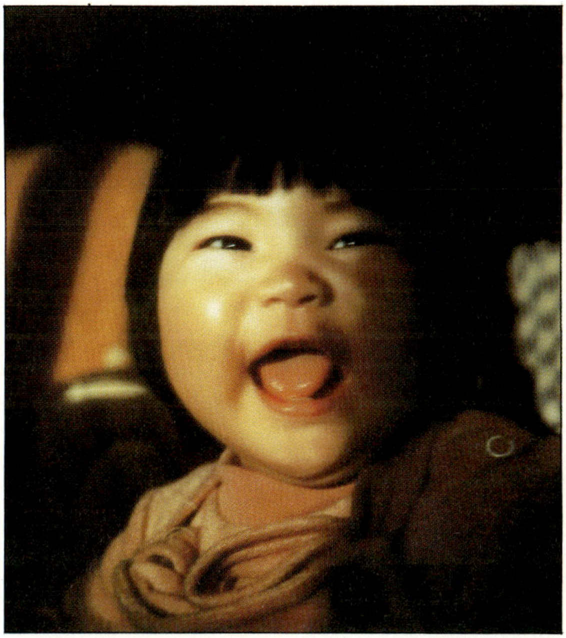

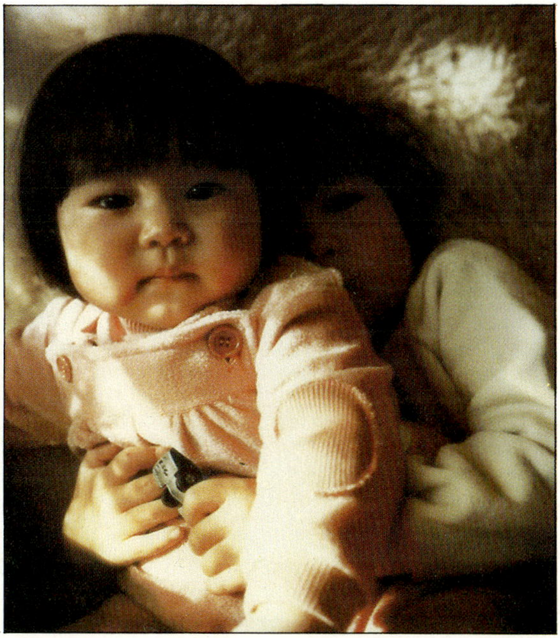

Introduction

This is the first practical handbook for people with instant cameras. It explains clearly and simply how to get the best out of these cameras, avoid mistakes, and make good use of the special qualities of this exciting medium. It also shows you how to take advantage of light, color, viewpoint, and composition and develop an eye for effective subjects – the heart of good picture-taking.

Ever since Edwin Land launched his first prototype camera and film, instant photography has delighted adults and children alike with its almost magical delivery – minutes after you press the shutter. This immediacy makes instant cameras ideal for learning – you can identify a mistake, and correct it while the subject is still available. Using your camera with this book, you will find that your picture-taking skill develops rapidly.

With today's instant materials and cameras you should get excellent results – films are improving, and cameras are more compact, with modern flash guns and autofocus devices. All pictures in this book were shot on various instant picture films; most are attainable with any instant camera, all of them with a single lens reflex type. But to get the best out of instant picture cameras, you must know their potential and limitations. The cameras have largely automatic controls, and some have limited exposure and focusing range. With many models, the viewfinder is separate from the lens which actually takes the picture. So you do not see the effects of focus in advance.

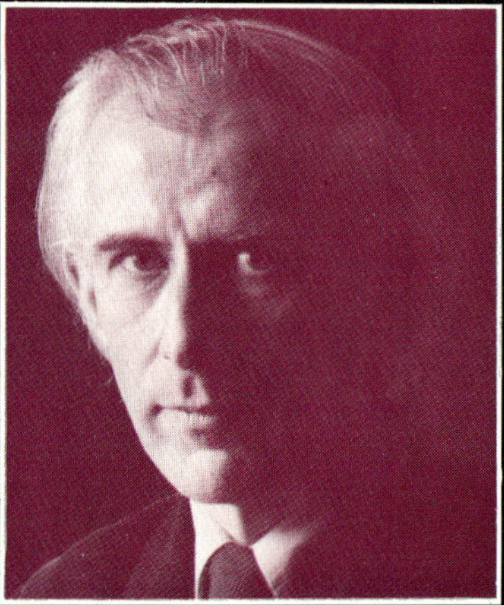

All these points are covered simply in the first part of this book, "Using your instant camera" (gray page borders). It looks at typical instant cameras and guides you through the basic routines for taking pictures.

The second section, called "Improving your pictures" (red borders), shows you how to use viewpoint, lighting, and composition, and how to handle night shots, moving subjects, and flash pictures.

The third section, "Handling different subjects" (yellow borders), looks at common picture-taking situations, from family groups to foreign vacations. It shows you how to make the most effective use of your camera, subject and location. The last section (gray borders) covers faults, accessories, advanced cameras, presentation, and special uses.

Michael Langford

Instant camera basics
A camera is a light-tight box with a hole in the front, covered by a lens. The **aperture**, adjustable in size, controls the amount of light entering the camera. The **shutter** controls the time light acts on the film. Together, aperture and shutter control exposure.

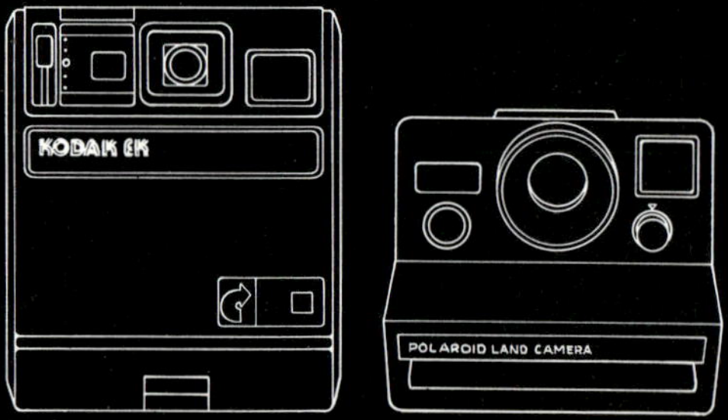

The **lighten/darken control** adjusts exposure. The **lens** makes rays of light from the subject converge to form an image on the film. Exposed pictures emerge from the **exit slot**. The **viewfinder** lets you compose your shot – most models use a separate window, but SLRs show the actual view of the lens.

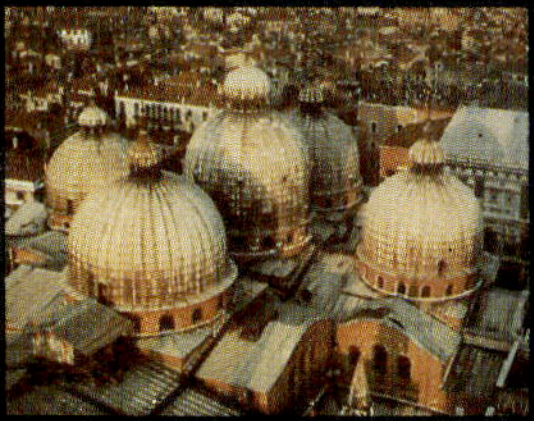
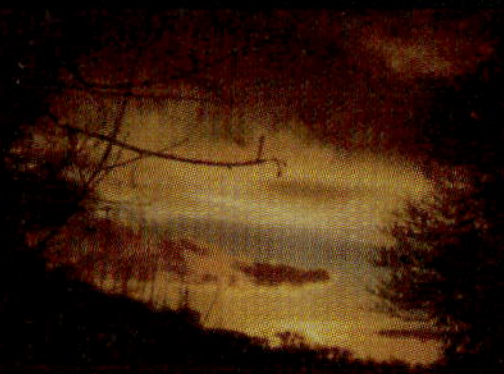
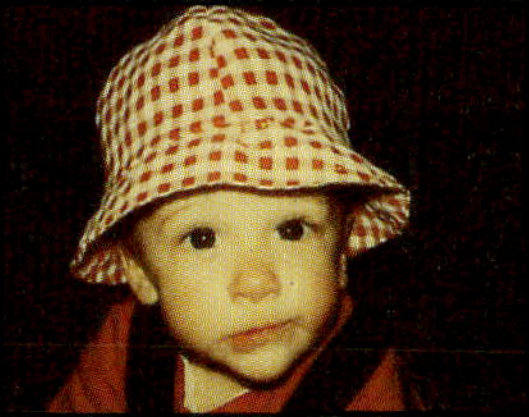
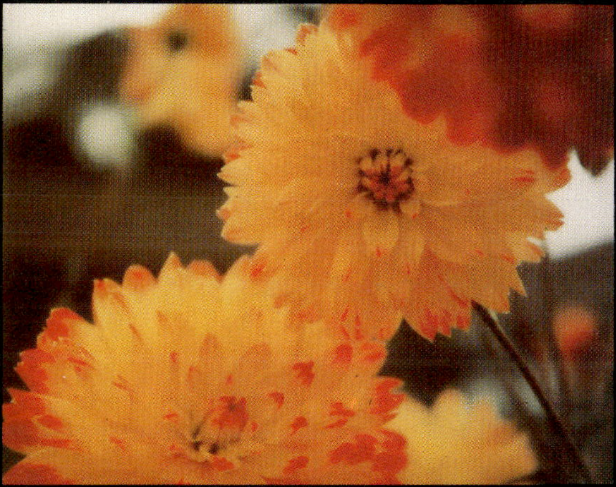
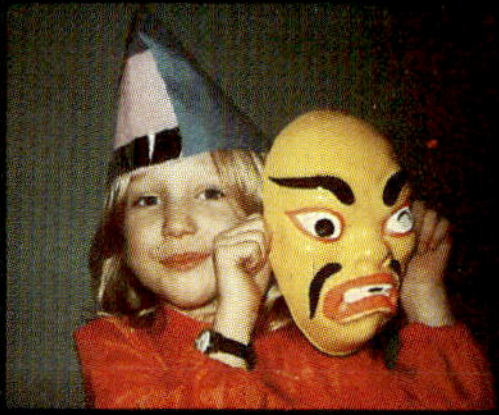
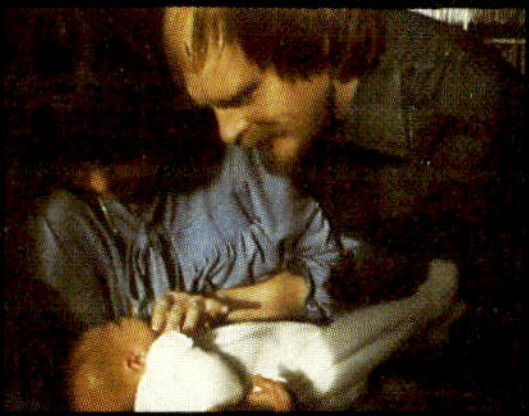
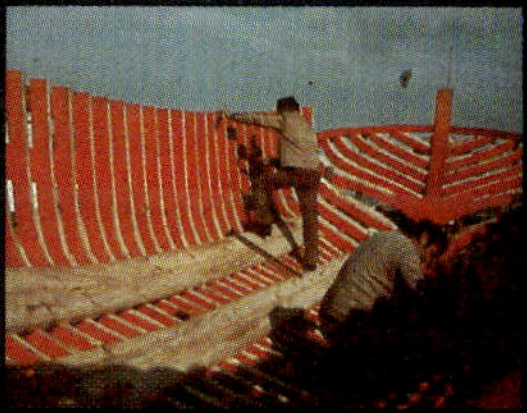
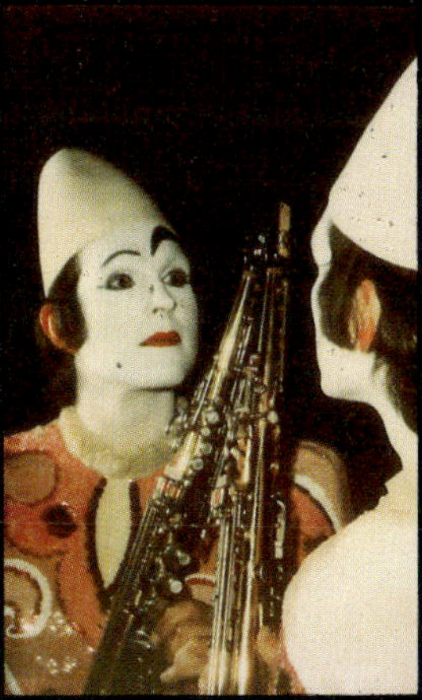
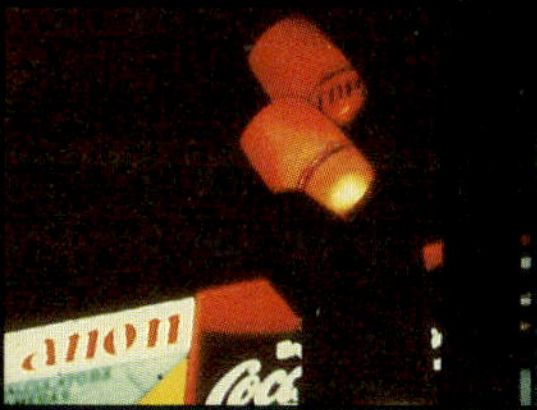
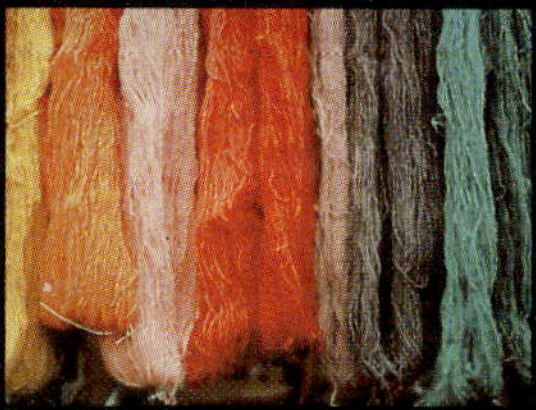
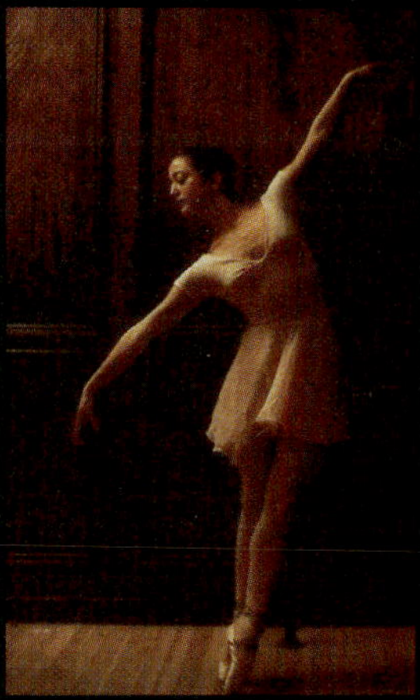
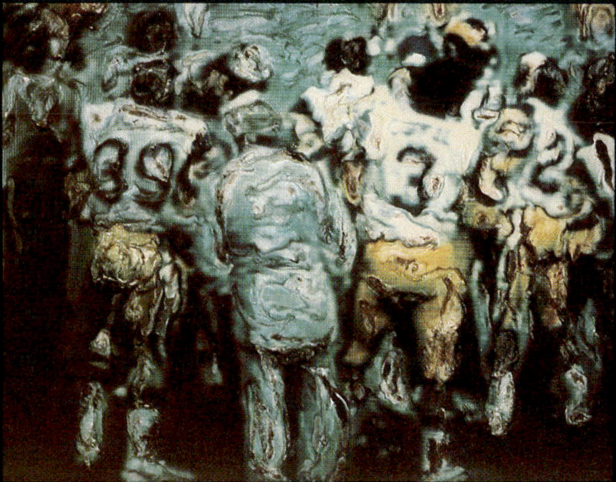

Simple cameras for peel-apart film

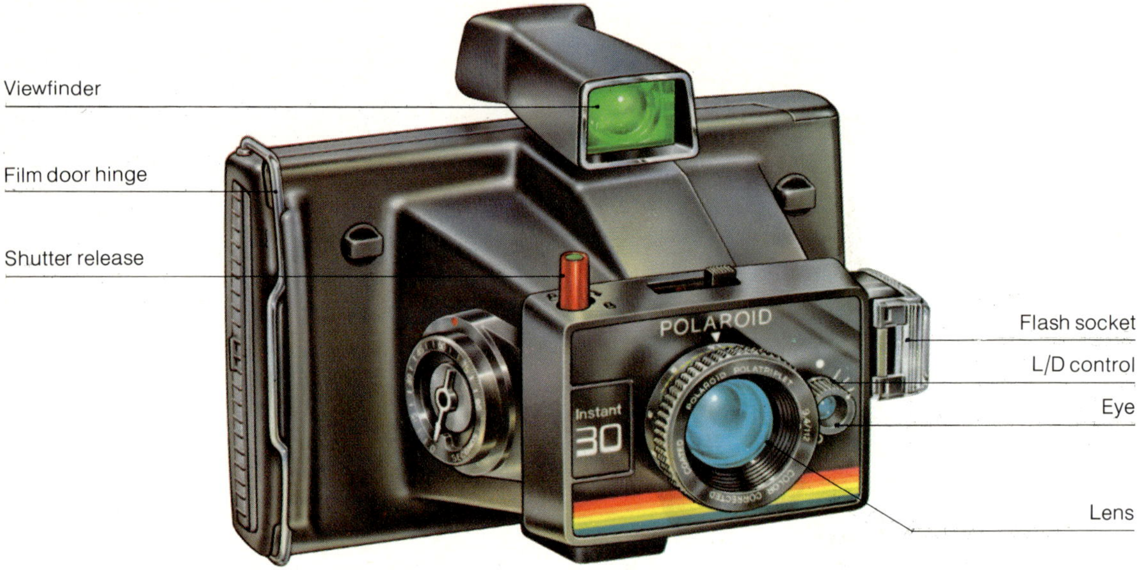

Peel-apart film enables you to take instant pictures at low cost, in black and white as well as color. After each shot, you pull the film out, between rollers in the camera, to set off development. Wait for the time recommended in your film leaflet (in the pack) and then peel off the backing paper (p.26). Cameras in the peel-apart range use batteries to power the shutter, flash and electric eye. They are direct vision models – you look through a window above the lens. Accurate framing takes practice (p.18).

Typical camera features

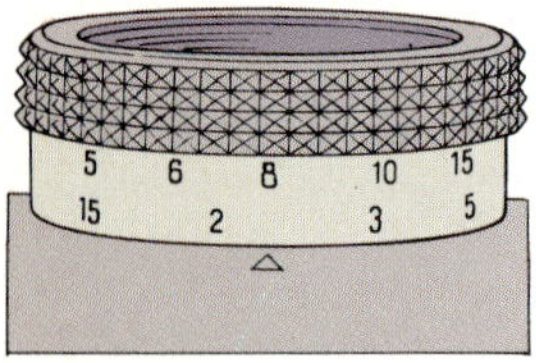

The lens
The lens on cameras for peel-apart film projects from the body and carries a manually set distance scale (p.19). The 'Polatriplet' lens will take sharp pictures from $3\frac{1}{2}$ ft (1 m) to infinity. Keep your lens clean at all times, see facing page.

Shutter lock and film speed selector
Turn the shutter button, below, clockwise to lock the release. Before using the camera, twist the button counterclockwise. Set film speed (ASA), right, at 75 for color film, or 3000 for black and white.

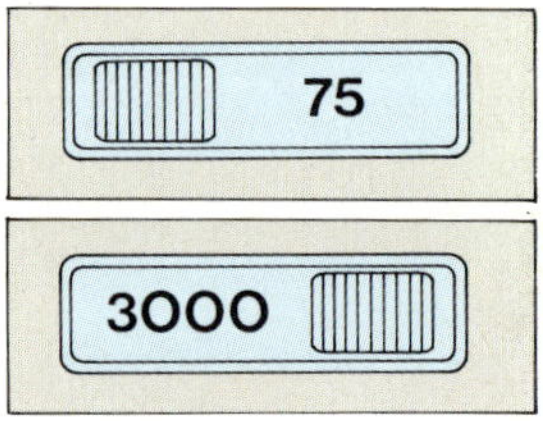

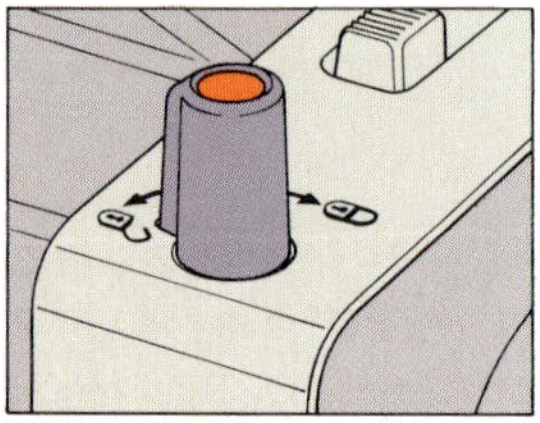

Electric eye and lighten/darken control
The electric eye measures the light level and sets the correct exposure automatically. In certain situations (p.21) the eye can be fooled, so use the L/D control to adjust the exposure level.

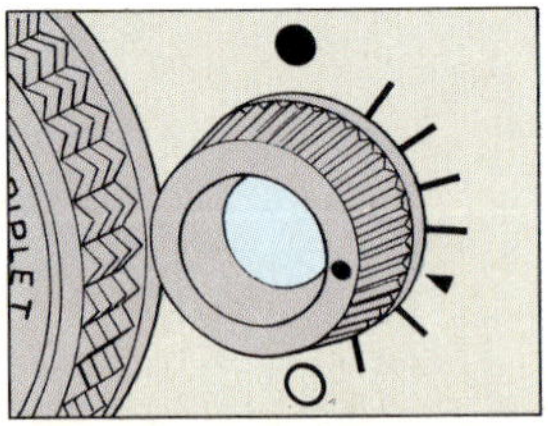

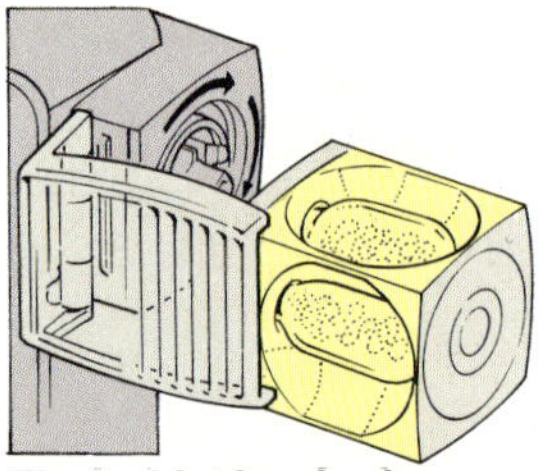

Flash shield and cubes
You can use regular or Hi-Power cubes (p.22). A used cube "reminds" you to remove it by locking the shutter release. To put in a new cube, swing out the shield and insert the cube at a 45° angle. Turn it clockwise until it stops.

The prints
Peel-apart film is available in square and rectangular formats, in black and white and in color. Black and white film which gives a retainable negative is also made (rectangular format only). The camera opposite is a versatile model, it takes any of these five types of film. The viewfinder adjusts automatically to suit a square or a rectangular format. Store peel-apart prints flat and out of direct sunlight. Avoid touching the print surface: you may mark the picture.

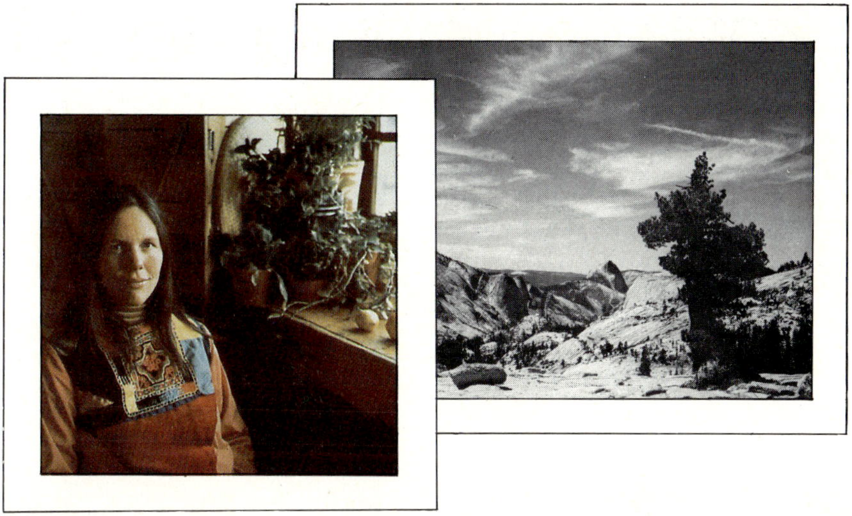

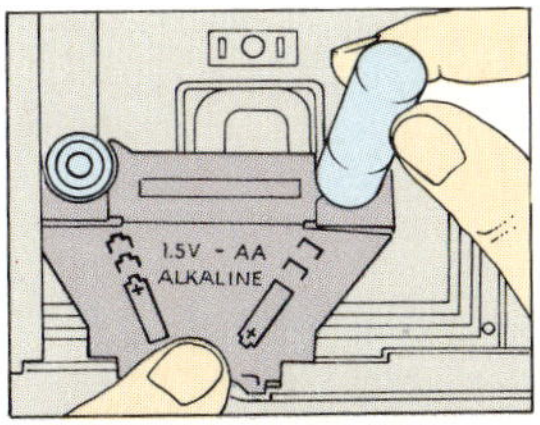

Annual battery change
Open the camera back and pull down the fingergrip. Match the + and — signs on the two 1.5 volt alkaline batteries to the camera markings.

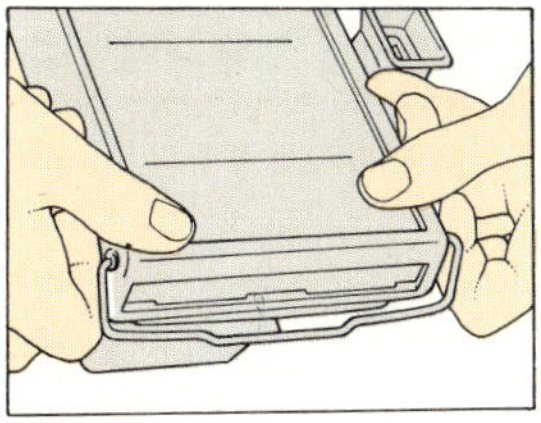

Opening the camera
To open the camera back, unlatch the metal hinge and then open the door carefully. If your camera is loaded, only open the back in dim light.

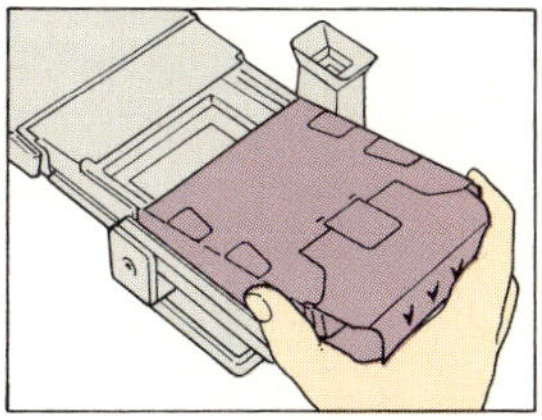

Loading the film
Insert the pack, holding it by its edges only. Make sure that you have not trapped any white tabs between the film pack and the camera body.

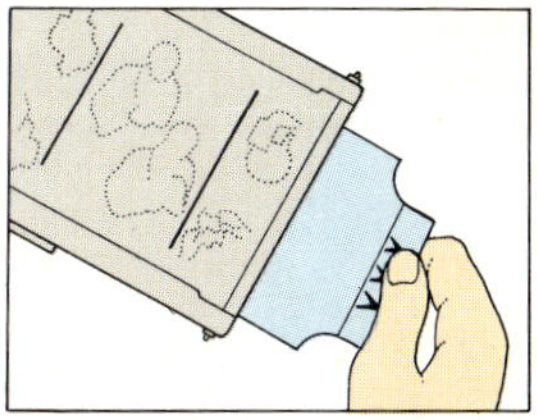

Ejecting the film cover
Close and latch the camera back. Pull the black tag (film shield) smoothly out of the camera. The peel-apart film is now ready to use, starting with tab 1 (p.26).

Camera care
You must clean the camera rollers regularly or you will get ugly specks on your pictures. The rollers are fitted in the camera door – to remove them just lift out by the metal loops. Then clean them with a damp cloth. To clean the inside of your camera hold it upside down and blow out dust with a puffer brush. To clean the lens use a puffer brush or a lens tissue. Do not use the chemically impregnated cloths intended for eyeglasses.

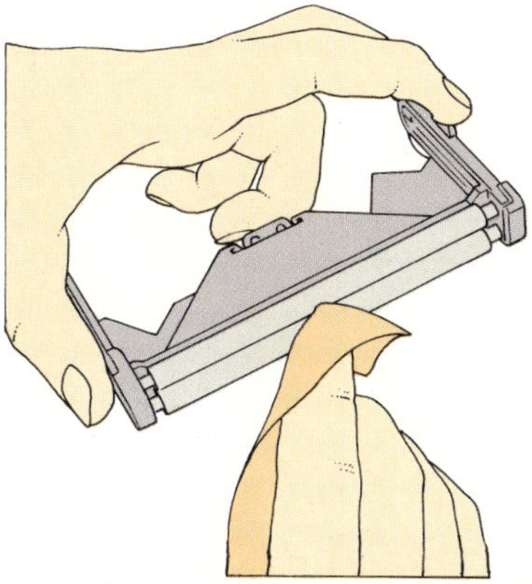

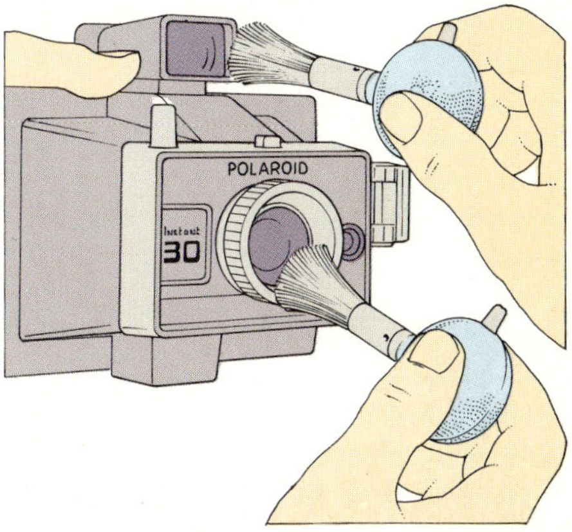

Simple cameras for integral film

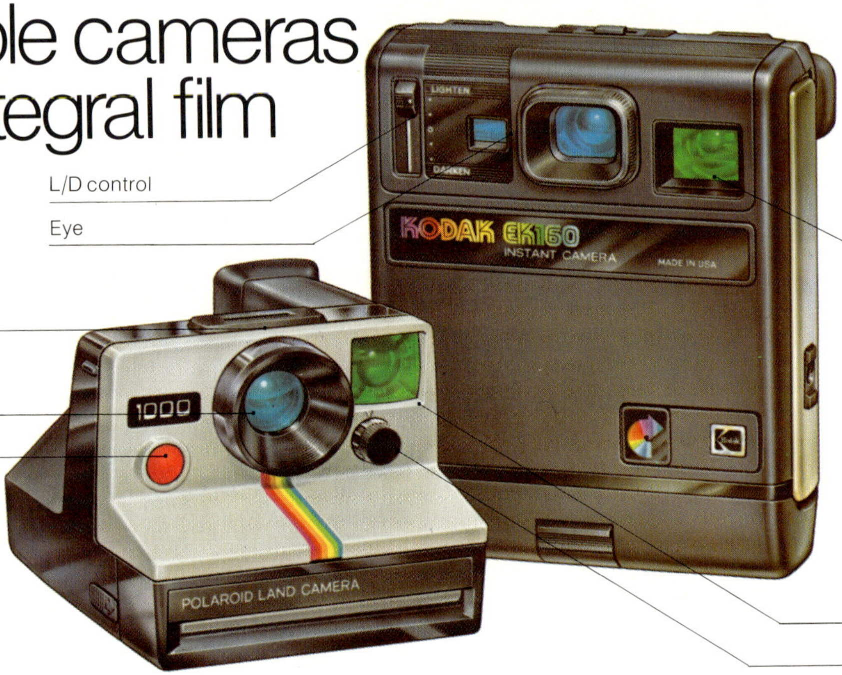

The integral system allows true instant photography – the image develops without your aid. Both Kodak and Polaroid produce integral direct vision cameras. But their systems differ, so you cannot use Kodak film in a Polaroid camera, or vice versa. Color results differ too (p.15).

Both cameras shown here are fixed focus: you do not have to set distance. (The minimum distance for sharp pictures is 6 ft, but sharp results are possible at 4–6 ft in bright light.) Other models have variable focus/autofocus (p.19). Most cameras have motorized print ejection.

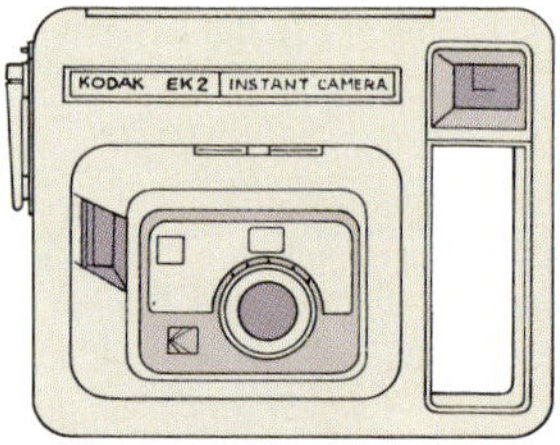

Typical camera features

Flipflash or bars

Use flipflash on Kodak cameras and flashbars on Polaroid integral models. If you take flash pictures regularly, electronic flash is a good investment (p.22). Some models have electronic flash built-in.

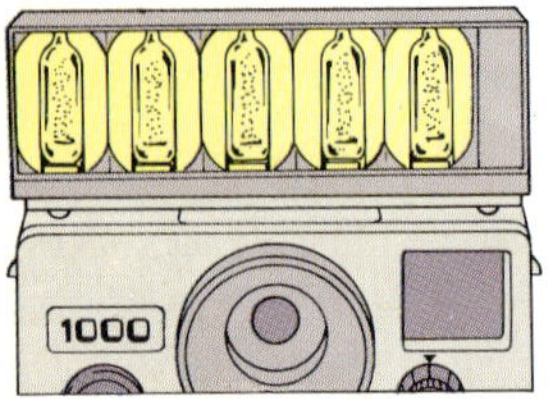

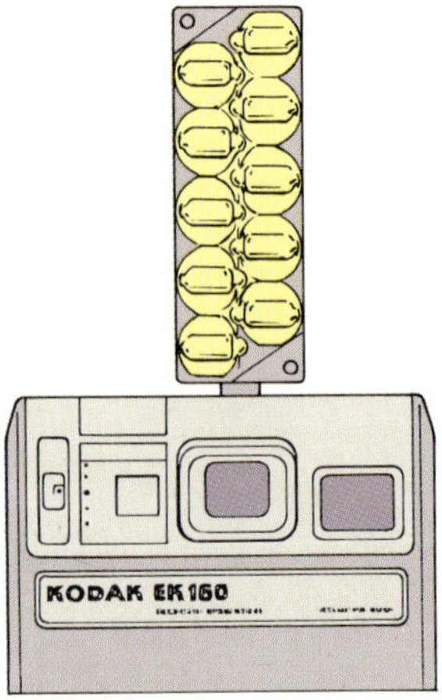

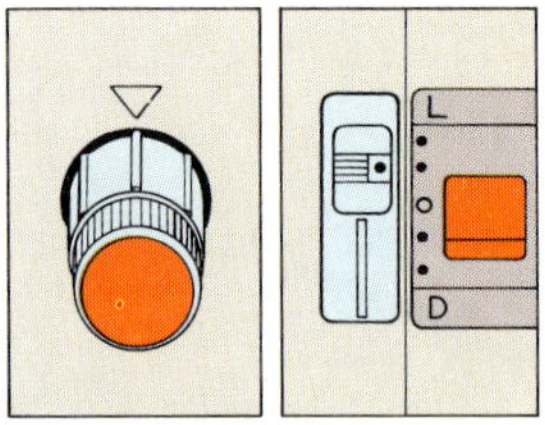

Lighten/darken control and electric eye

The "eye" measures light reflected from your subject, and exposure is set automatically. In some situations, the eye can be biased (p.21). Then you must use the L/D control to compensate.

Hand-cranked cameras

Some Kodak models, such as the Handle 2, above, are not motorized. To eject the print you must crank the handle at the side of the camera. You must use one continuous, smooth motion, as shown below.

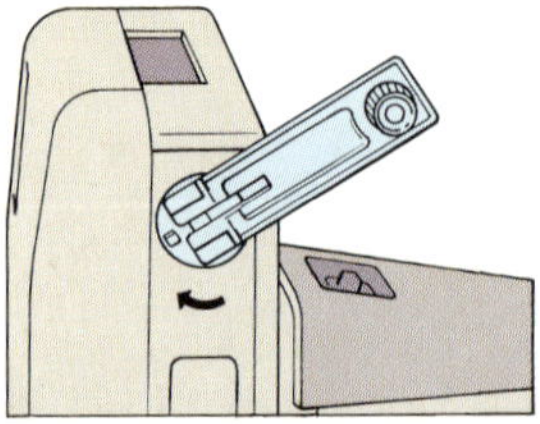

Integral prints
Fully formed prints are full color and sealed in protective plastic. Polaroid prints are square and Kodak are rectangular. They have different color characteristics too (p.15). Decide which you prefer before you choose your camera. Never bend, cut or fold an integral print or you will damage the image. If you get fingerprints on the image area of an integral print, "mist" the surface with your breath, and polish with a soft cloth.

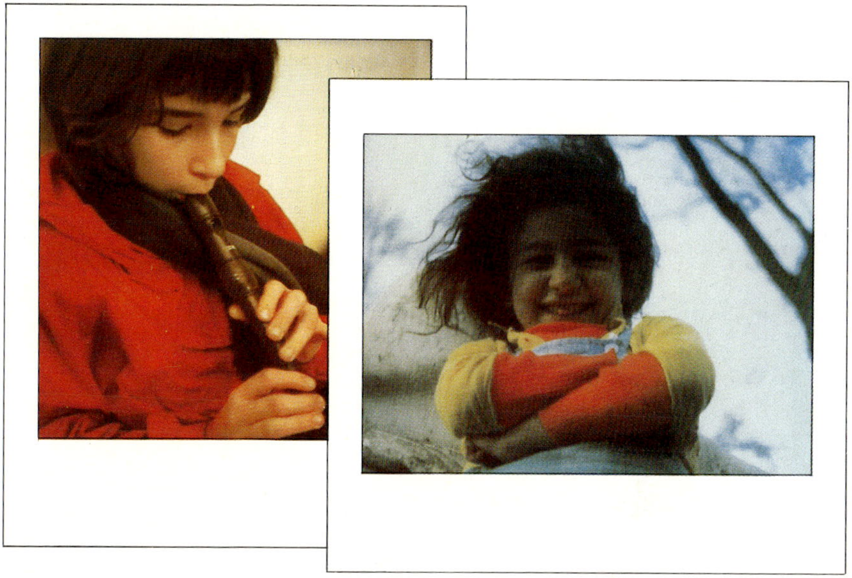

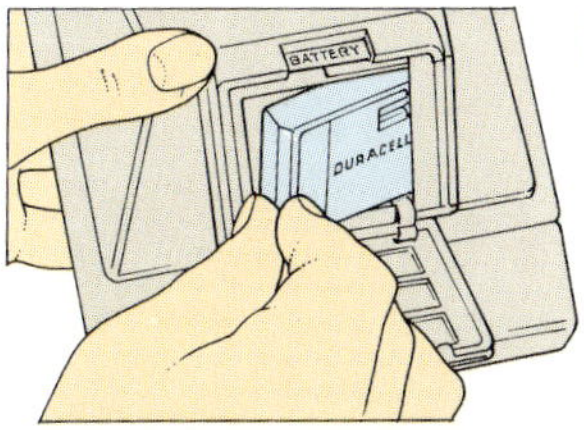

Batteries – Kodak models
Push in a size J battery, angled corner first, until the notch fits behind the holding lug. Remove the batteries before storing the camera.

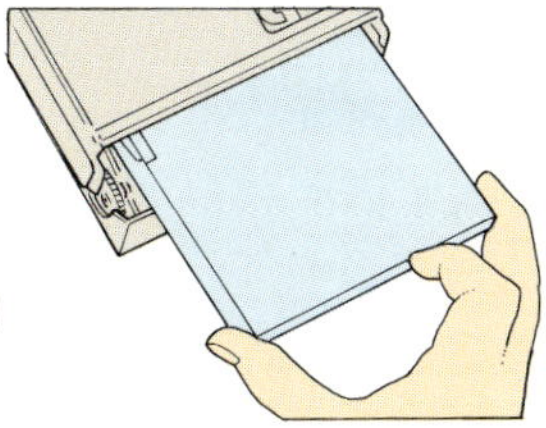

Loading Kodak film
Insert the pack, thin end first, lining up its orange stripe with the orange line on the camera. Close the film door and press the shutter to eject the cover.

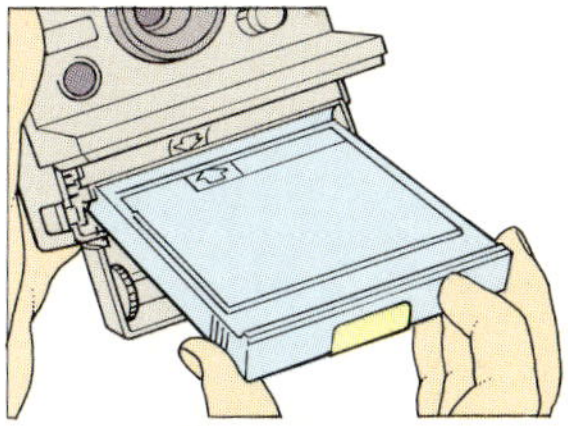

Loading Polaroid film
Insert the film pack with the colored tab toward you, and push it in until the strip on the pack front snaps open. SX70 covers eject automatically.

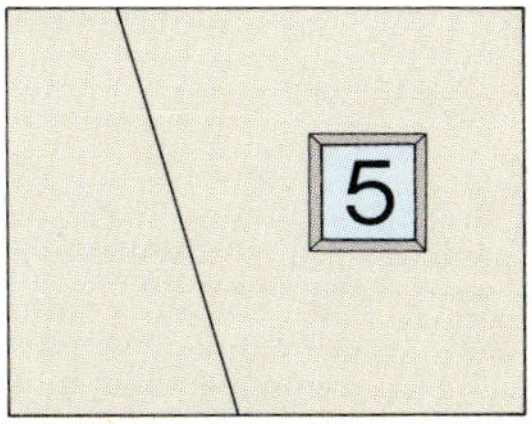

Picture counter
Cameras that take integral film have a counter that starts at 10 with a new film pack and *subtracts* each shot until it reaches 0.

Print ejection
After you have pressed the shutter release you must still hold the camera steady. If your camera is motorized, the print will appear automatically. With a non-motorized model you must use the hand crank, see facing page, to eject the print. On some Polaroid models a black film shade comes out over the print as it emerges. Do not touch the shade – it will spring back into the camera automatically.

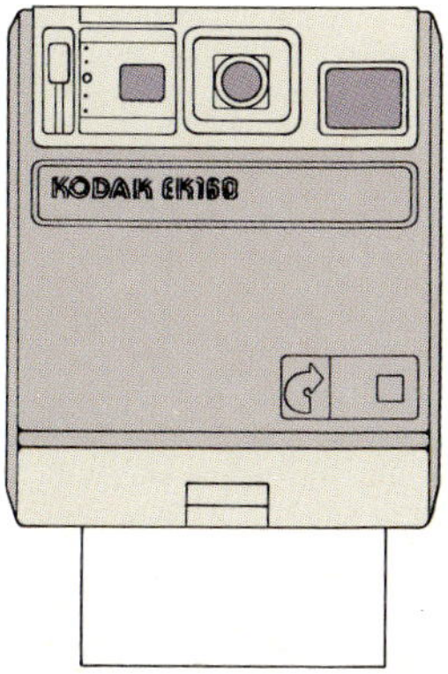

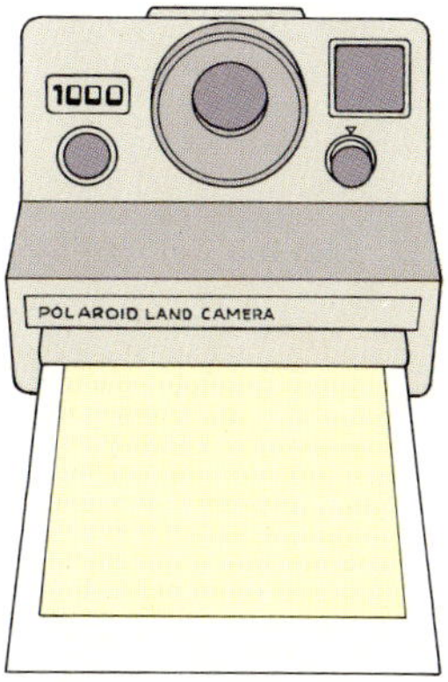

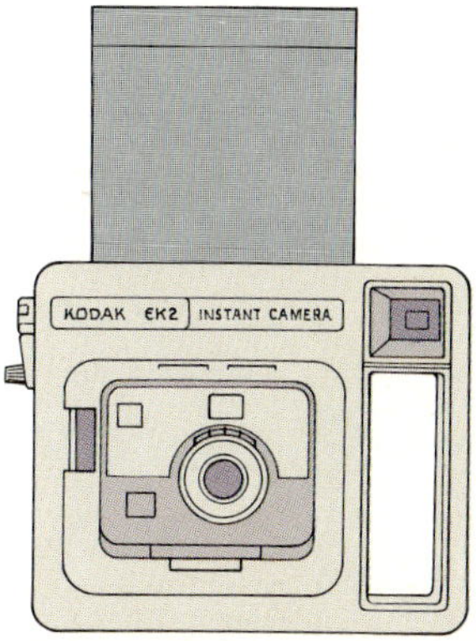

SLR cameras for integral film

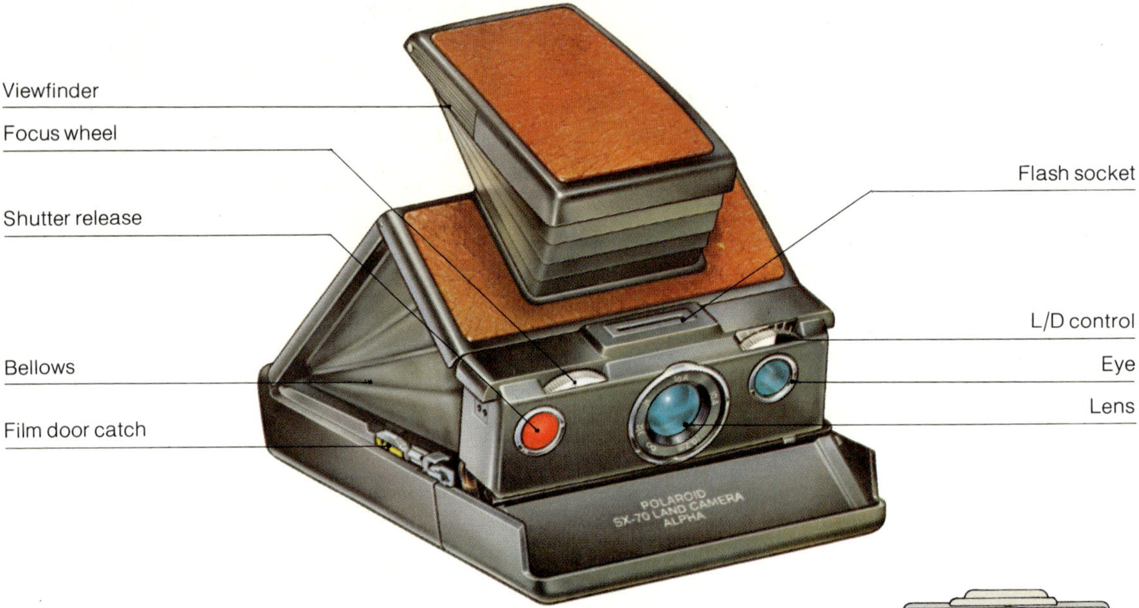

SLR cameras enable you to see the exact effects of framing and focus before you take a picture. With the aid of a series of mirrors, you look through the lens itself. Polaroid SLR cameras have elegant, folding bodies and use motorized print ejection. It takes practice to use the viewfinder eyepiece comfortably (p.18) – keeping the camera still, move your eye until you can see all four corners of the black frame. The sonar autofocus models are simpler to use than manual focus ones, ensuring sharp pictures.

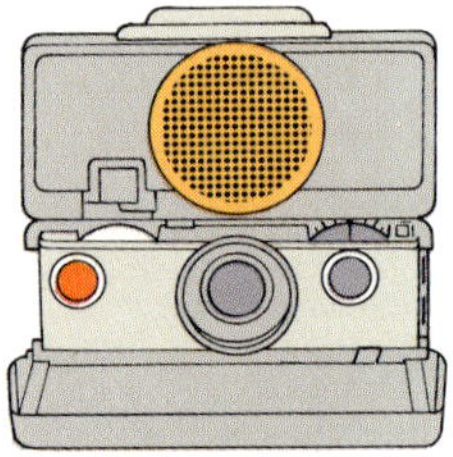

Typical camera features

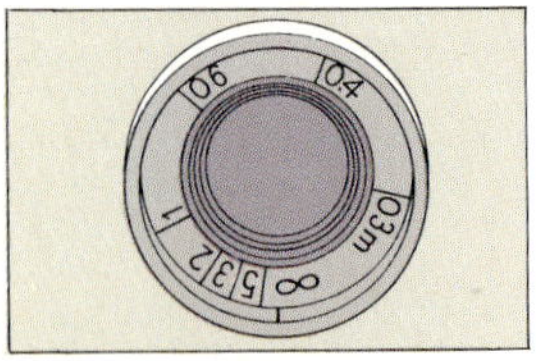

The lens
With an SLR camera you see in your eyepiece exactly what the lens sees. Unlike conventional SLR cameras, which accept a range of lenses, instant SLRs have only one lens. Close-up and telephoto attachments are made.

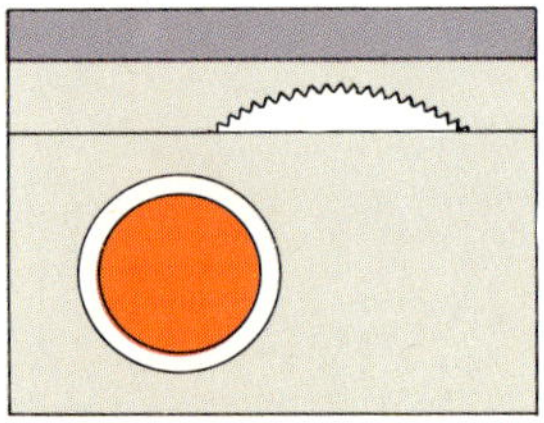

Focusing aids
When you press the shutter on an autofocus model, above, sound waves measure subject distance (p.19), then the camera focuses the lens. On a manual model you focus the lens yourself (p.19): rotate the wheel, left.

Flash
All models accept flash bars, right, or an electronic unit. If you use flash often, an electronic unit will cost less in the long term. The cameras have a flash range of 11 ins–12 ft (26 cm–3.7 m), and take a flash bar diffuser (p.22).

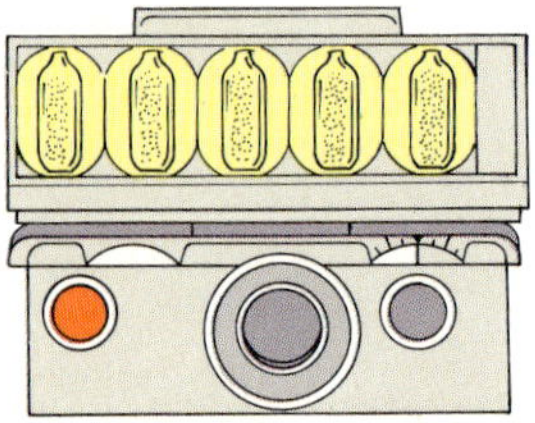

Lighten/darken control
You can use the L/D control to adjust exposure in certain conditions (pp.20–1). Each mark on the control darkens or lightens the picture by the same amount. For most pictures leave the control at the center setting.

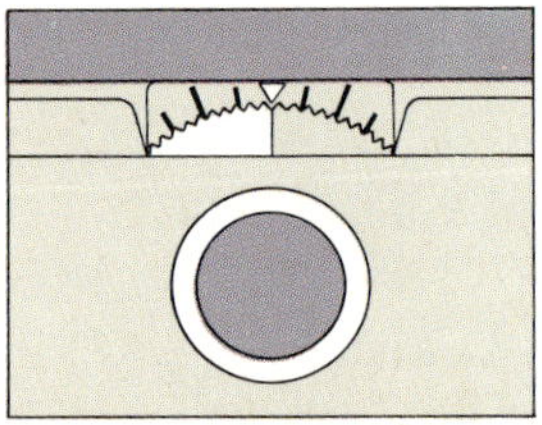

Prints and print ejection
A few seconds after you have pressed the shutter release, the print will be ejected from the exit slot (at the bottom of the camera). For a perfectly sharp picture, you must hold the camera still until the print is ejected. You have nothing to do once the picture has emerged from the camera. Just wait a few seconds and the image will start to appear. Soon you will have a finished print. Never cut, bend or fold your picture. You can clean SX70 prints by "misting" the surface with your breath and then wiping with a soft cloth.

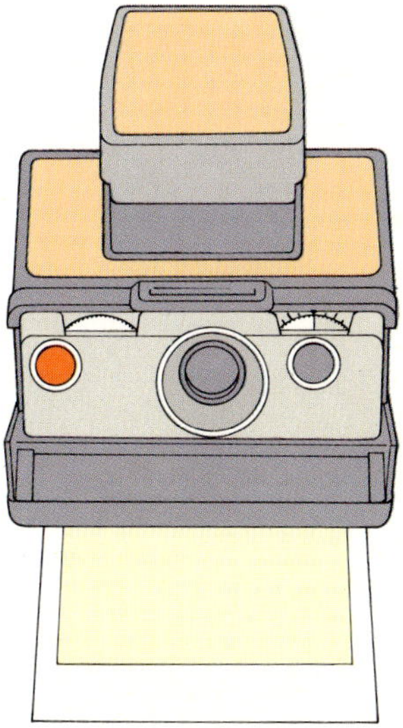

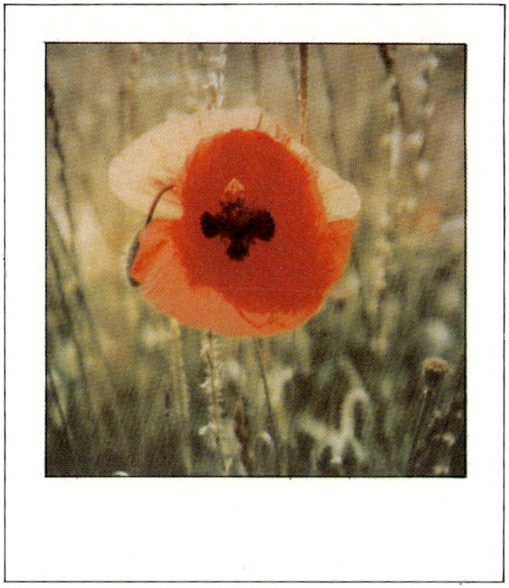

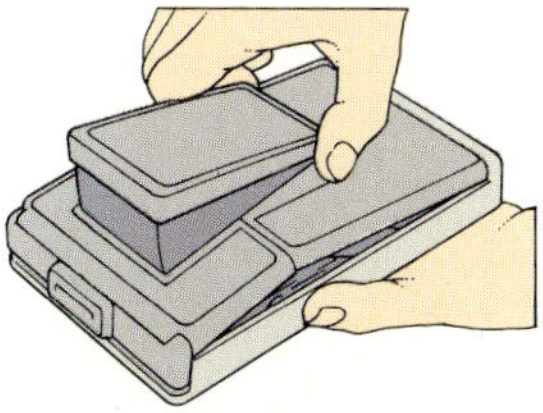

Opening the camera
Hold your camera in your palm, and pull up the thin end of the viewfinder cap on top of the camera.

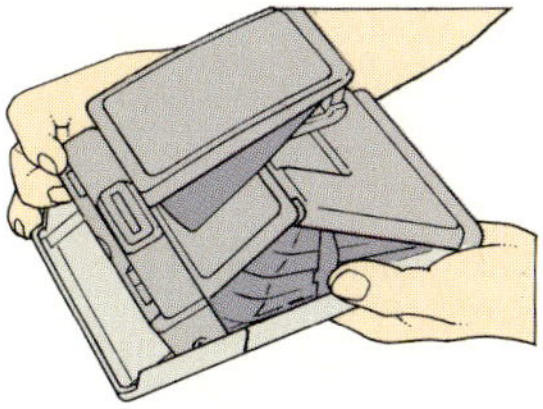

Metal cover support
Push the cover support toward the front of the camera, until it locks in position.

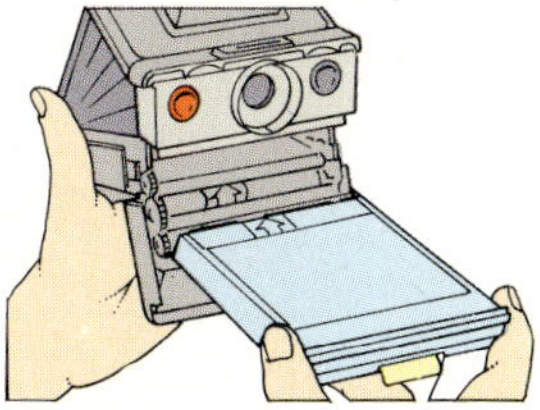

Loading film
Hold the film pack by its edges only, with the colored tab on the pack facing toward you.

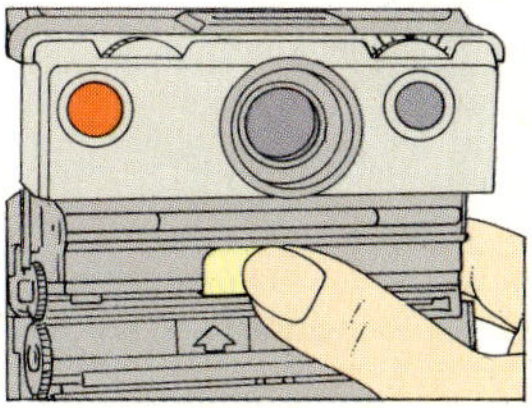

Pushing film in
Press the film pack all the way in so that the thin black strip on the pack front snaps open.

Choosing a camera

All the models shown here can be used with flash bars or electronic units. Before you choose a camera consider what you will use it for – an inexpensive direct vision model (pp.10–11) will suffice for family snapshots, but for a wider range you will need an SLR

Key to symbols
A Sonar autofocus
DV Direct vision camera
R Rangefinder camera
S Sunny conditions only
+ Greater focus range
SLR Single lens reflex
● Acceptable pictures

	Polaroid cameras					**Kodak cameras**		
	1000 ONE-STEP	2000 PRONTOS!	5000	SX70 ALPHA RANGE	600SE	EK160 COLORBURSTS	EK8	EK2 HANDLE 2
Photographic situations	**DV**	**DV**	**DV A**	**SLR A**	**DV R**	**DV**	**DV R**	**DV**
Outdoor pictures	●	●	●	●	●	●	●	●
Indoors (natural light)	S	S	●	●	●	●	S	S
Portraits	●	●	●	● +	● +	●	● +	●
Night pictures		●	●	●	●			
Action shots		S	S		●	S	S	
Close-up pictures				●	●			

Instant picture film

Instant pictures use a unique principle – as the piece of film leaves the camera, chemicals are released. They develop the image – causing the dyes to move through the layers to form the picture. On integral prints you can watch the image forming; on peel-apart you cannot. Instant color pictures have their own special qualities. The rich dyes give best results with subjects in bright, even light and within the right temperature range (pp.62 and 69).

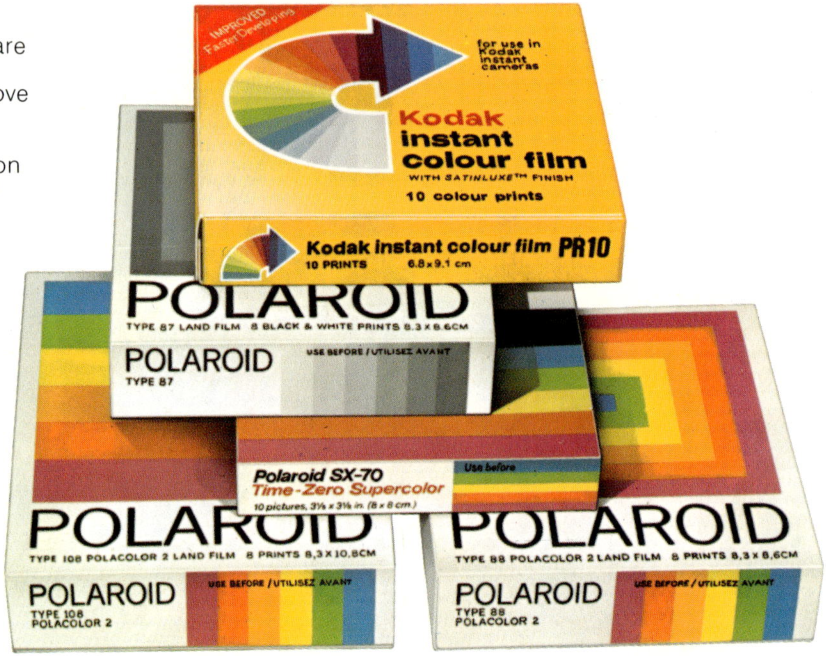

Film types
Kodak and Polaroid films are not interchangeable. Both make integral color films, and Polaroid also make peel-apart film in color, black and white (pp. 40–1), positive/negative (p. 41) and professional types (p. 88). Choose a type and format to suit your camera and check the expiry date on the pack.

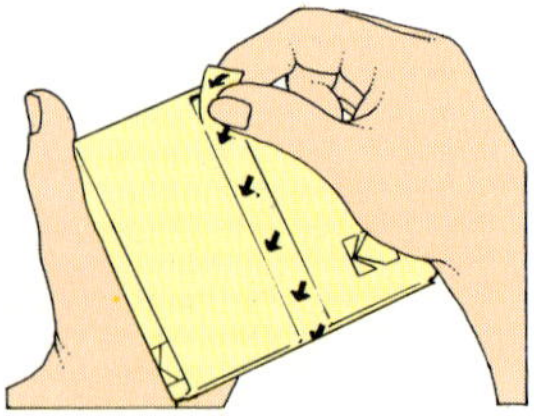

Opening Kodak film
Remove the yellow wrapper gently, tearing the middle strip in the direction of the arrows. Always hold the film pack by its edges only – pressure on the middle of the pack will harm the film and you may damage several shots.

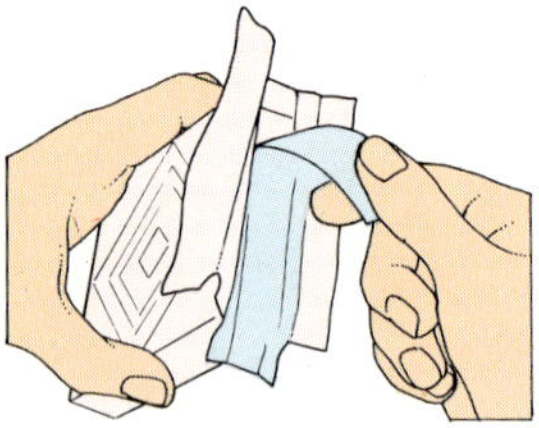

Opening Polaroid film
Open the carton carefully, tear off the foil seal and take out the film pack, holding it by its edges only. Do not touch or squeeze the middle of the pack – you may damage several shots. Once open, use film immediately or store in a refrigerator.

Film Type	Format		Color		B/W	
	Sq.	Rect.	Peel-apart	Integral	Peel-apart	Pos/neg.
87	●				●	
107		●			●	
665		●				●
88	●		●			
108		●	●			
SX70	●			●		
PR10		●		●		

Polaroid SX70 integral film
Colors are strongest in bright sunlight or flash. This film gives very successful reds, blues and yellows. Flesh tones are realistic, and greens are acceptable. Pastel colors are sometimes washed out in flash shots. The new SX70 Time Zero film (available from late 1980) gives you brighter colors faster – the image starts to come up after 15 seconds. And the new film can cope with a greater range of light and shade. Direct flash shots indoors may look cold – use natural light or diffuse your flash (p. 23) for warmer colors.

Daylight

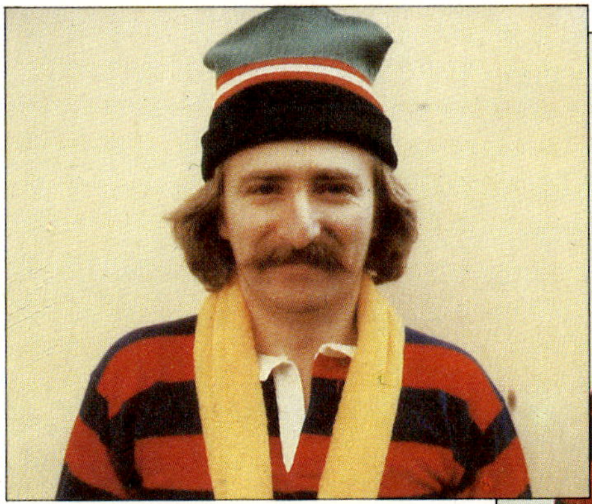

Flash

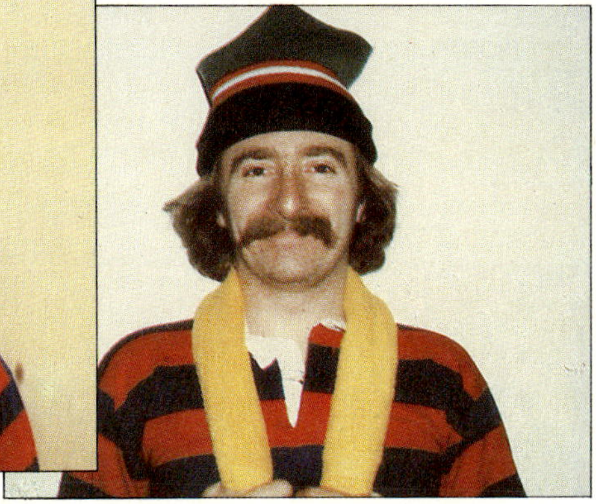

Daylight

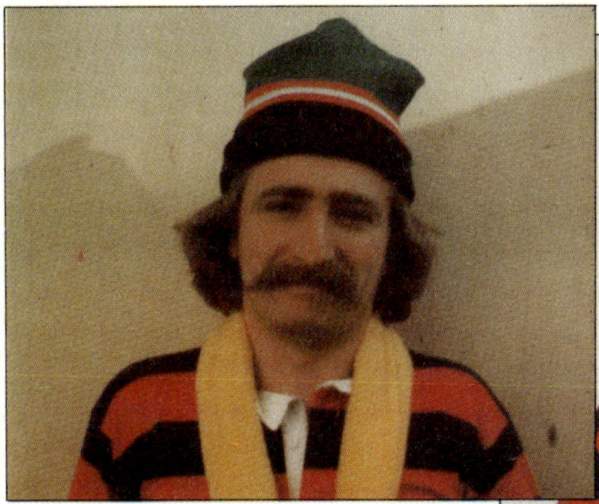

Flash

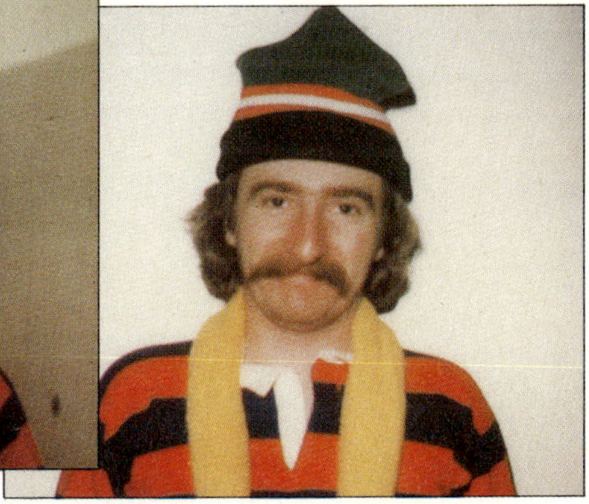

Kodak PR10 integral film
Colors are strongest in bright sunlight or flash. Kodak film colors are soft. Reds, greens, yellows and blues are most successful and flesh tones are acceptable. Direct flash shots with Kodak film have warm colors. You may get a washed-out result when you shoot pastel colors with flash. If you diffuse your flash (p. 23), you will get a more natural result but you will lose color (see p.48).

Polacolor peel-apart film
Colors are strongest in bright sunlight or flash. Flesh tones, reds, blues, greens and yellows are all successful. Colors are truest outdoors. Flash results are very warm. You may get a washed-out result when you shoot pastel colors with flash. Try to use natural light – indoors and out – wherever possible. Peel-apart film produces thinner prints than integral – they are more like conventional color prints.

Daylight

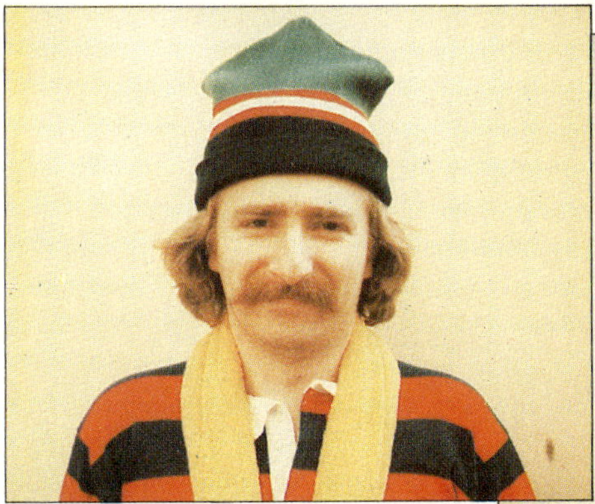

Flash

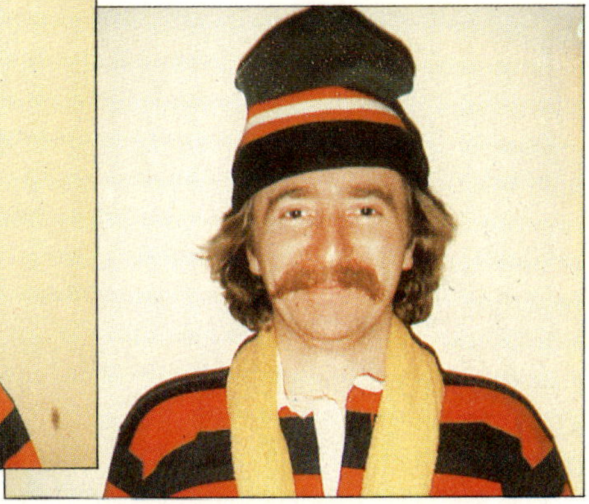

Holding your camera

To take sharp pictures you must hold your camera still – if you shake the camera your picture will be blurred. Stand firmly, feet apart and elbows tucked in, and grip the camera steadily. Place your fingers so you can set the controls quickly, using your right forefinger for the shutter release, but take care not to obscure the lens, eye, or film exit slot. With integral shots, continue to hold the camera still until the print has emerged, or your picture will not be sharp.

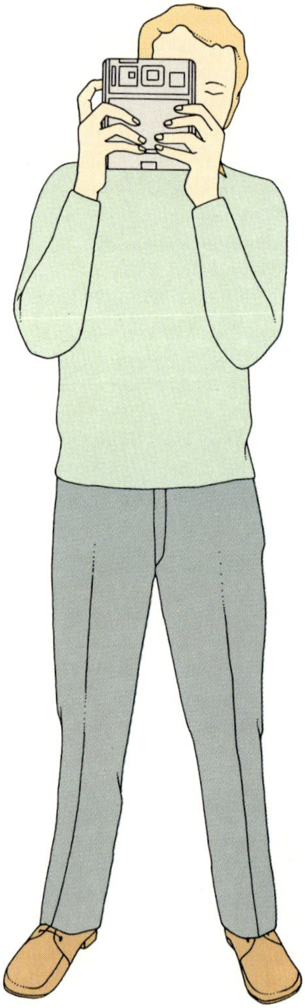

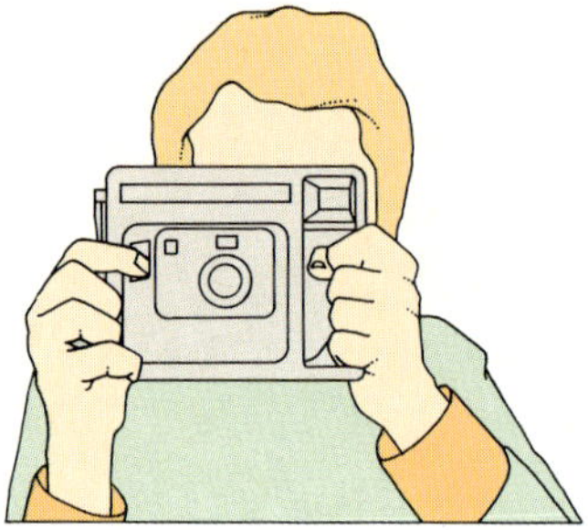

Kodak EK 2 or Handle above
Grip the handle with your left hand. Press your right thumb against the back and curl fingers around the body.

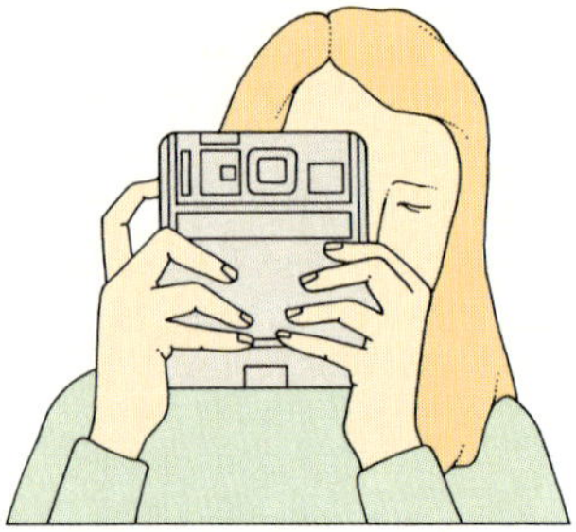

Kodak motorized cameras above
Grip each side of the body. Use your thumbs as supports at the back, and curl your fingers around the front, clear of the slot.

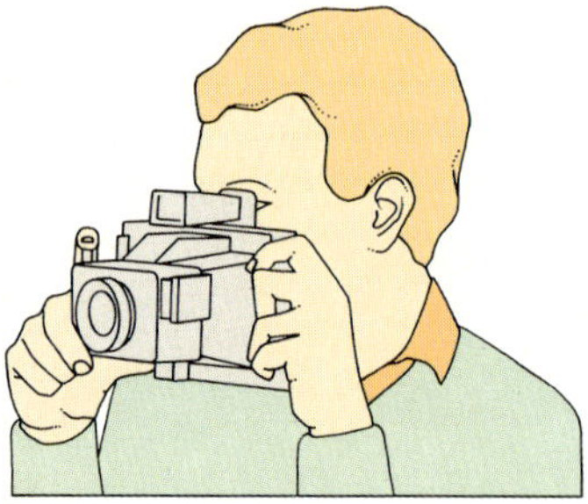

Polaroid peel-apart cameras above
Grip the body with your left hand, supporting the camera front with your right thumb. Curl spare fingers around.

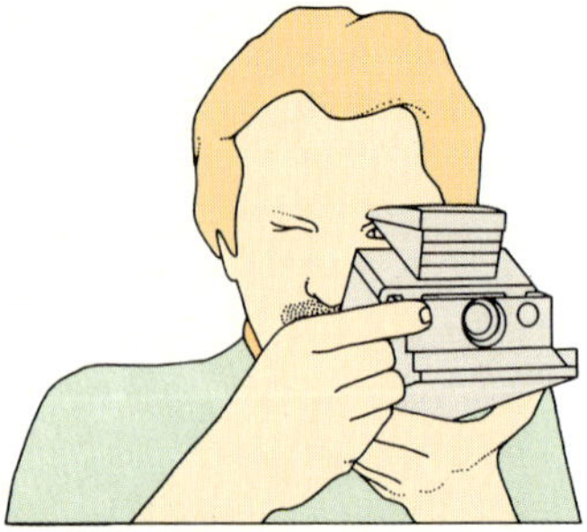

Polaroid SX 70 cameras
left and right
Hold the camera in the palm of your left hand. Use your right thumb as a support, right forefinger on the shutter release. Curl spare fingers into your palm, taking care not to obstruct the bellows on the Alpha.

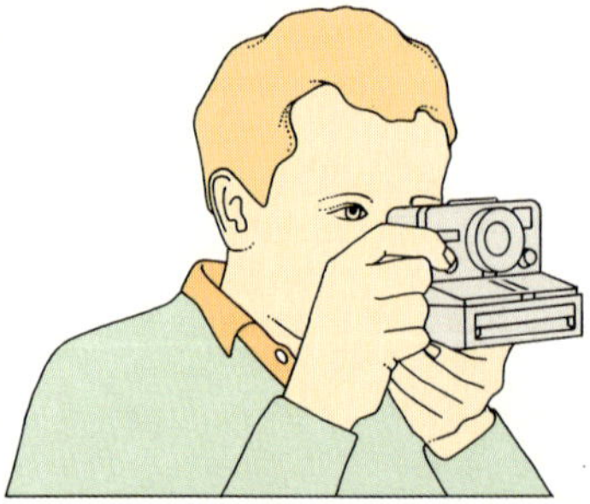

Supporting your camera
Camera shake will cause blurred or tilted pictures, as below. To avoid it, use a support to steady your camera. Lean against something firm, such as a wall, right. For low viewpoints, rest your elbows on your knees, or lie flat with elbows supporting you, see below. Take care not to obstruct the exit slot. If light is dim, rest the camera on a flat surface, see far right, or use a tripod.

Check in the viewfinder to see that the camera is level and steady before shooting.

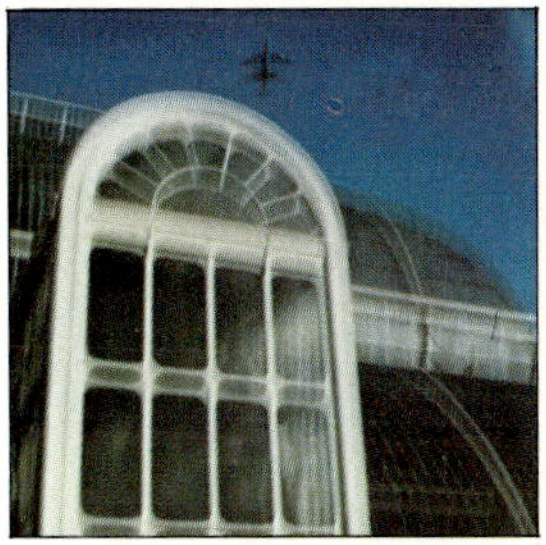

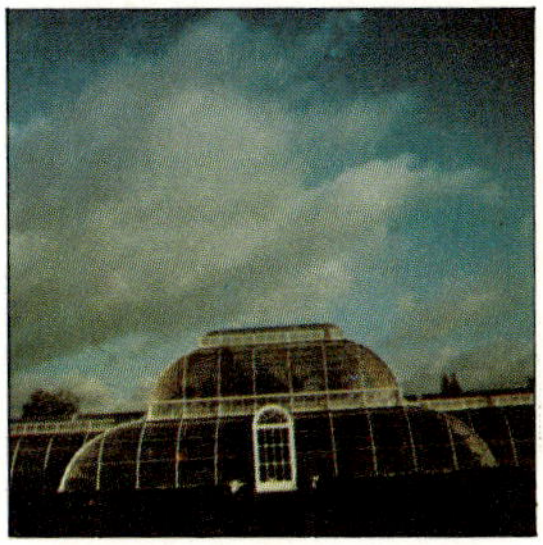

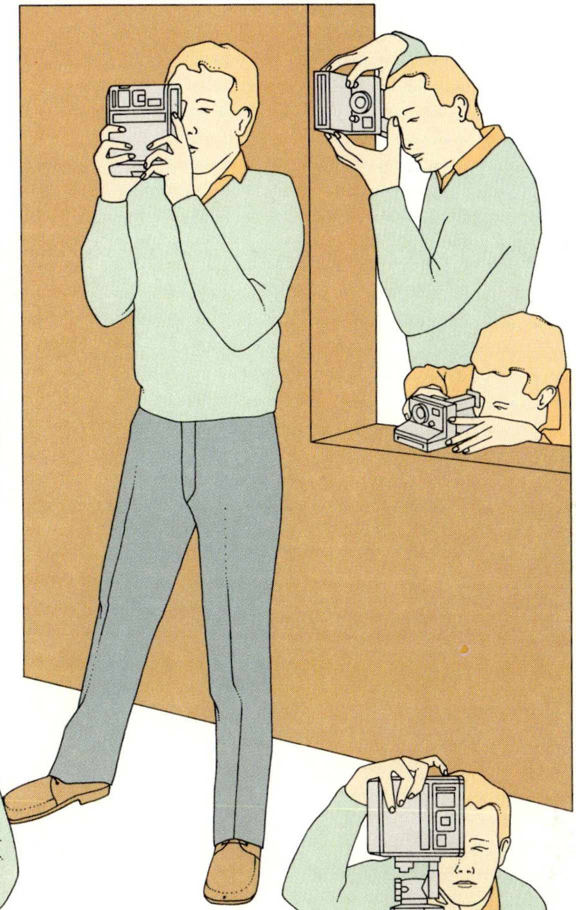

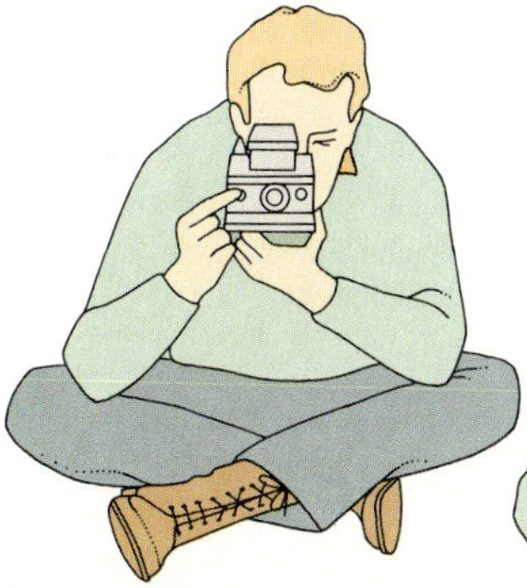

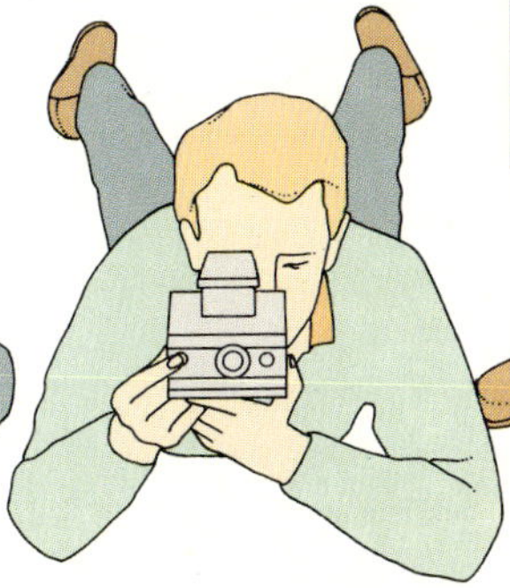

Releasing the shutter
Never "stab" the shutter release, or press too hard. Press gently with your right forefinger. At the halfway point, watch for any low light warning (and wait for autofocus models to focus) before shooting.

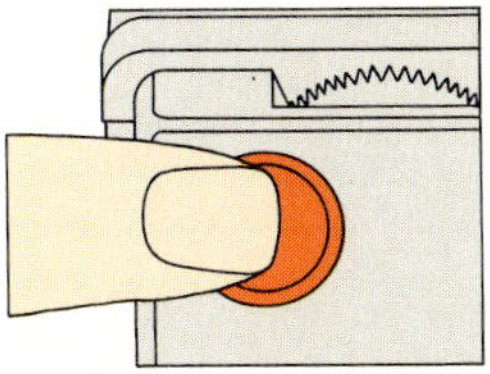

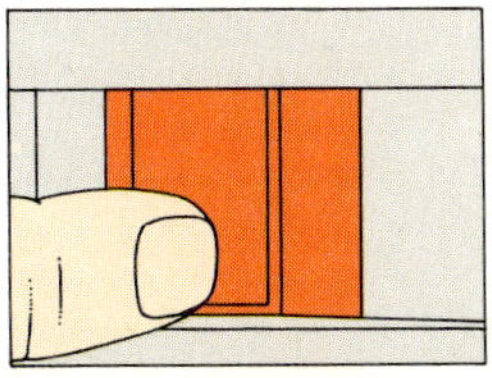

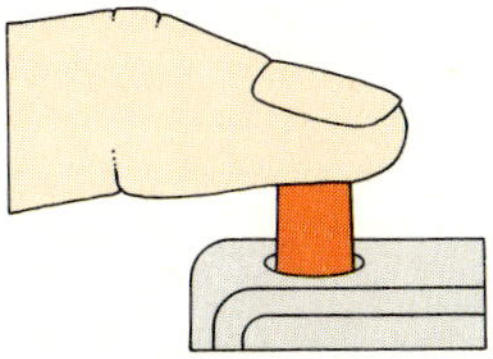

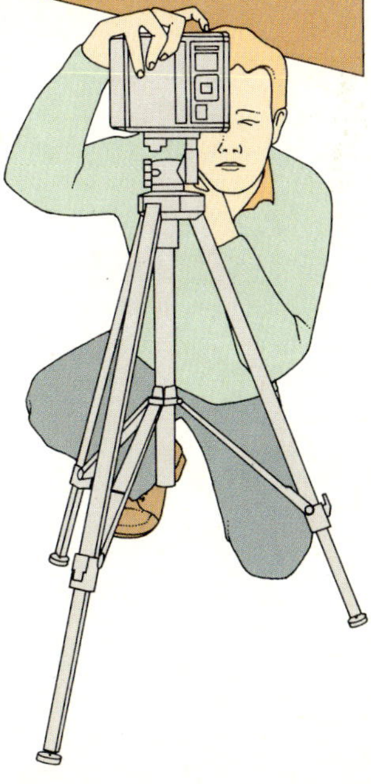

Using a tripod
In dim light your camera will select a slow shutter speed. Any movement of the camera (or your subject) while the shutter is open will result in a blurred picture. Some cameras have a low light signal which shows in the viewfinder, warning you to support the camera. To steady your camera, attach it to a standard tripod, or set it up on a table. Tripods can be adjusted to different heights. Use a cable release, plugged in to the remote shutter button, and avoid touching the camera while the shutter is pressed.

Viewing and focusing

For well framed shots, you must use your viewfinder accurately. And for sharp pictures, the camera must be focused – the lens must be set for the camera-to-subject distance. With SLRs, framing is quite accurate once you have your eye in the right position, and you can see the effect of focus in the finder. Direct vision viewfinders do not show the effect of focus, and can be inaccurate close up. Take a few shots with your own camera to check its framing. Fixed focus models will take sharp pictures from 4 ft (1.2 m) to infinity. With these, and with autofocus cameras, you do not have to focus.

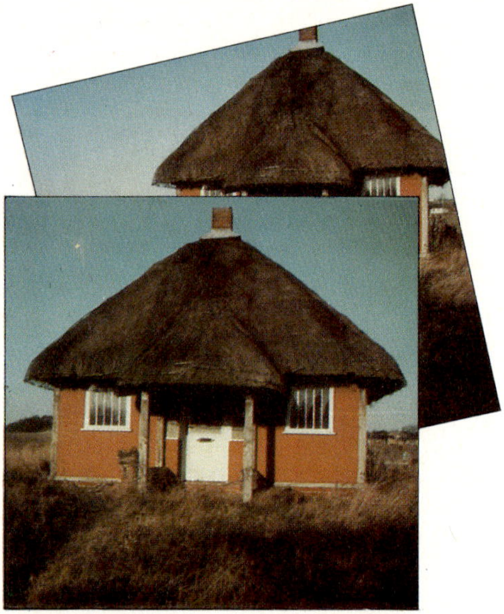

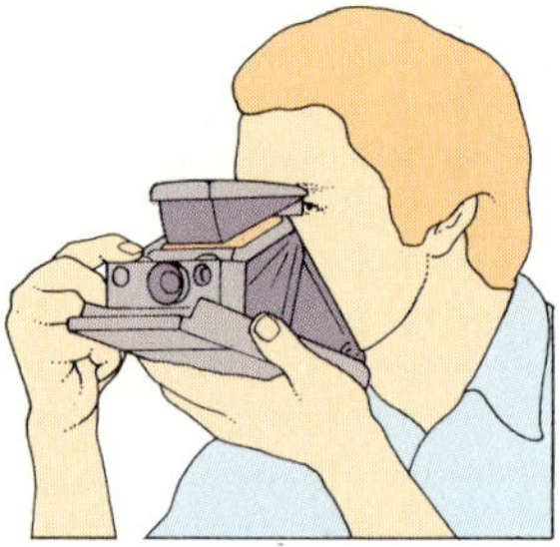

Framing your picture
Use the viewfinder frame to help you to avoid crooked or cropped-off pictures, left. Keep the horizon and vertical lines parallel with the edges. And make sure that your subject fills the center, but does not touch the sides or top.

Close-up error (parallax)
Some direct vision finders are inaccurate for subjects closer than 6 ft (2 m). You may find you are cropping off heads or arms, as right. To correct this, frame your close-ups with more space at the top or side of the subject, as shown far right.

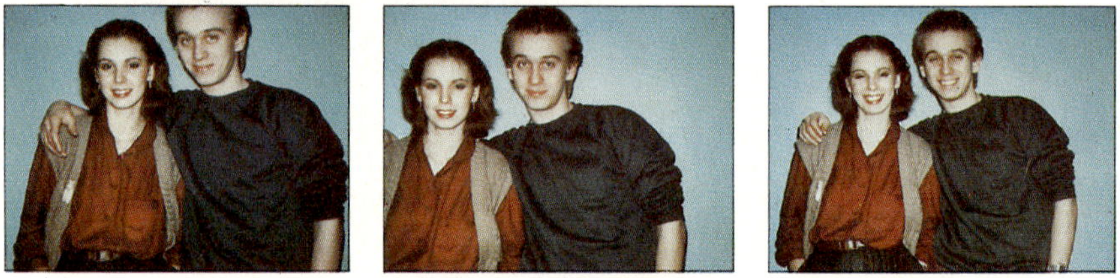

Using your viewfinder
It takes practice to get your eye in the correct position for accurate use of the viewfinder. You should be able to see all four sides of the finder frame, or all of the bright inner frame lines if these are present. On models without an eye cup, you will get a vignetting effect, top right, if your eye is too close (or too far or at the wrong level). Move your eye back until you can see all four sides clearly, below right, before framing or focusing.

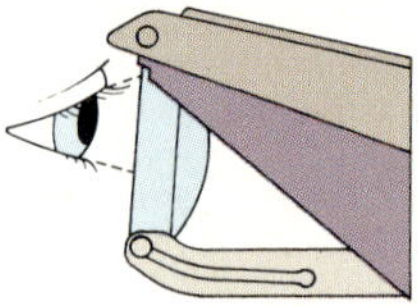

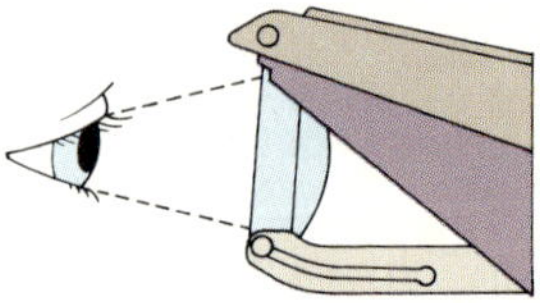

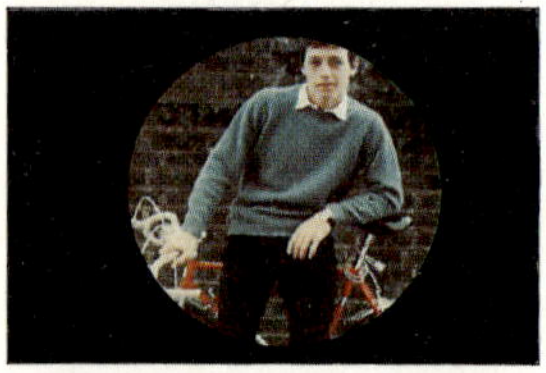

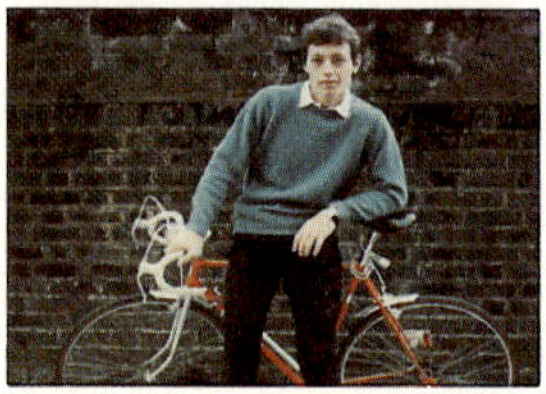

Using the eyecup
If your camera has a rubber or plastic eye cup to assist viewing, put your eye right up to it. You should be able to see all four sides of the frame, or all of the bright-line inner frame.

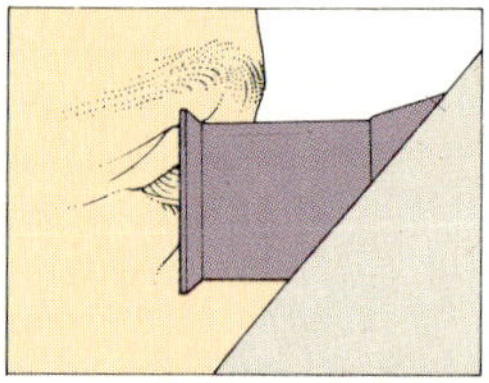

Focusing aids

Foot/meter scale

Some cameras are focused by adjusting a foot/meter scale on or near the lens. Assess your distance from your subject, and set the scale. Take care with subjects under 12 ft, or your shot will be out of focus.

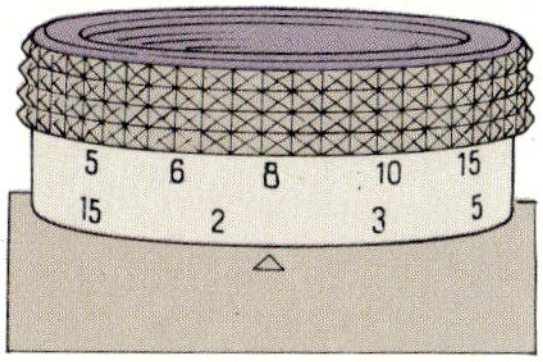

Distance symbols

Some cameras have a set of symbols to help you focus. Use the head-and-shoulders symbol for subjects 4–5 ft (1.2–1.5 m) away, the people symbol 5–12 ft (1.5–3.6 m) away, and the mountain symbol beyond 12 ft (3.6 m).

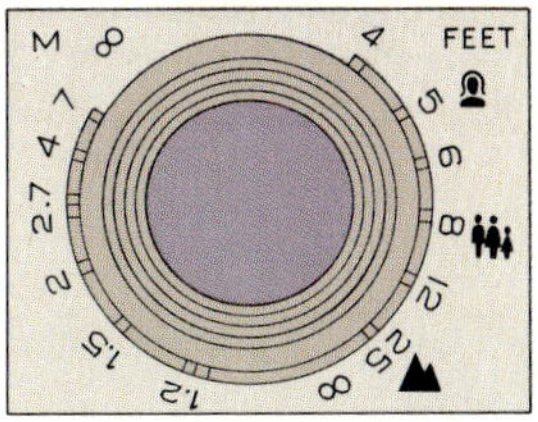

Split circle

Place the circle over a vertical line in your main subject. If the line is not continuous, right, the subject is out of focus. Roll the focus wheel until the line re-unites, and is continuous, as shown by the faint lines, right.

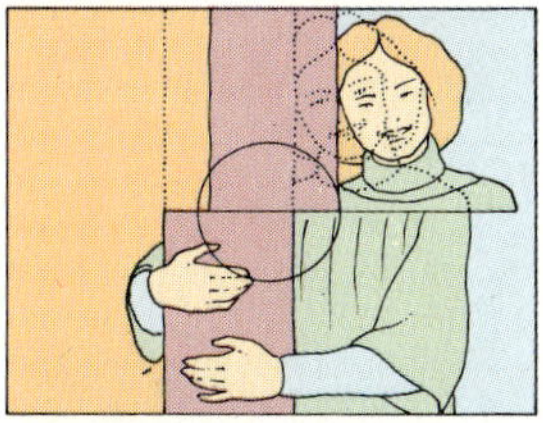

Zoom circle

Some models have a zoom circle in the finder to help you focus. This changes size as you move the focus slide. When the circle exactly fits around your subject's head (with adults), your picture is correctly focused.

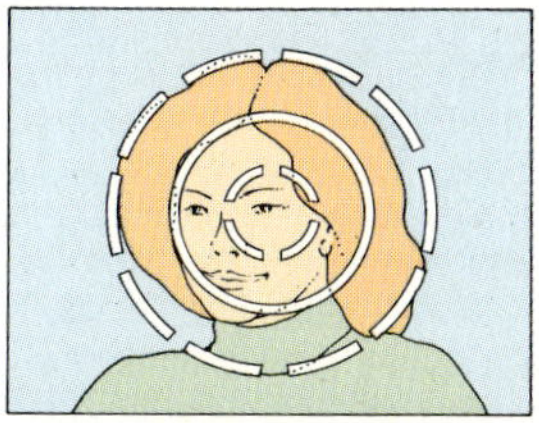

Focusing results

A well focused picture presents the main subject in clear outline and shows good detail, as in the picture far right. In bright light, your picture should be sharp overall. But in dim light, you may get only the main subject sharp, and the rest blurred. A badly focused picture will have fuzzy edges on the main subject and appear indistinct all over, as shown above right. With a direct vision camera you cannot take sharp pictures closer than 4 ft (1.2 m). SLR cameras give a sharp picture as close as 11 ins (28 cm). With an autofocus model, you must wait for the lens to stop moving before pressing the shutter all the way down, or your picture will be blurred. The camera will focus on the nearest large object in the center of the frame. If your subject moves, don't forget to reset the lens.

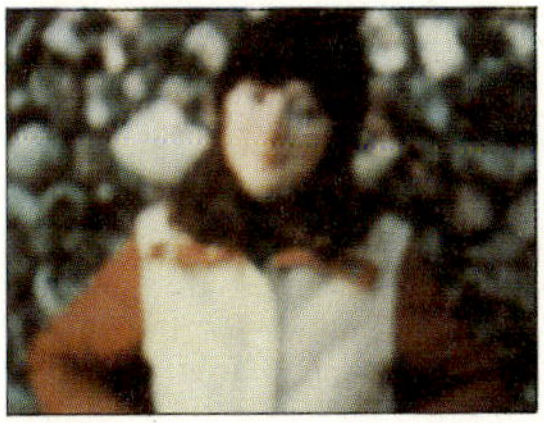

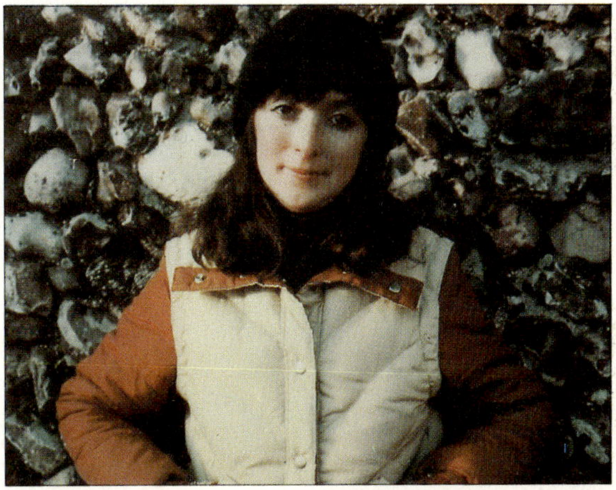

Viewing checks

Unwanted elements

Look around the frame and make sure that you have not included any objects in the background which could spoil the shot, or give an odd effect. The camera faithfully records every element of a scene, whereas you notice only the subject that interests you. A common picture-taking error is to have some object, such as a lamp, apparently growing out of someone's head, as in the top picture, right. You can avoid this by moving your camera position, as for the lower picture.

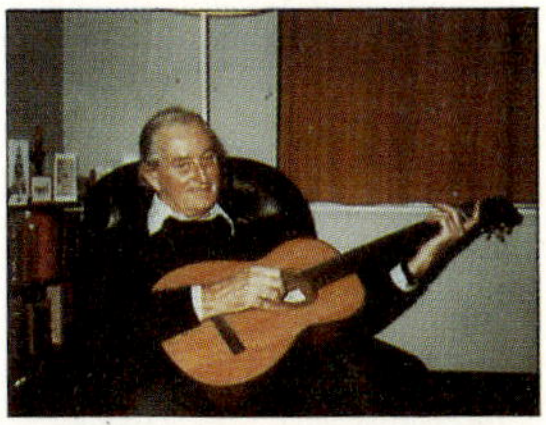

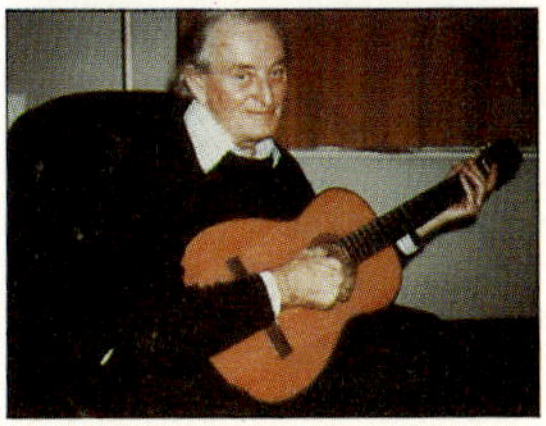

Backgrounds

Check that you have chosen a simple background at the right distance from your subject. If the background is too far from your main subject, particularly with flash, much of your picture will be dark. An elaborate or confusing background will overpower most subjects, as in the top picture, right. Only choose this sort of background if it suits the subject. In order to avoid a confusing background you should either move in close, or alter your position or your camera angle, as in the lower picture.

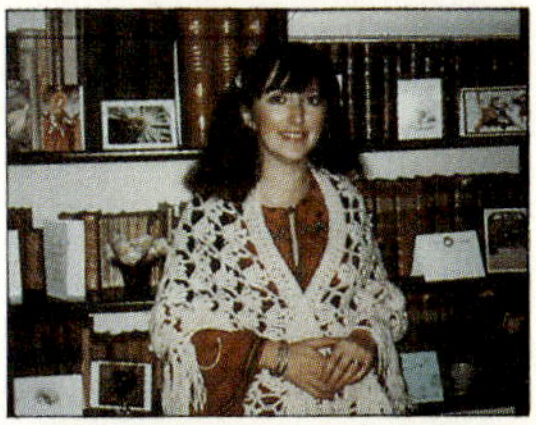

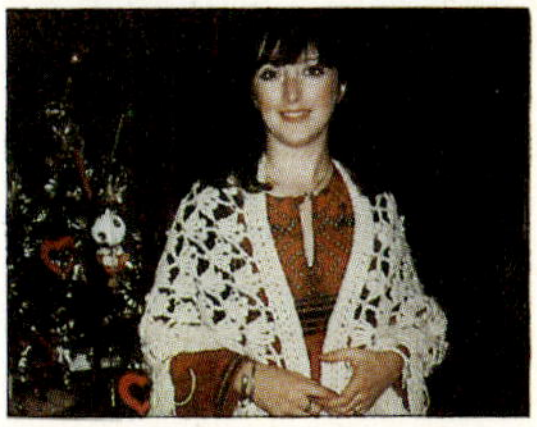

Getting the right exposure

After you have framed and focused your picture, you are ready to expose the film. The electric eye measures the light in your subject, and the camera sets the lens opening (aperture) and shutter speed so that the right amount of light reaches the film when you press the shutter release. When a slow speed is set, the shutter is open long enough for subject or camera movement to cause blur. Some cameras give a low light warning (slow speed) and you should use flash, or use a tripod and keep the subject still. A large aperture also affects the image – less of it will be sharp, and foreground/background may be blurred. Focus accurately in dim light and keep your background close to the subject if you want it to be sharp. The lighten/darken control allows you to vary exposure, to compensate for the effects of temperature (pp.62 and 69) or lighting conditions which mislead the eye, as shown on the facing page.

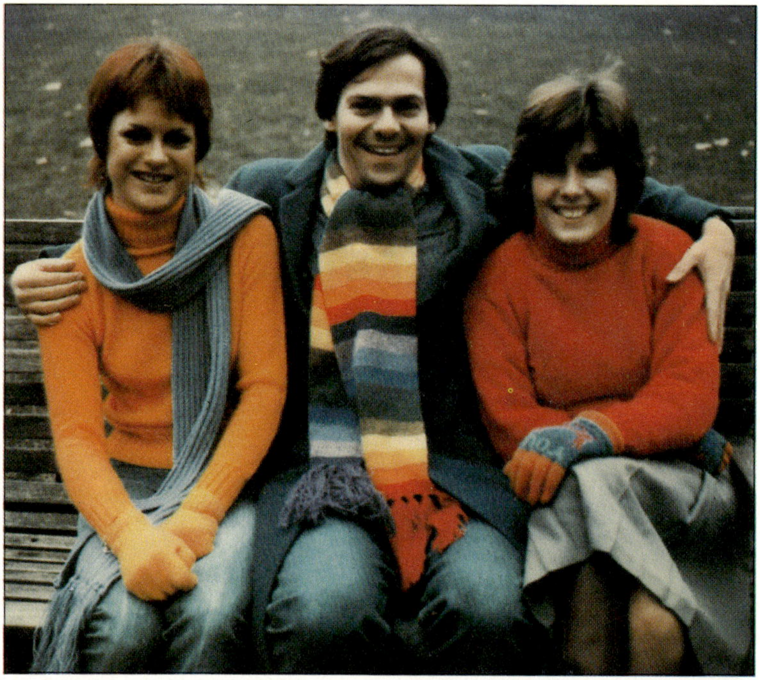

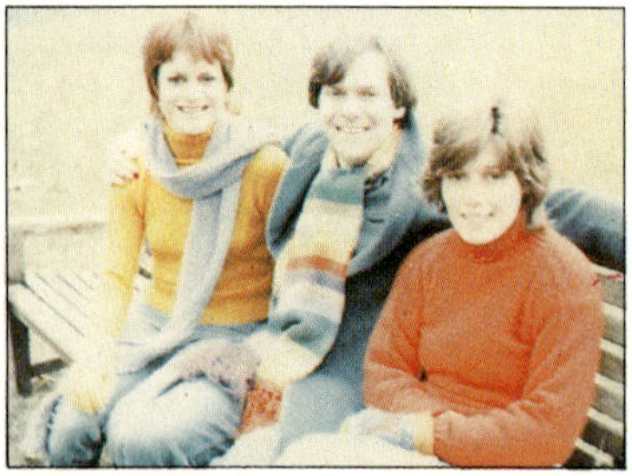

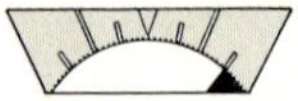

Lighter
To take a lighter picture, move the control toward lighten. Remember to move the control back to the center position after taking the picture.

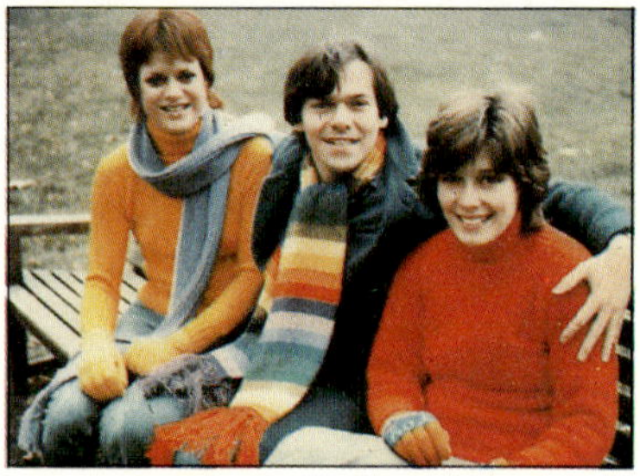

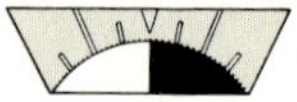

Normal
The center position is correct in most situations. Study the light in your subject and background (see facing page) before using the L/D control.

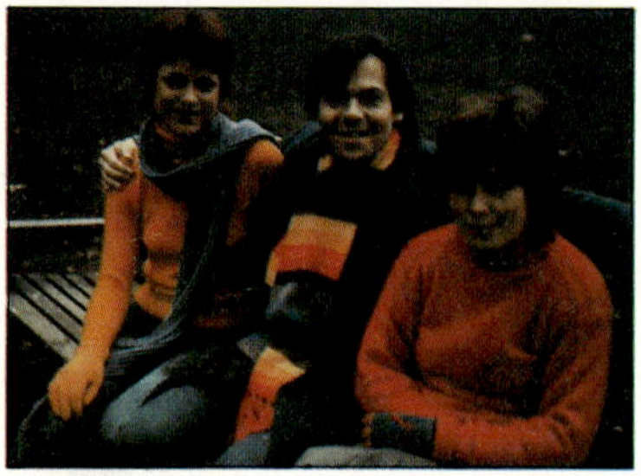

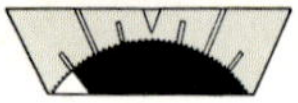

Darker
To take a darker picture, move the control toward darken. Move it back to the center once you have taken your picture. A darker picture can be dramatic (p.51).

Back-lighting
Subjects lit from behind will fool the electric eye – it will set the exposure to cope with the bright background light, and your subject will be dark (underexposed), above right. To avoid this, set the L/D control toward lighten, below right, or change your position so that the light is behind you. But if your subject would be effective as a silhouette, take advantage of back-lighting, and leave the L/D control at normal. Results can be dramatic, far right.

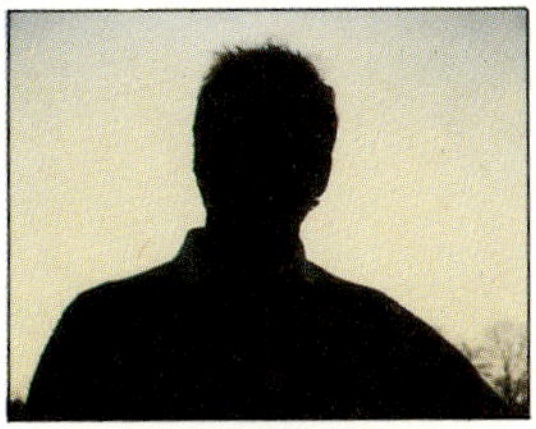

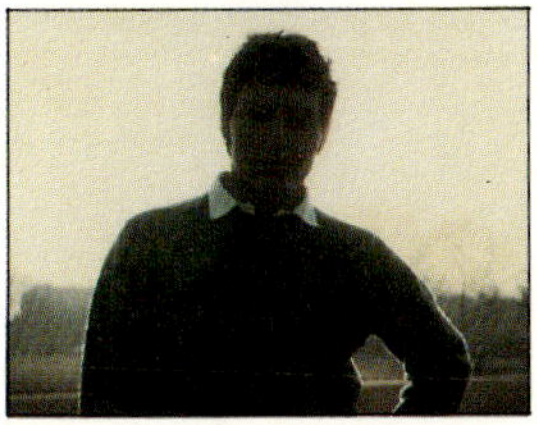

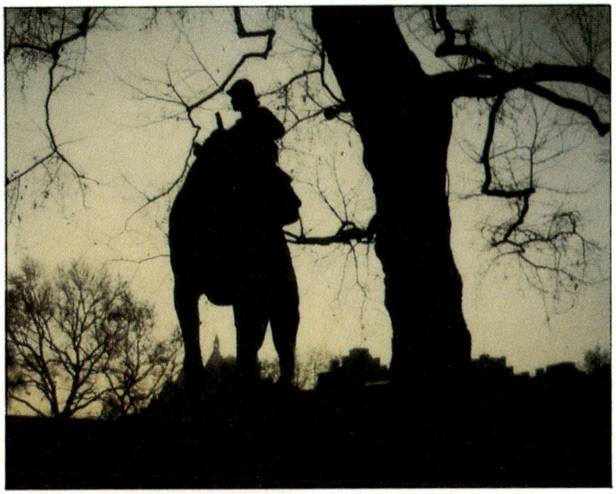

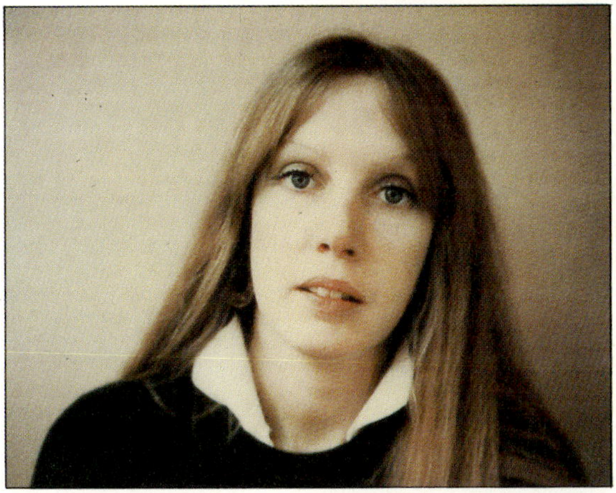

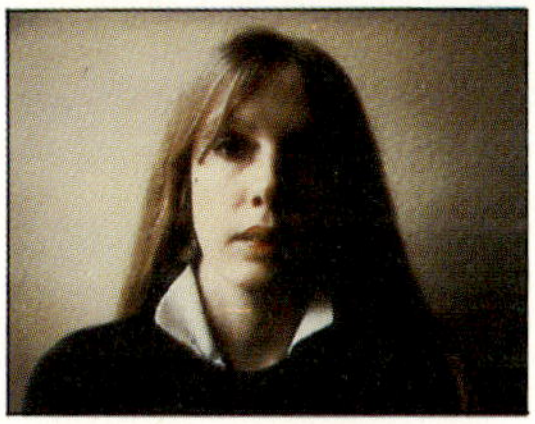

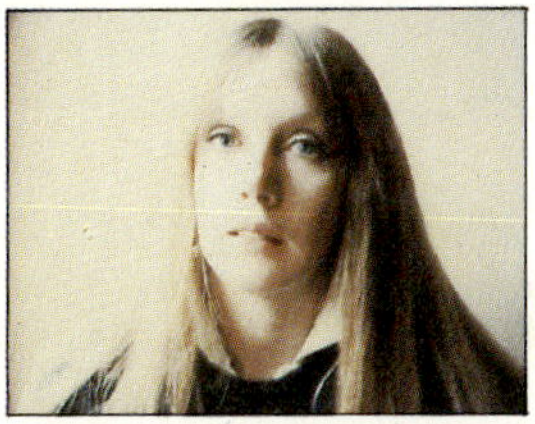

High contrast
If you have very light and very dark elements in one subject it may fool the electric eye and/or be beyond the capabilities of the film (p.37). To avoid a picture with under- or overexposed elements you must reframe your picture (for example, move in close to eliminate most of the background). In the shots, left, the range of light is too great. As a result some areas lose detail, at both L/D settings. You should change your position or your camera angle, far left, to get a better result.

Dark backgrounds
A background that is too dark will "fool" the electric eye – it will set the exposure for the background and you will get a pale, overexposed subject. Large areas of shadow in the background may have the same effect. To avoid the result, top right, set the lighten/darken control toward darken, far right, or move in close in order to eliminate the background, as in the picture below right. (Very light backgrounds, such as white, brightly lit walls, may have the opposite effect. The subject will be too dark.)

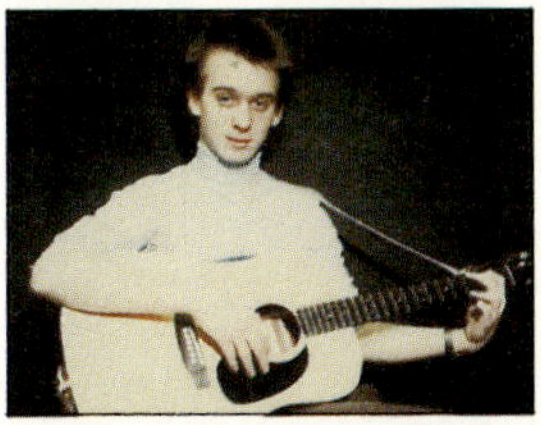

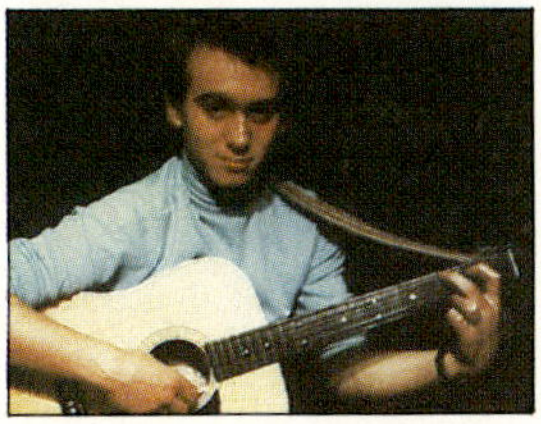

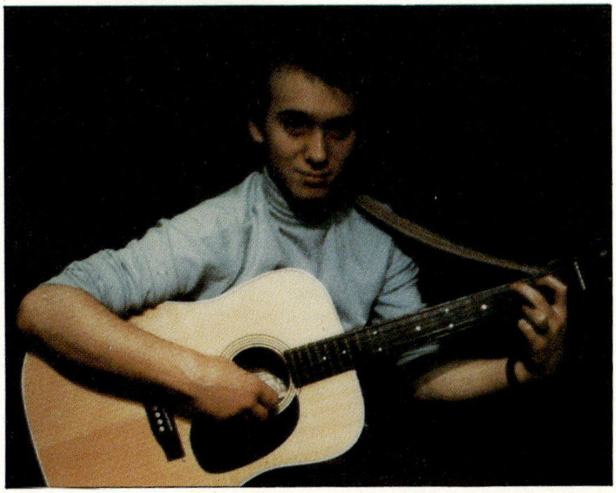

Flash – how it works

A flash attachment for your camera allows you to take pictures anywhere, day or night. For most indoor color shots you must use flash to get good results. Outdoors, you can use it to brighten a dull or shadowed scene. If you use flash often, buy a compatible electronic flashgun: it will light the subject more evenly than a cube or bar, and prove more economical per shot. Some Kodak cameras have electronic flash built in. With the peel-apart system, you can only use flash cubes.

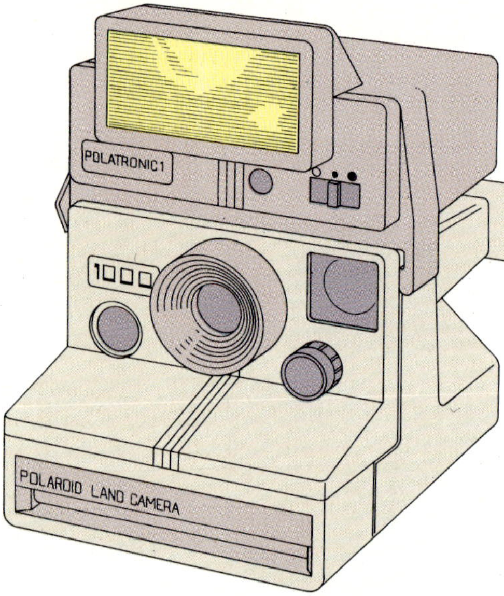

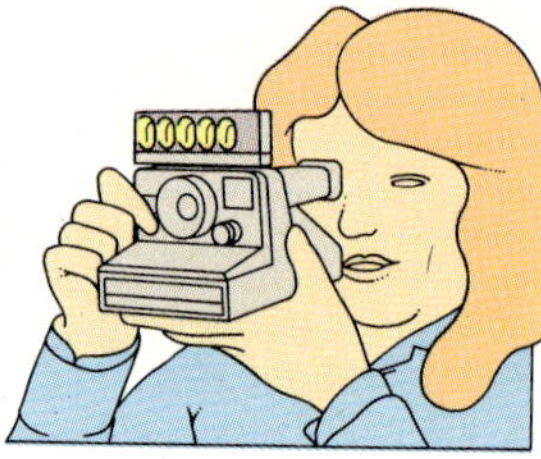

Choosing flash
Most instant cameras give you a choice between flash bars, above, or a compatible gun which fits on the camera, left. Some cameras take one type of cube only. Before buying, check which type and model of flash your camera will accept.

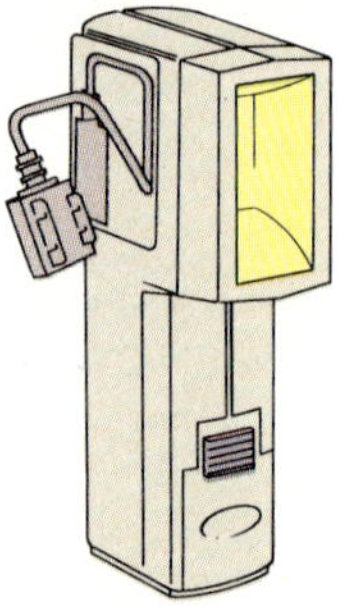

Flashguns
Consult your camera manual before choosing a gun – an incompatible model can damage your camera. Most guns have a firing interval of about 10 seconds, with fresh batteries. In some cases there is an L/D control on the gun.

Renewing batteries
Guns require batteries, and give about 100 flashes per set. (Built-in flash takes power from the camera batteries.) If the firing interval slows down, renew the batteries. Match the + and — marks to those in the battery compartment.

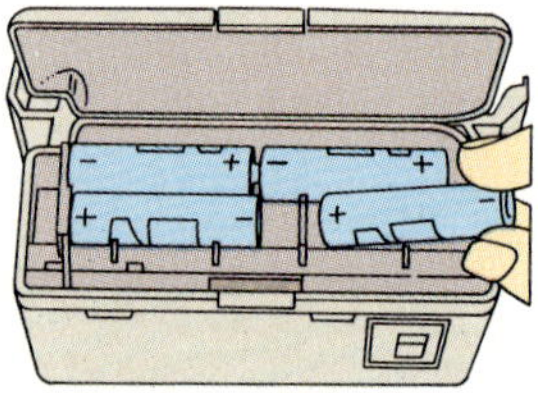

Flash cubes and bars
Cubes hold 4 bulbs and rotate automatically. Bars hold 8 or 10 bulbs, and you turn them around after 4/5 shots. With Philips' flipflash bars you can fire 2 or 3 bulbs at once. You can buy a diffuser, shown below, for flash bars, to cut down glare. Cameras that take cubes may have a flash shield built in.

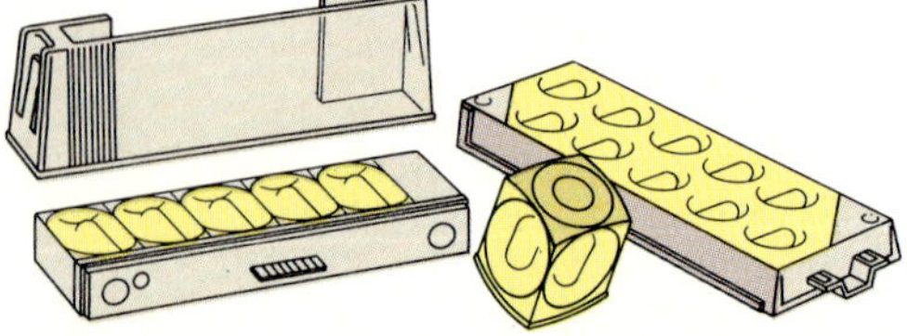

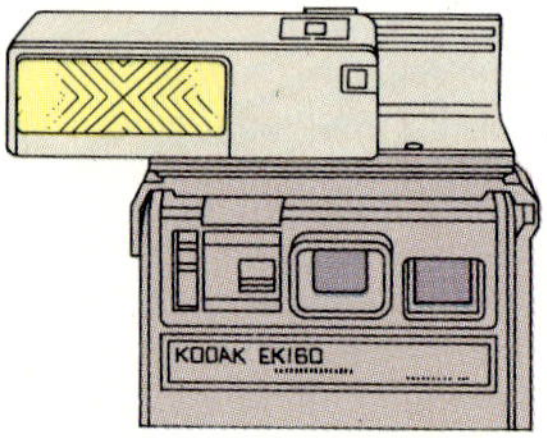

Turning on the flash
Some guns and built-in units have a simple on/off switch. Others slide out to the side of the camera (this helps to cut out "red eye", facing page). Be sure to switch off your flashgun when you finish shooting.

Ready light
Most guns and built-in units have a ready light which begins to glow when your flash is fully charged. If it is slow to light, replace the batteries.
Always wait for the ready light before pressing the shutter for a flash shot.

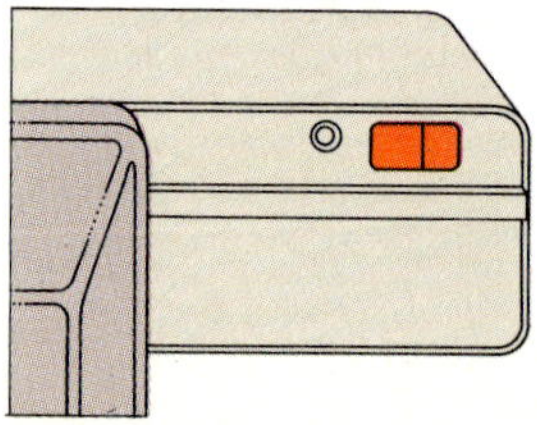

Flash faults

Reflections

Avoid reflective surfaces, like windows or mirrors, in the background – the resulting glare spot may spoil your picture, right. If you cannot avoid a shiny background, take the shot from an oblique angle.

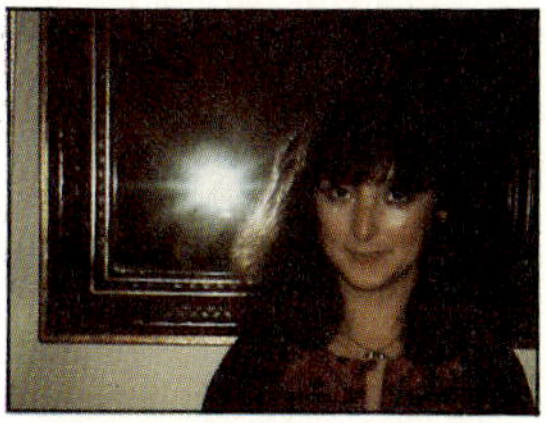

Red eye

Flash portraits may show bright red eyes, as right – the flash has reflected off the retina of the eye. The effect is worst in dim light. To minimize it, shoot in a brightly lit area, and ask your subject to look slightly away.

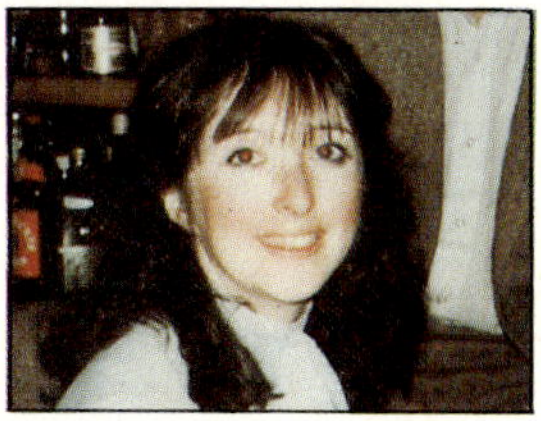

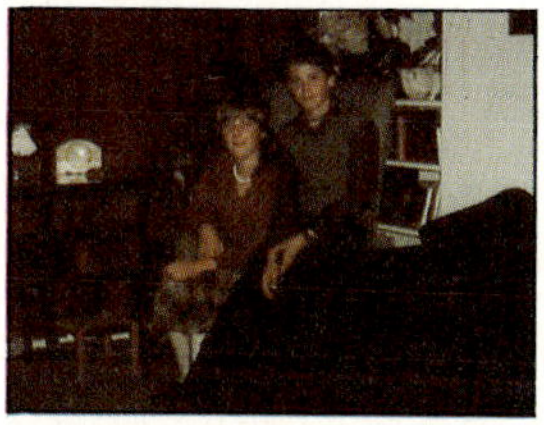

Too far away

Generally, flash will not give enough light to scenes more than 10 ft (3 m) away. The picture will be dark and your L/D control will not be able to correct this. If you cannot move in closer, use a long exposure on a tripod (pp.44–5), instead of flash.

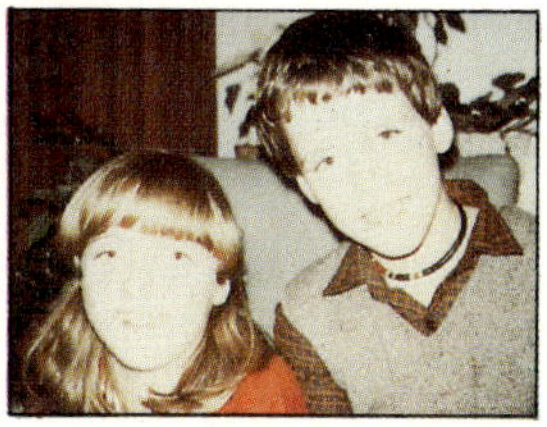

Too close

In general, you cannot use flash closer than 4 ft (1.2 m). The picture will look bleached out and foggy, and you will hurt people's eyes. But, SLRs with a gun and diffuser allow you to take flash close-ups down to 11 ins (26 cm).

Flash quality

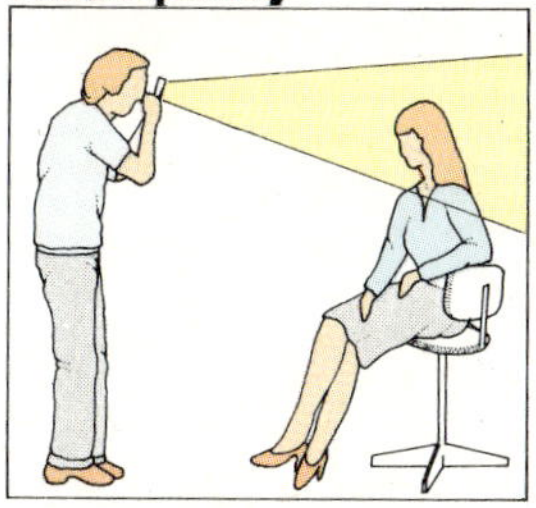

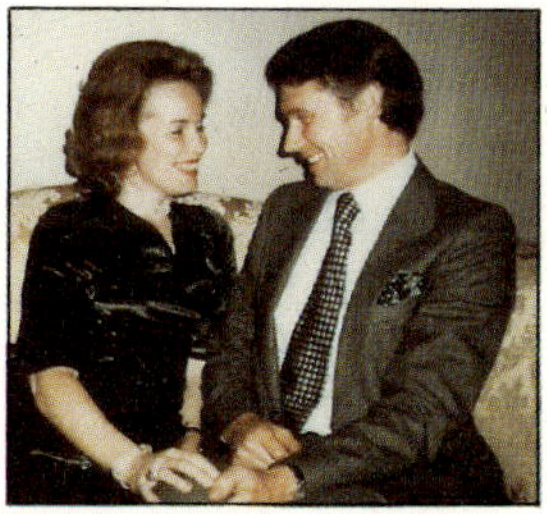

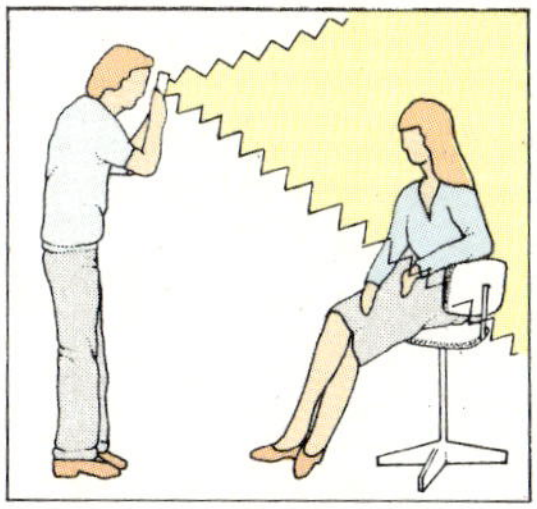

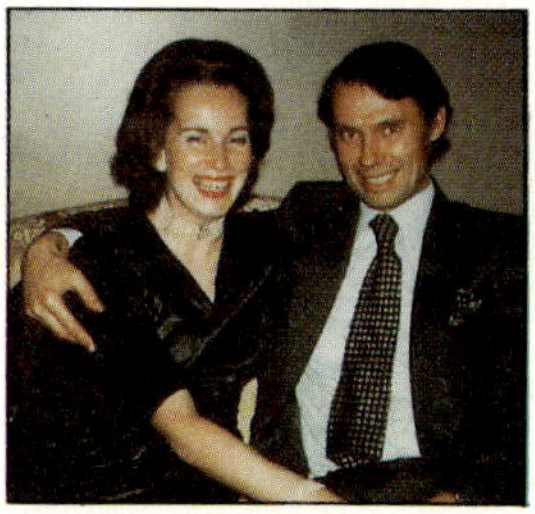

Direct flash

Direct (undiffused) flash can be harsh. The light travels straight toward the subject, as shown above, and reflects back off pale or shiny areas. The flash has the same quality as bright sunlight. Like the sun, it shows up strong colors, but bleaches pale colors and skin tones, and may produce ugly, black shadows as above.

Diffused flash

A diffuser scatters the light from your flash, as shown above, giving softer, more even illumination. Soft light is important for instant pictures, especially for portraits. Shadows are less obtrusive, and pale areas stronger. Cubes and bars have their own diffusers. With a gun, use a tissue over the flash. You can also buy "softlight" guns.

Flash range chart

Flash range – the distance within which the flash will illuminate your subject correctly – varies according to your camera and flash unit. Within this range, flash "fall-off" (p.35) may make subjects further away appear darker than those close up. Focusing cameras may adjust exposure to suit the flash-subject distance, so focus carefully. Hi-Power cubes, or two flipflash bulbs fired at once, give you $3\frac{1}{2}$ ft (1 m) more than normal. It is dangerous to fire bars or cubes when the subject is less than 4 ft (1.2 m) away.

Cameras	Cubes	Bars	Guns
Polaroid Peel-apart range	● 4–8 ft (1.2–2.4 m)		
Polaroid 1000/ One-Step range		● 4–8 ft (1.2–2.4 m)	● 4–8 ft (1.2–2.4 m)
Polaroid 2000/ Pronto! range		● 4–9 ft (1.2–2.7 m)	● 3–12 ft (1–3.7 m)
Polaroid SX70 Alpha range		● 4–12 ft (1.2–3.7 m)	● 11 ins–12 ft (26 cm–3.7 m)
Kodak cameras		● 4–9 ft (1.2–2.7 m)	● 4–9 ft (1.2–2.7 m)

Before you press the shutter

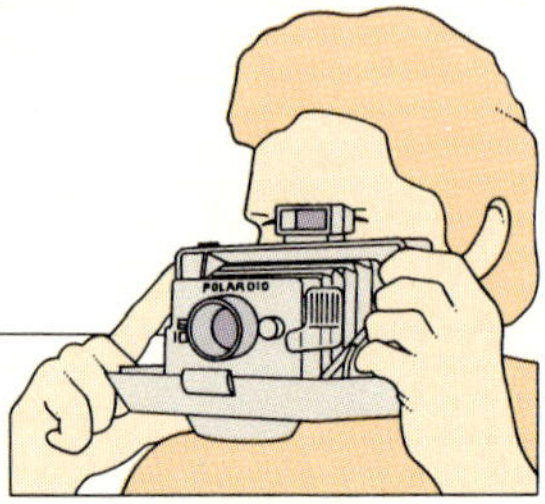

S

Set the controls

There is no focus control to worry about with fixed focus or autofocus cameras. On other cameras make sure that you have set the distance scale/rotated the focus wheel (p.19) to get a sharp picture. Check that your L/D control is set correctly, and that you have set the correct ASA (p.8) to match your film.

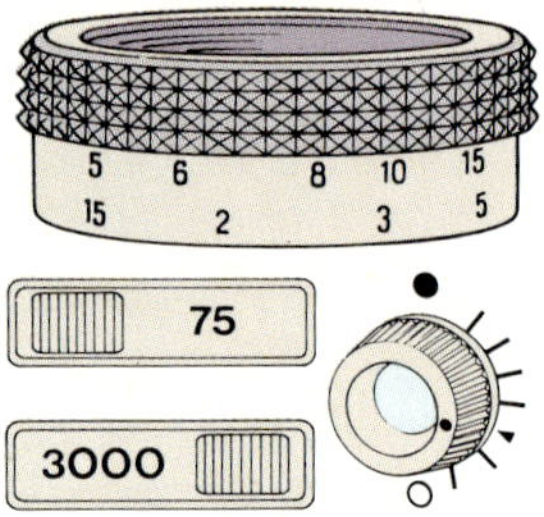

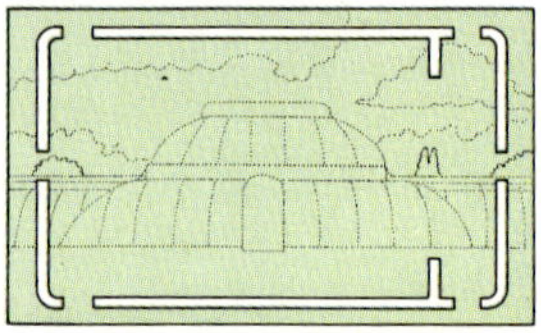

N

Nothing obscuring view

Make sure that you are not obscuring the camera's viewing and exposure system. If you cover the lens or electric eye with your finger/the camera strap you will get an obscured or black picture. You should also check that you are not blocking the bellows or exit slot, see facing page.

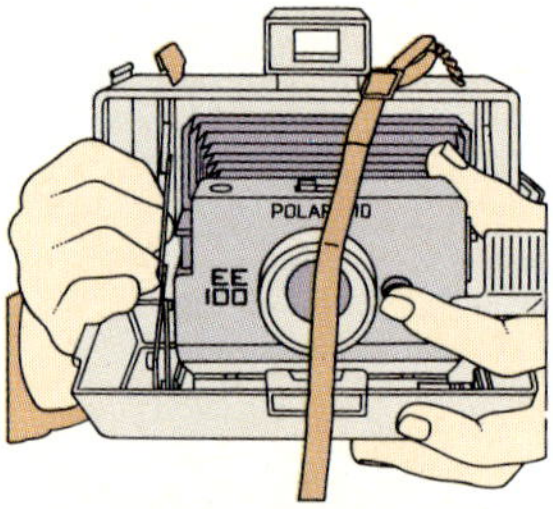

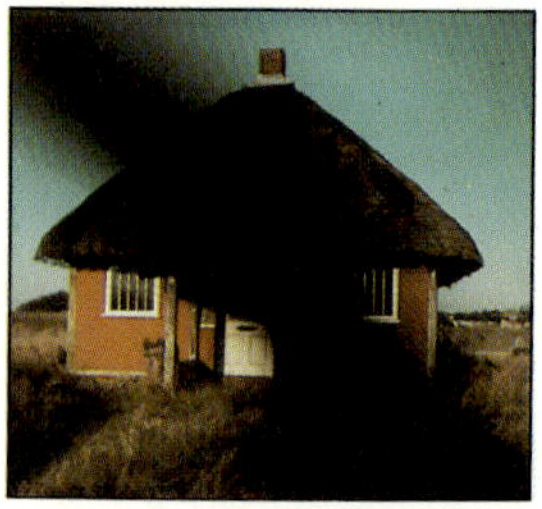

A

Aim accurately

Hold the camera steady (p.16) and frame your picture well (pp.18–19). Make sure that the horizon is straight in your picture – if it is crooked your camera is tilted. Watch out for distracting elements, such as trees growing out of heads or confusing backgrounds, that will spoil your picture.

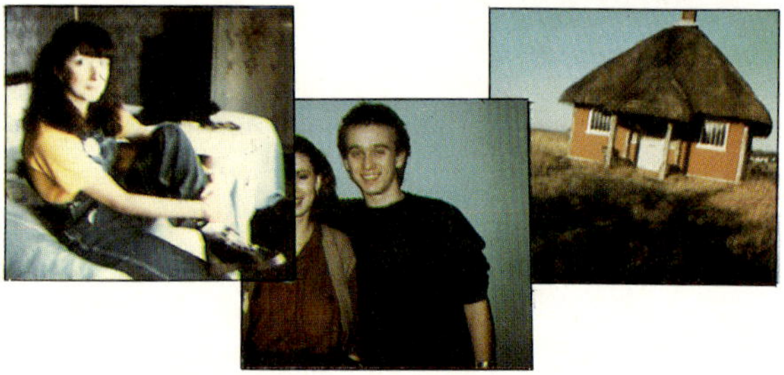

P

Press gently

You should hold your breath while you gently press the shutter release or you risk shaking the camera. With an autofocus model, press halfway to focus, then all the way to fire. If a red light (low light warning) appears as you start to press the shutter, use flash or a tripod.

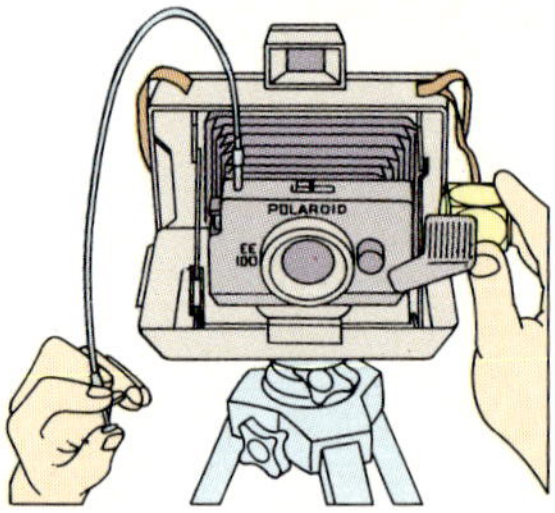

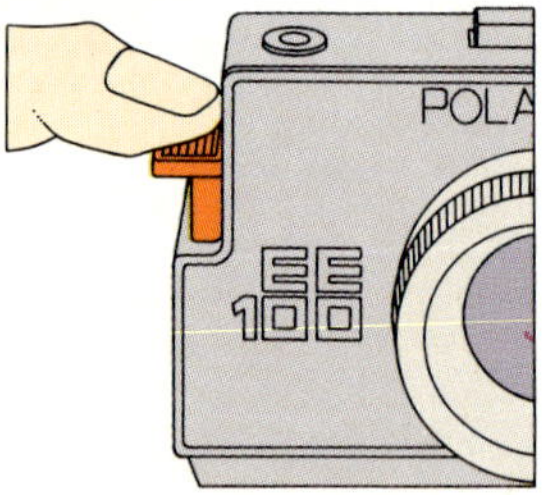

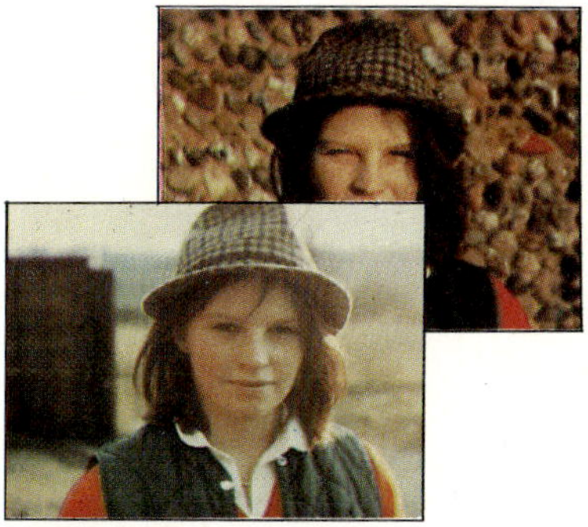

Check your subject
Place your subject against a simple background and make sure that her face is evenly lit and that she is not squinting.

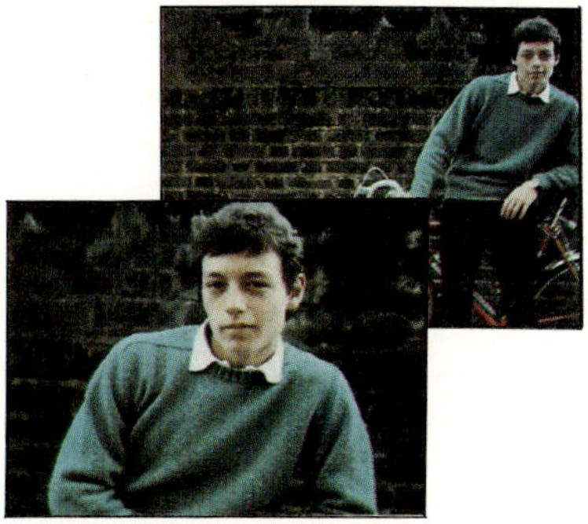

Check your composition
The simplest way to compose a good instant picture is to choose a colorful subject and make sure that it fills the center of the frame.

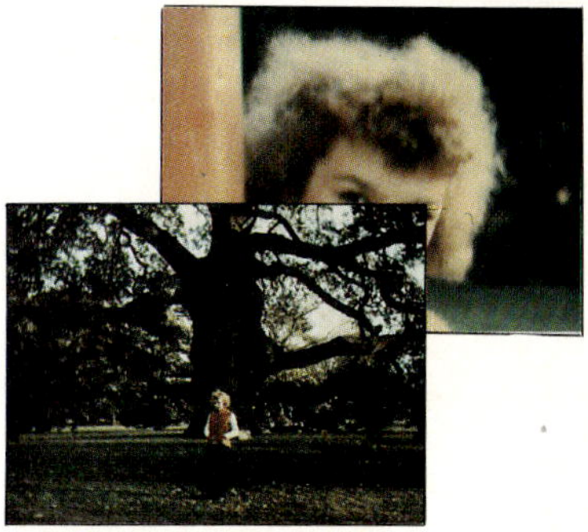

Check your distance
If you are too close, your subject may be out of focus (or too near the flash), too far and it may look too small (or be out of flash range).

Finger in the bellows
The bellows on SLR models are part of the camera's mechanism. If you obstruct the bellows, either your current or following shot will be fogged or completely white. Check the position of your hands before shooting.

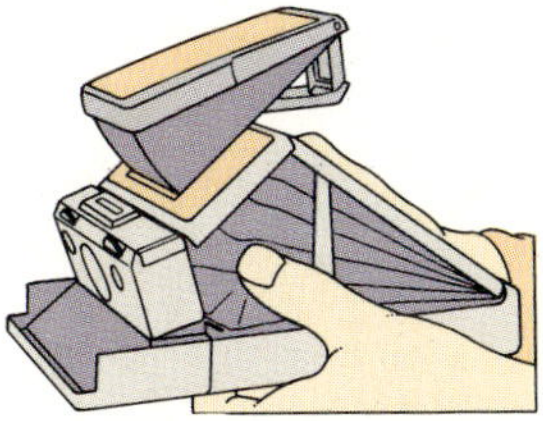

Finger over the exit slot
If your finger blocks the exit slot of an integral camera the picture may become jammed inside. To remove it, open the film door and rotate the rollers. The picture will probably be spoiled by creases or streaks across the image.

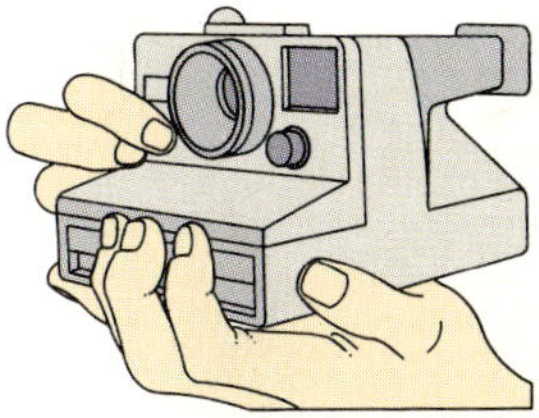

Shutter fails to work
There are several reasons why a shutter fails to work on an instant camera, see left, but the usual reason is that the batteries that power the camera are not working. With Kodak cameras and peel-apart Polaroid models you should change the batteries (pp.9 and 11). Polaroid integral models, on the other hand, are powered by a fresh battery in each film pack. If your film pack is faulty, remove it and insert an empty pack – reserve power in this pack will enable the camera to complete its cycle. *Now* insert a new film. (If you insert new film when the cycle is incomplete you may lose several shots.) Some models lock the shutter if the light is low: you should check your camera manual for full details.

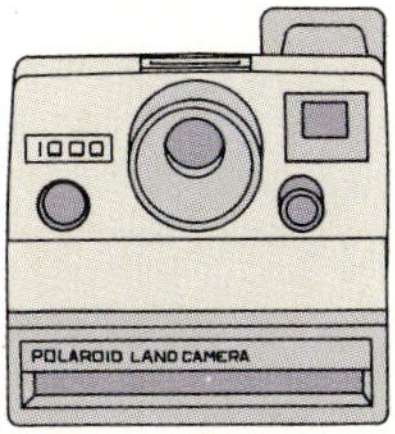

Polaroid 1000/One-Step
- Low light
- Flash faulty/finished
- No film in camera

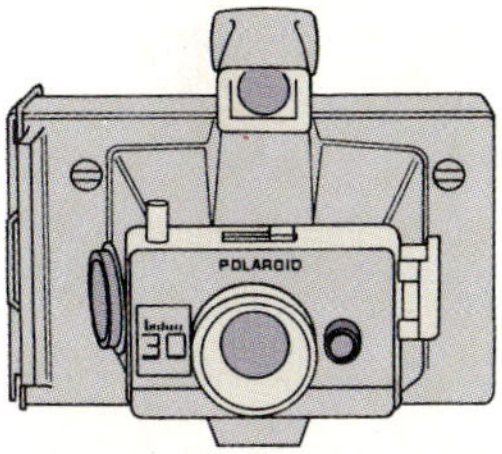

Polaroid 30/Minute Maker Plus
- Transport lock on
- Batteries dead

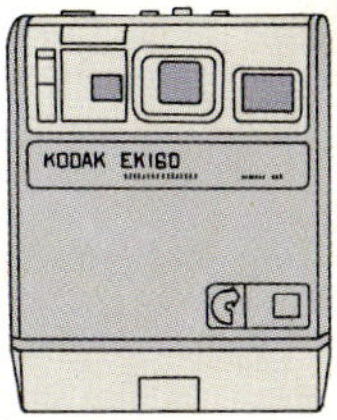

Kodak EK 160/ Colorburst 50
- Batteries dead
- Film pack empty

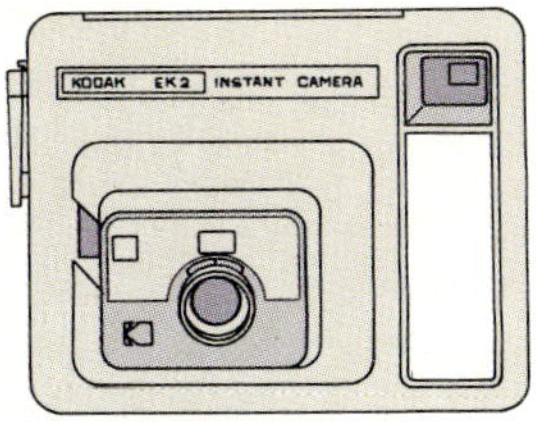

Kodak EK 2/Handle 2
- Batteries dead

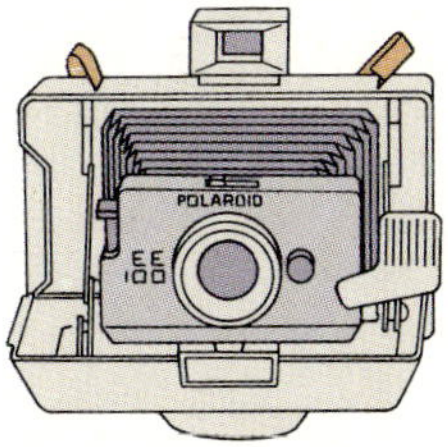

Polaroid EE100/The Reporter
- Batteries dead

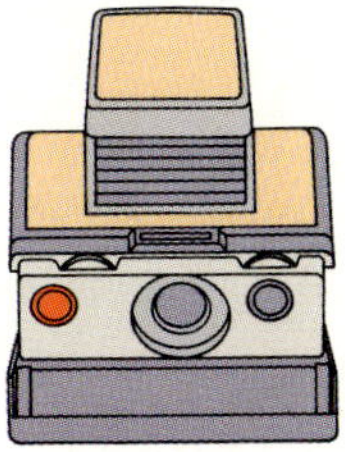

Polaroid SX70 Alpha
- Flash faulty/finished
- No film in camera

After you press the shutter

When your integral picture emerges from the camera, handle it by its white border. The picture area is white (Kodak) or off-white (Polaroid) at first. After 60 seconds the image starts to form, and five minutes later your instant picture is completely developed. Be careful not to bend or flex the print during or after development, or you will spoil the image. Follow the advice for mounting and storing prints given on pp.84–5.

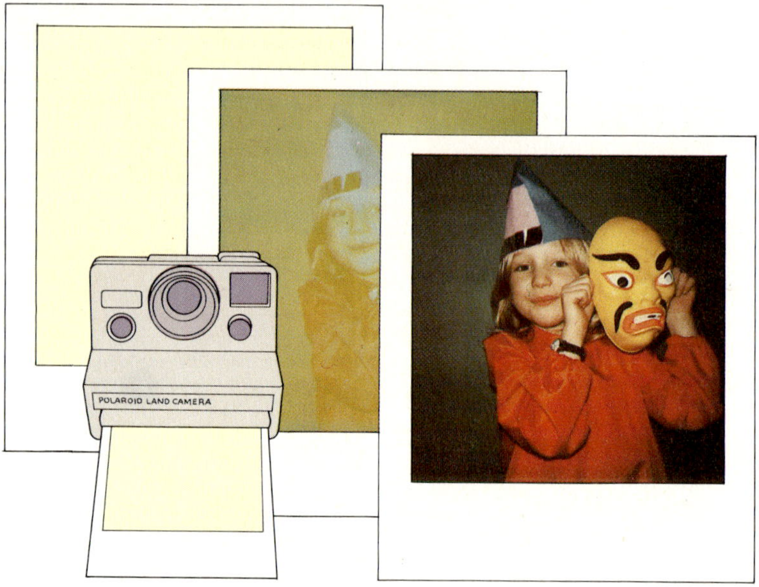

Peel-apart prints

Tab-pulling sequence
With peel-apart film you have to participate in the development process. Make sure the temperature is right (pp. 62 and 69), then follow the step-by-step instructions, right, for accurate development. Never pull the tabs at the bottom before those above. The correct tab-pulling sequence is 1–8, in order.

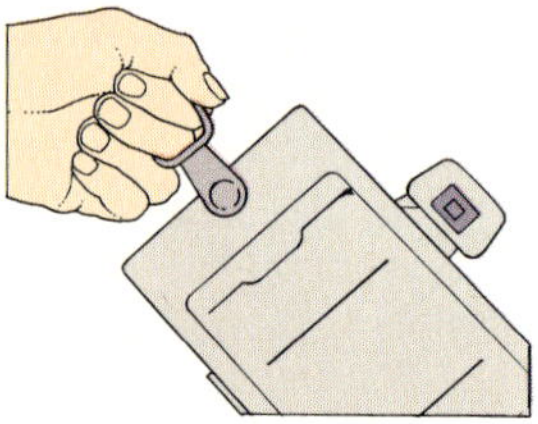

1 Hold your camera firmly by the ring or T handle on the back of the camera.

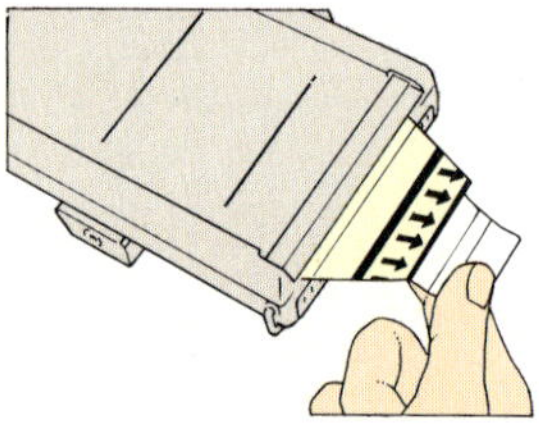

2 Grip the middle of the top white tab and, keeping it straight, pull it out smoothly.

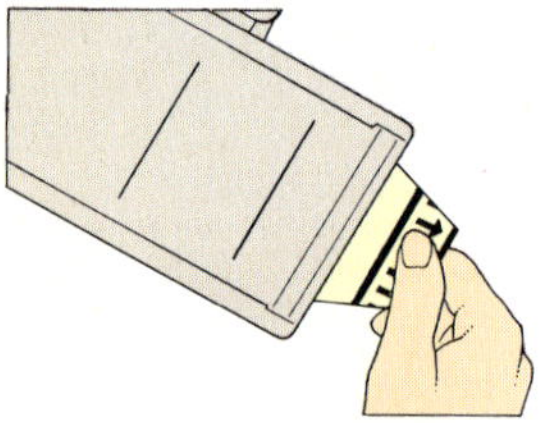

3 Grip the yellow tab in the middle. Pull it straight out in one slow, smooth movement.

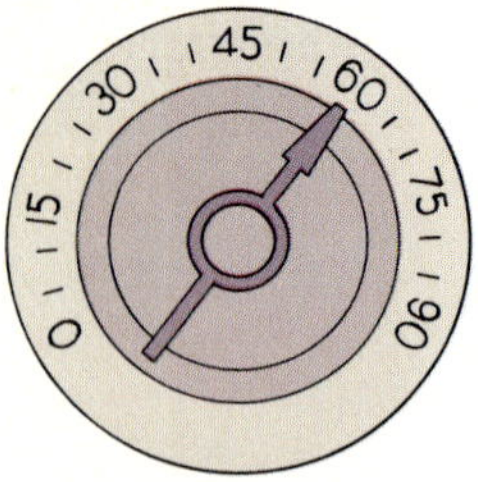

Developing color pictures
Set your clock for 60 seconds and start timing development immediately.

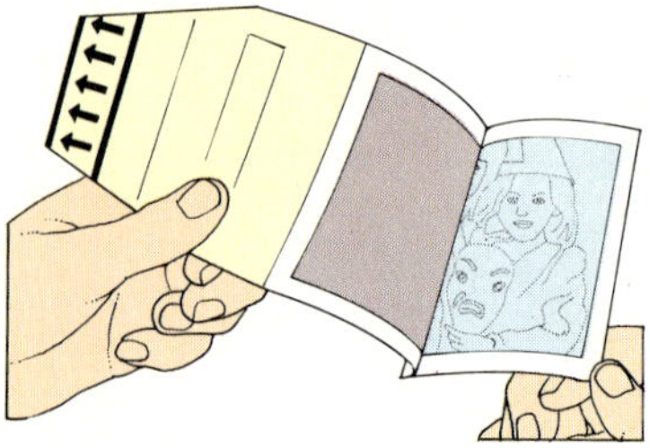

Peeling apart
When the time is up, peel off the backing paper for a finished print, right.

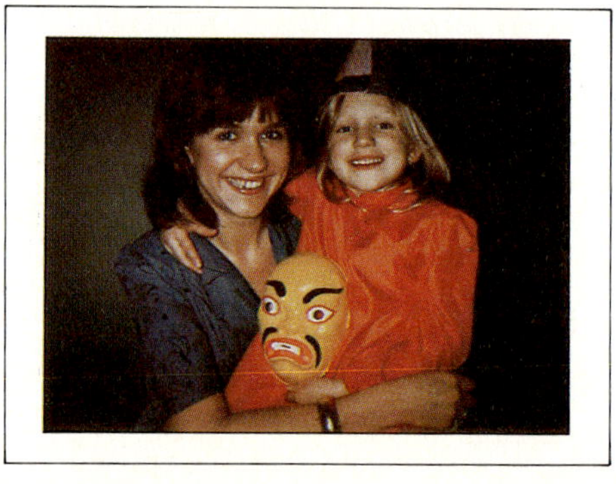

Print ejection faults
If the negative portion of the film alone comes out of a peel-apart camera, the picture paper has jammed inside. Open the camera and straighten the tabs, see below. If you get a picture with a mottled impression of a tab, or a black image or a line on one edge, far right, you have pulled the wrong tab. Always pull the white tab first, then the yellow tab. If a tab jams, do not pull another; correct as shown below. If you get the result, right, with an integral camera, you have blocked the exit (p.25) or cranked the handle unevenly (p.10).

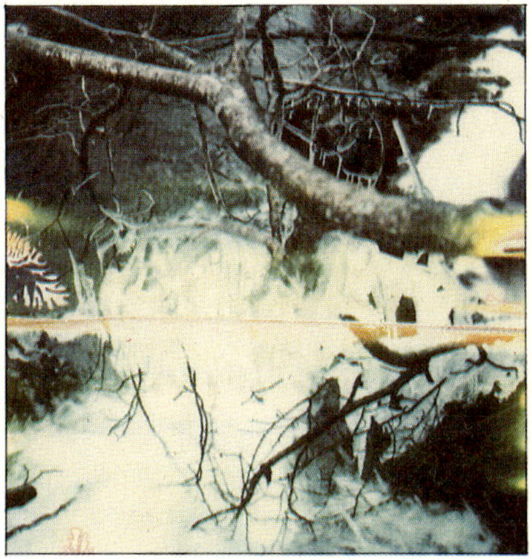

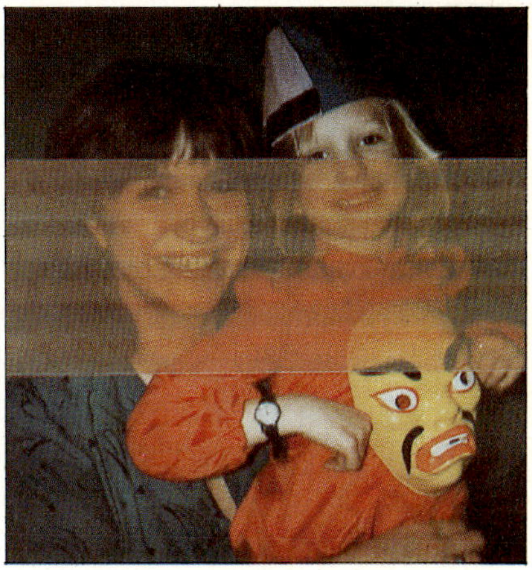

Correcting tab errors

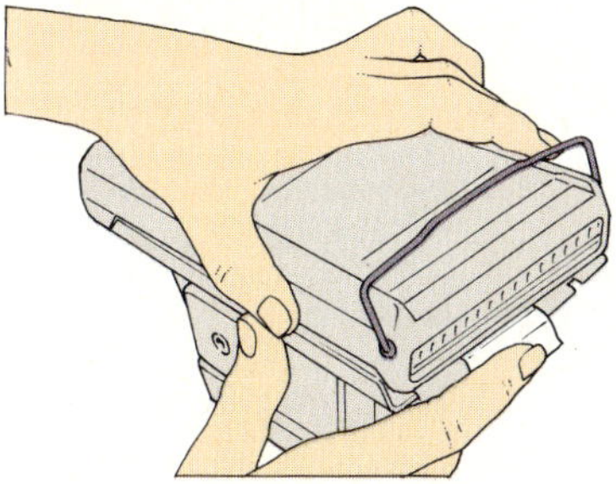

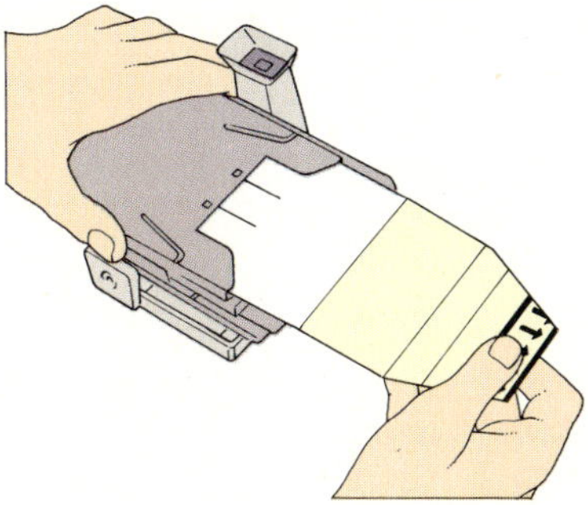

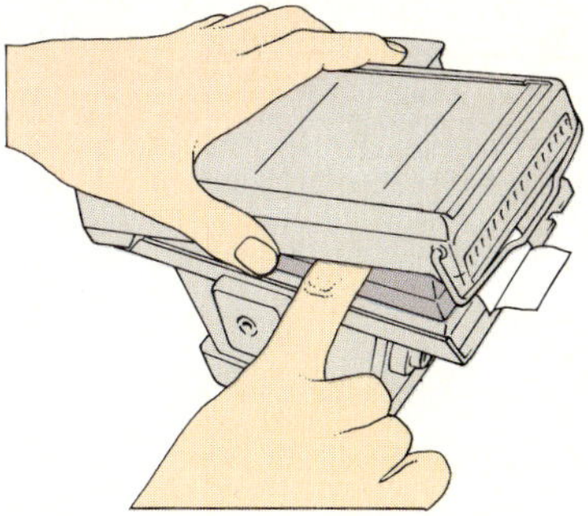

1 Open the camera in dim light, holding the edge of the film pack in position with your fingertip. Take care not to put pressure on the pack (p.14).

2 In the dark, remove the top yellow tab and any torn paper, as above. But in dim light keep the camera back partly closed, as above right. Clean the rollers (p.9).

3 Unfold the top white tab. Close the camera with all the white tabs sticking out between the camera front and the metal hinge.

Processing faults

Three very common processing faults are shown here. For information on several other faults see p.91. To avoid spoiling your pictures, follow these simple camera and film care tips: Always clean the rollers on peel-apart cameras before loading a new pack of film. Clean rollers on integral models at least once a year. Handle the film pack by its edges (p.14) and pull tabs in the right order.

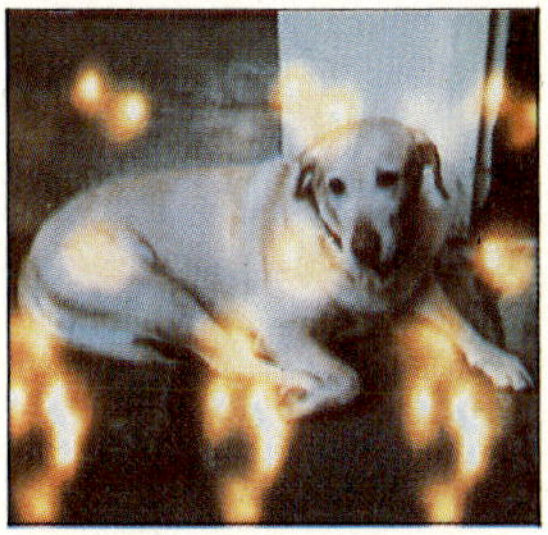

Dirt on the rollers
Specks or bars across the image are caused by dust and development fluid on the rollers. You must clean the rollers regularly.

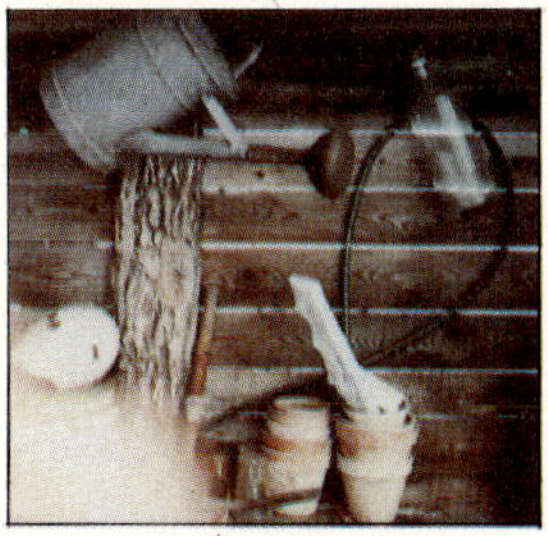

Pressure on the film
Never squeeze a film pack or you will lose part of your picture. Always hold the pack by its edges (see p.14).

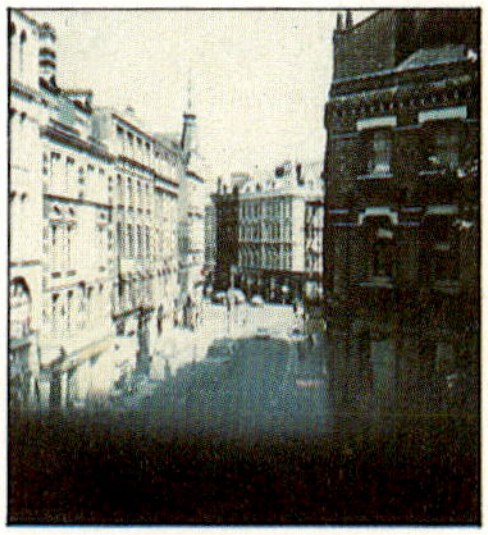

Fogged film
If light reaches the film you will get a whitish, fogged result. You should never open the film door in the light.

Choosing your viewpoint

There are endless ways of photographing a subject, so before you shoot, move around and examine it from different angles and heights. Notice how the image in your frame is affected. The background changes, and altered perspective influences the subject's shape. Whichever viewpoint you decide on, always make sure that your subject fills up the frame. The most obvious viewpoint of our subject, top right, was from the side, at normal height. The result is a straightforward record, but it lacks imagination. A closer view from the same angle, below right, fills the frame with color but it lacks impact. The oblique view, far right, gives the most dramatic, lively result.

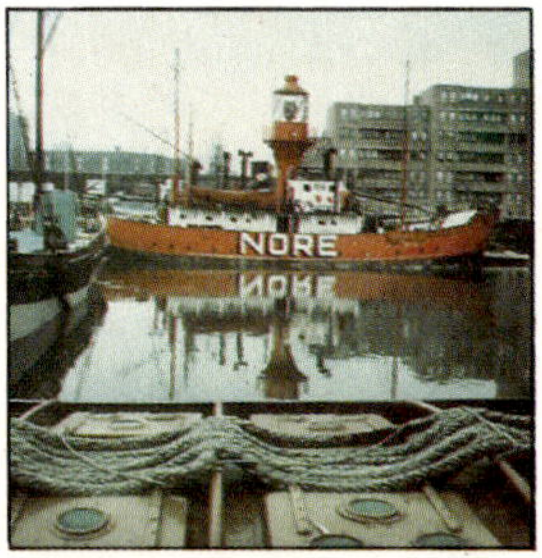

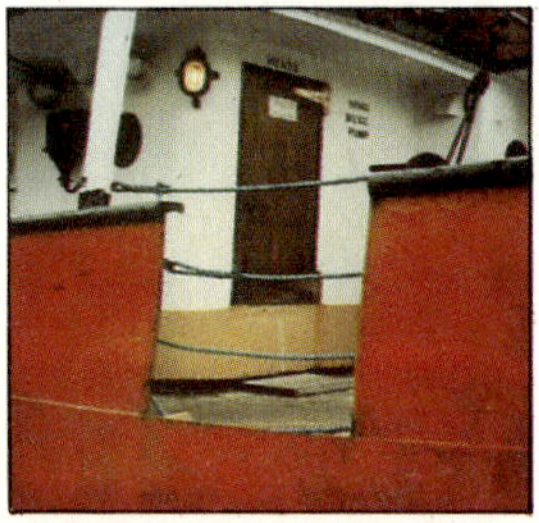

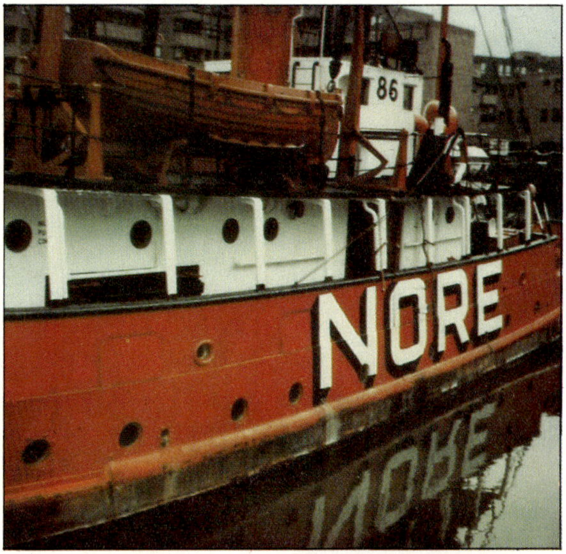

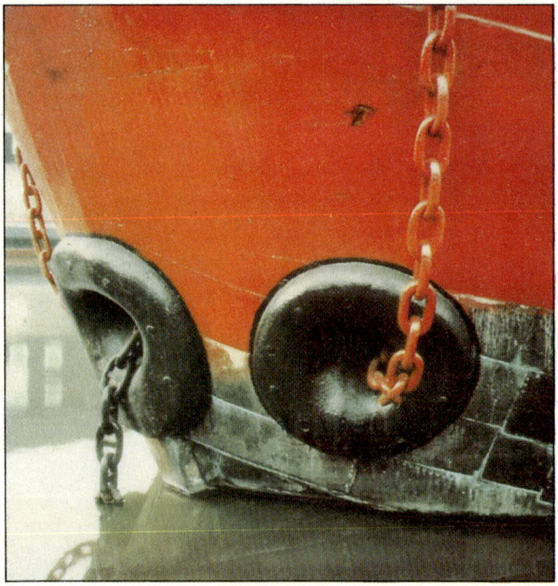

Unusual viewpoints
Use an unusual view to emphasize qualities or features of the subject that particularly appeal to you. Taking the boat from a low viewpoint, looking up, fills the frame with color and gives an impression of size and strength, as left. By contrast, a high viewpoint looking down, top right, has a busy atmosphere – it emphasizes the pattern and groupings on the deck. A head-on view at normal height, bottom right, flattens the boat – its verticals are exaggerated, but its shape is lost. In general, low and oblique views tend to dramatize a subject and steepen perspective whereas high views diminish a subject, but reveal unexpected pattern and groupings.

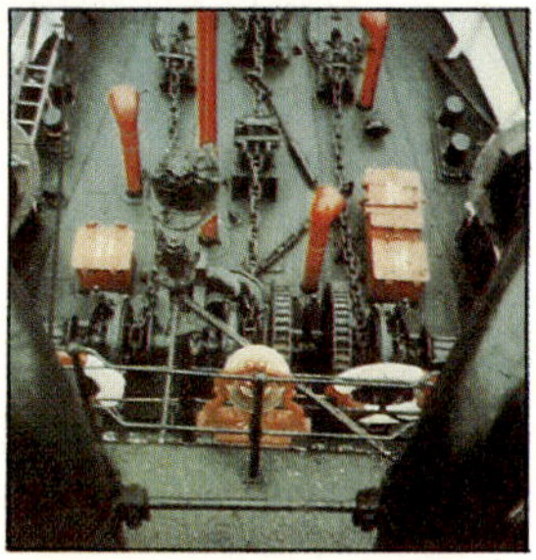

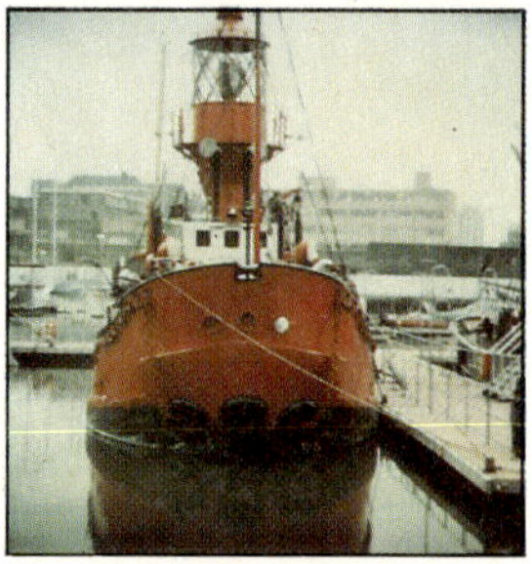

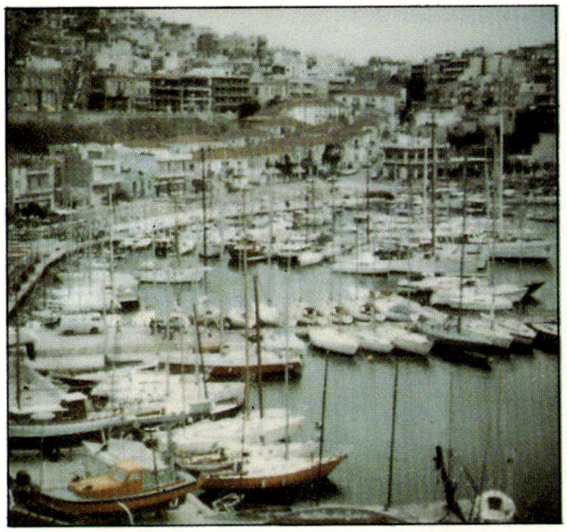

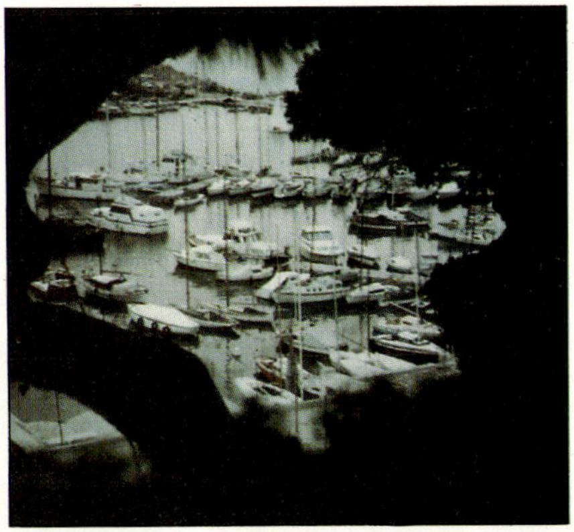

Viewpoint from a distance
A distant view of a scene is often very flat, particularly on a dull day, far left. If you get this type of result, look around for something, like the low-hanging foliage left, to frame your shot with. The irregular shape of the dark frame highlights the clusters of boats in the harbour, and turns the blue colors of an overcast day into a feature of the picture. Including a foreground object, figure, or frame adds depth to a distant scene.

Filling out the frame
The most effective instant pictures have a clearly defined subject, which fills the frame, against a simple background. When you are taking a middle distance view, right, it is difficult to avoid including extraneous objects in the frame, and getting a muddled result. Outdoors, make use of repetitive background shapes, below right, or foreground reflections, above right and far right, to fill out the frame. Indoors, make use of props – seat your subject in a high-backed chair, for example (see p.51).

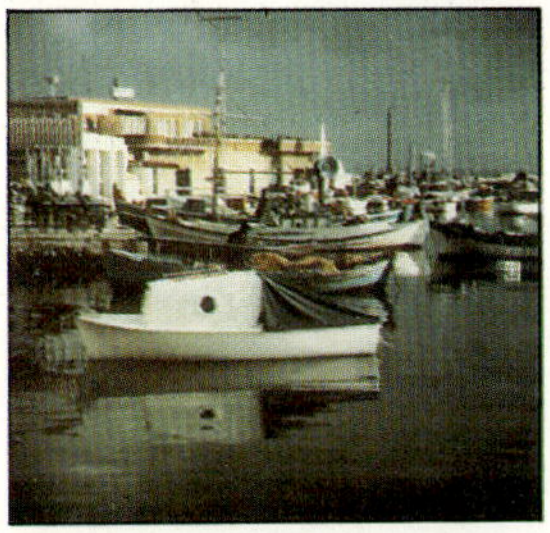

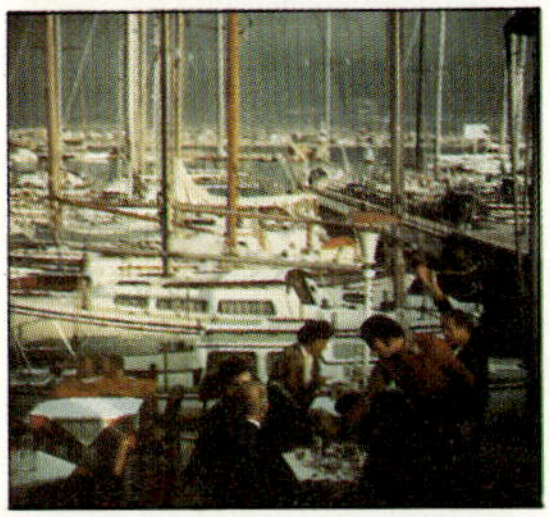

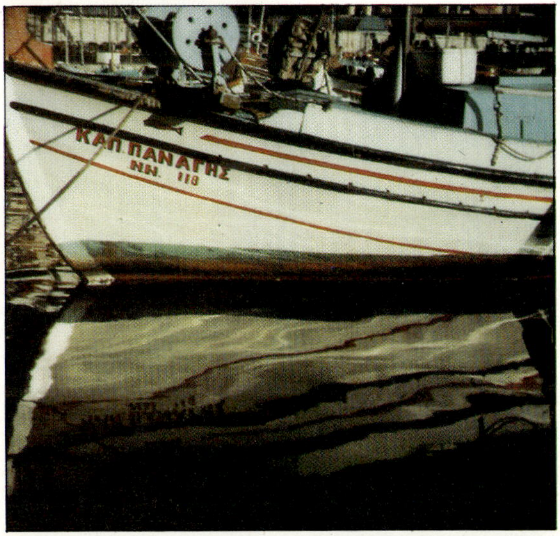

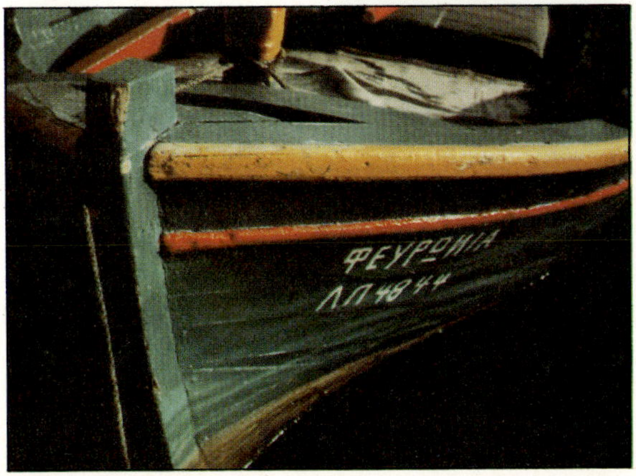

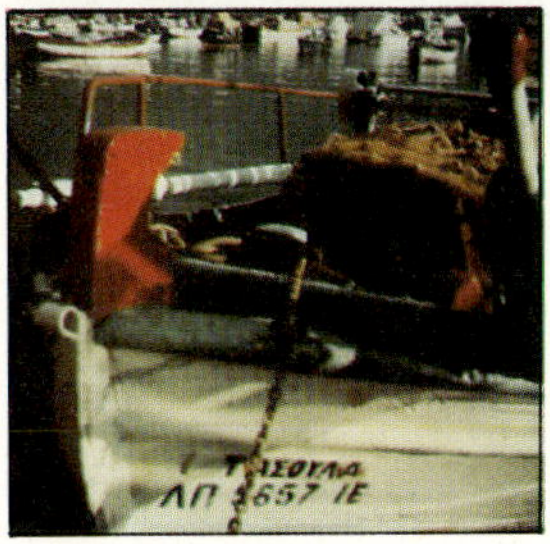

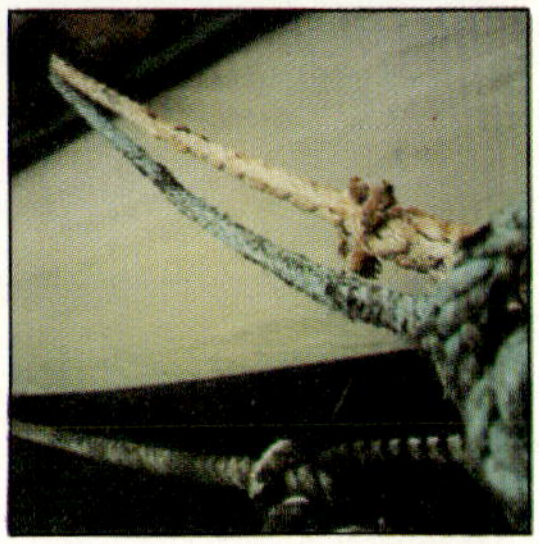

Close-ups
You may find, even after you have moved around the subject and examined it from different angles, that you cannot clear a muddled background. Instead of attempting to show all the subject, try moving in close and shooting one part only. Keep beyond your camera's minimum distance (p.79).

Composing your picture

Your instant pictures will be much stronger if you take care with composition. First consider different viewpoints (pp.28–9). Then decide where to place the main subject or point of interest within your picture – centrally or elsewhere – and check how it relates to the background. If your film is rectangular, you can hold the camera vertically or horizontally to suit the subject – with a square picture, try a diamond-shaped shot for fun. Look around the frame to see if you could improve the way the colors, shapes, lines, highlights and shadows work together. And wait for the right moment to shoot.

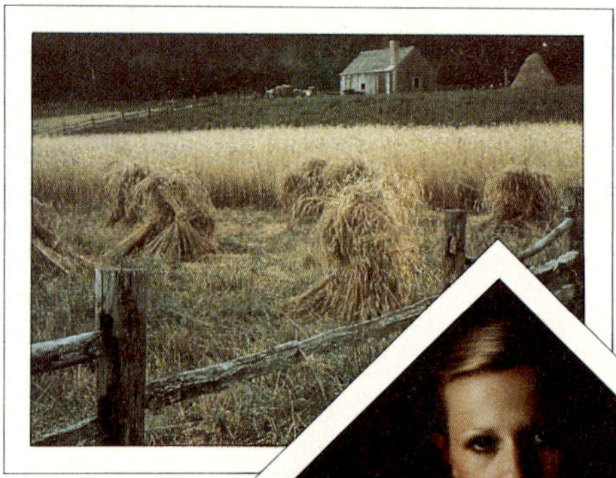

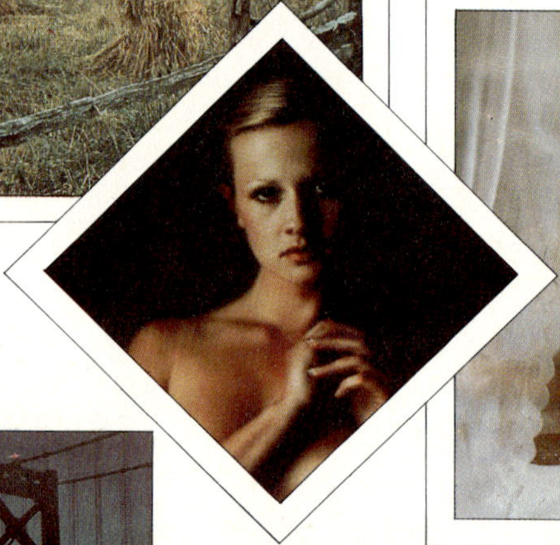

Choosing your framing
Choose your framing to echo the dominant shape or lines of your subject. This will enhance its mood, as these examples show.

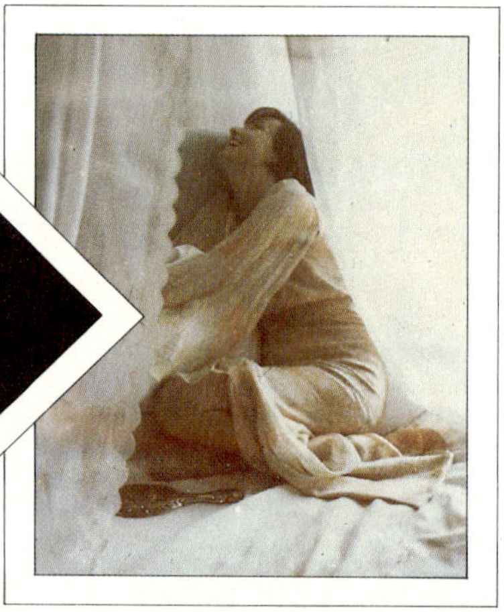

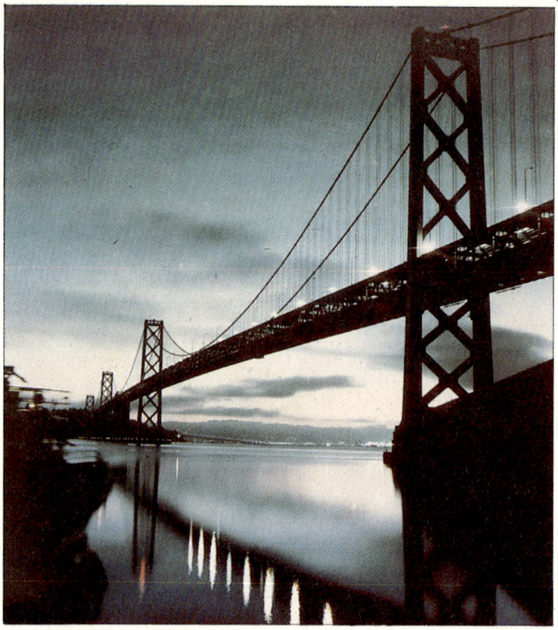

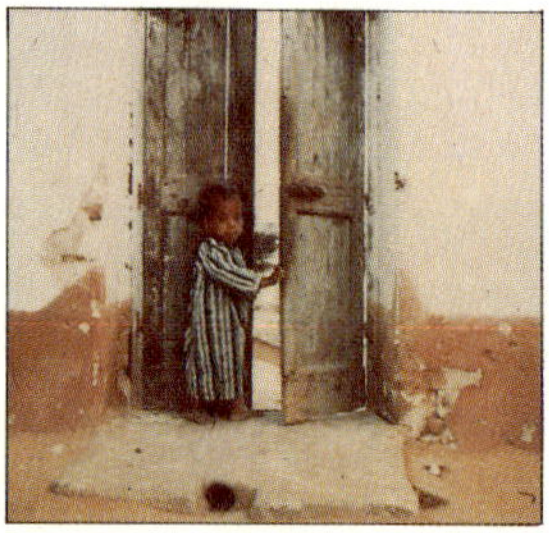

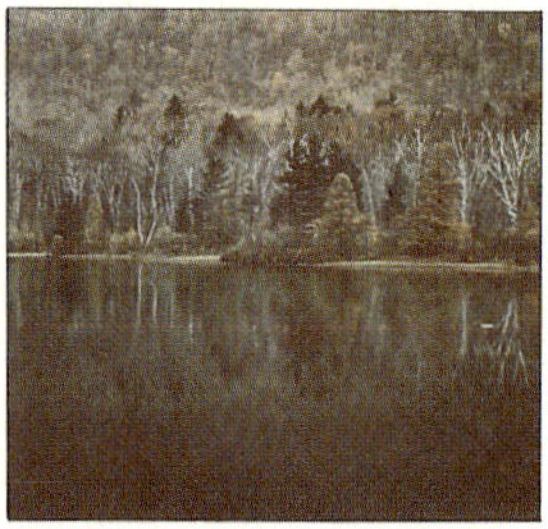

Making use of line
Diagonal lines, left, emphasize depth and give a three-dimensional feel, or sense of perspective to a picture. Diagonals are restless and dynamic in mood. Vertical lines suggest height and grandeur – use them to frame an impressive landscape, or to emphasize the small size of a child, above left. Horizontal lines convey balance and calm, as in the tranquil scene above. By changing your viewpoint and framing you can convert horizontals to diagonals and verticals, and vice versa. Or you can make lines lead to the subject, drawing the eye toward it.

Arranging picture elements

The way your subject is set within the four sides of the frame has a great effect on the success of a picture. With single subjects, like portraits, you can fill the center of the frame. But for more complex scenes, a subject placed in the center can look dull. Try dividing the picture into thirds, as shown below, to create balance. Or use a framing device, bottom right. Generally, you should avoid splitting your picture across the center with a horizon or vertical line – place horizons high or low in the frame instead (see p.67), unless you want to stress symmetry, right.

Symmetry
Reflections in water are useful to balance shapes in your pictures. If a scene and its reflection are perfectly symmetrical, you can break the usual rule, and place the horizon in the center of your frame, right. Symmetry can also create abstracts out of ordinary subjects – the outlines of the subject and its mirror image merge, to make a single shape.

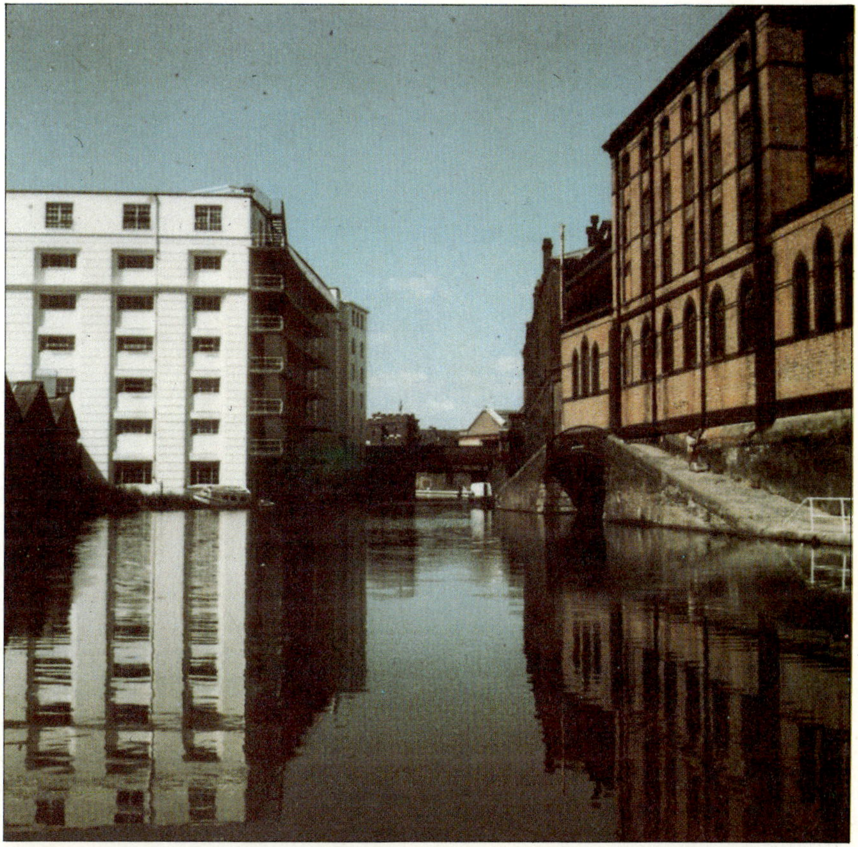

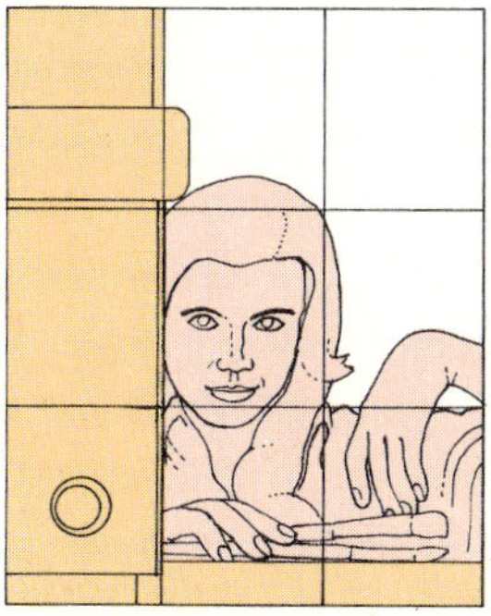

Using thirds
The shot, right, uses the "rule of thirds", above. Try imagining lines dividing your picture into thirds. Here, the lines of the easel, and the hands, suggest the use of thirds.

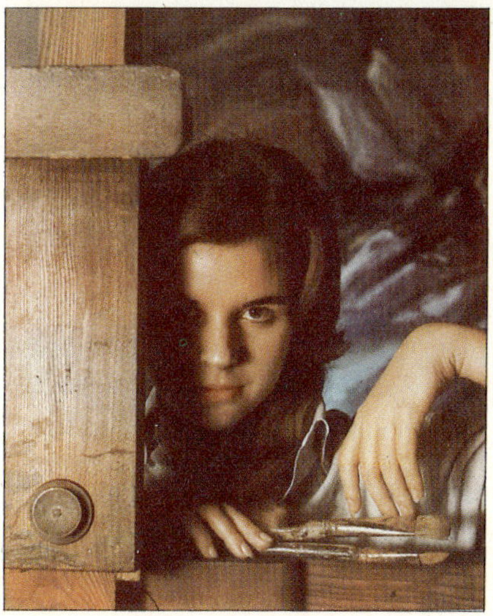

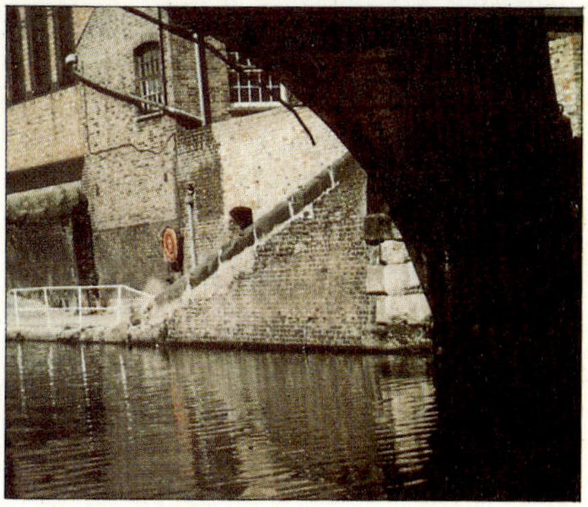

Filling the foreground
An empty or cluttered foreground will weaken a picture. Use the foreground to create depth and emphasis in your shots. Try shooting through an arch or window, above.

Making use of natural light

Natural light is perpetually changing – in color, direction and quality. It changes with season, latitude and climate, and varies hour by hour throughout the day, as the weather and the sun's position affect it. And in changing, it alters the appearance of the world about us. Light will affect color – early morning light gives a blue or yellow tone, midday light is white, and mid-morning or afternoon light is warm and golden. And light may be either soft or hard, depending on weather and time of day. When the sun is filtered by cloud, mist or rain it gives soft light which mutes color, right. When the sun is bright and direct, it gives hard, contrasty lighting with sharp-edged shadows and bright colors, far right. Learn to recognize the type of light that will enhance the qualities and mood of your particular subject.

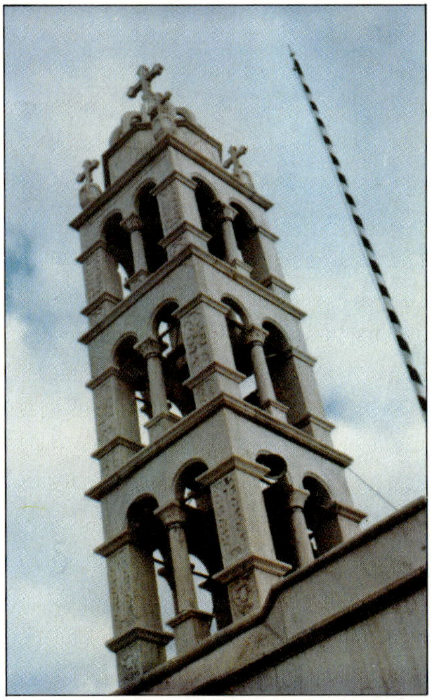

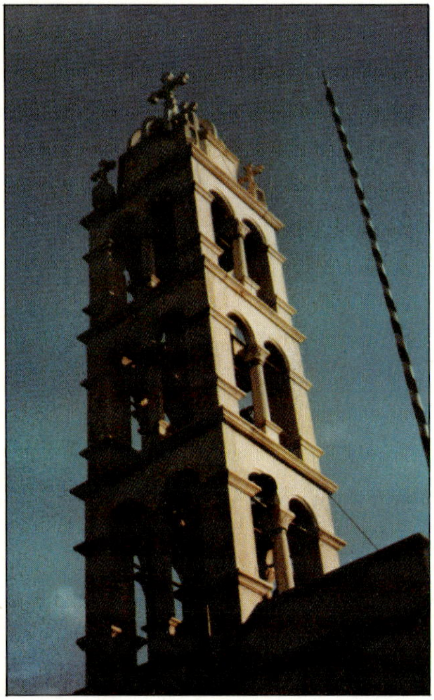

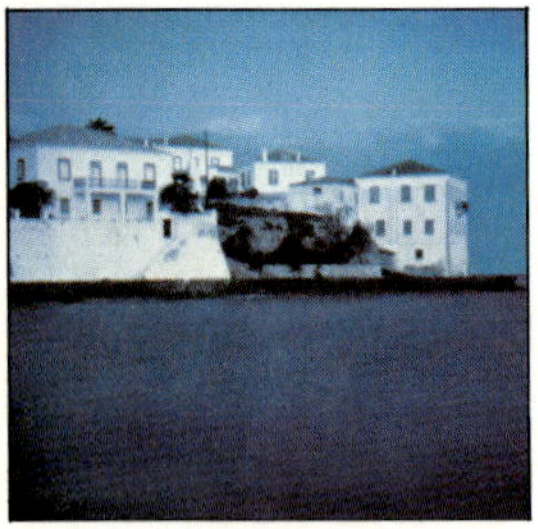

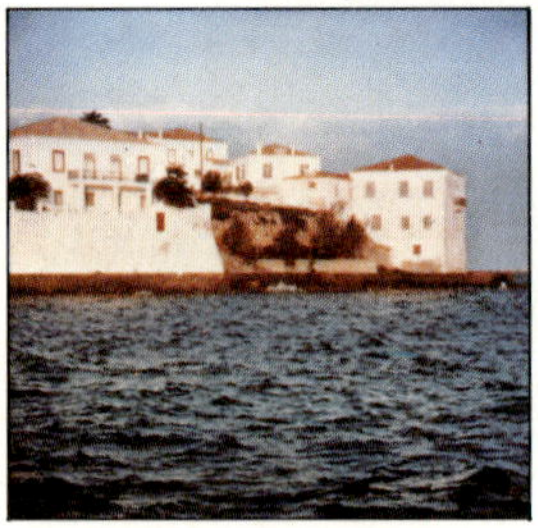

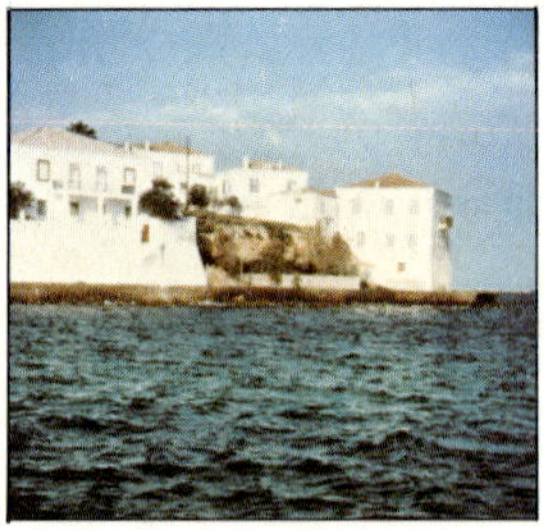

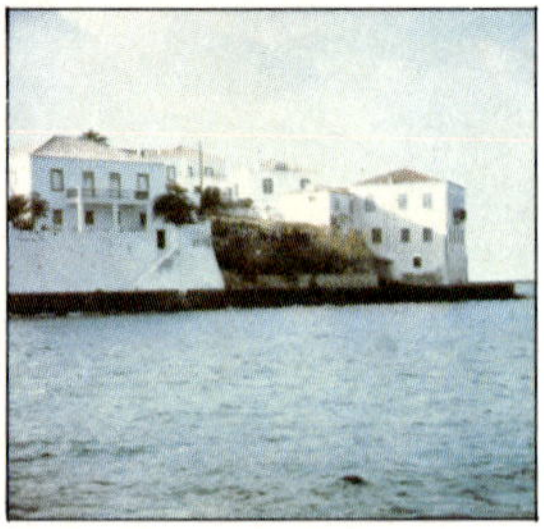

Time of day
Between sunrise and sunset daylight presents a range of colors and moods. At 7 am, above, dawn light produces cold, blue tones and blurs shapes.

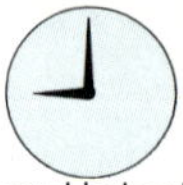

By 9 am the sun is casting strong, golden light on the scene and bringing out detail. Mid-morning and afternoon light are best for instant photography.

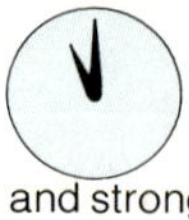

At noon the sun is overhead, giving hard-edged shadows and strong colors. Highlights will start to burn out on instant picture film if the sun is very bright.

The setting sun casts long shadows and detail starts to disappear in shadow areas. After the sun has set, colors become muted and cold.

Light and instant color
Colors vary according to the type of light that your picture is taken in. Summer afternoon light gives a golden tone – use it with bright colors, right, for a warm effect. Bright light brings out strong colors, below. Dim light mutes colors – use it with harmonious colors to enhance mood, below left. On dull days find bright colors to lift your picture or you will get a flat result.

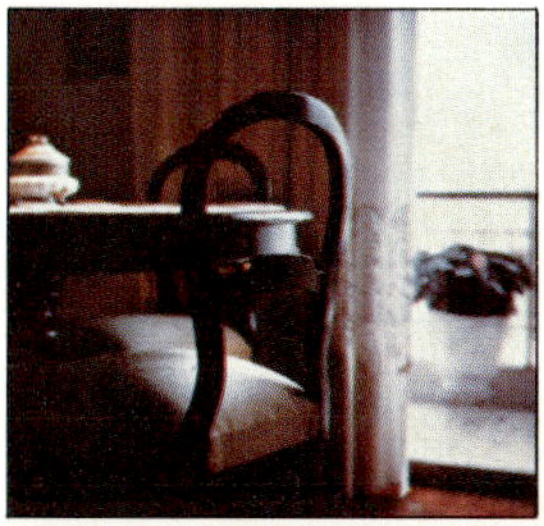

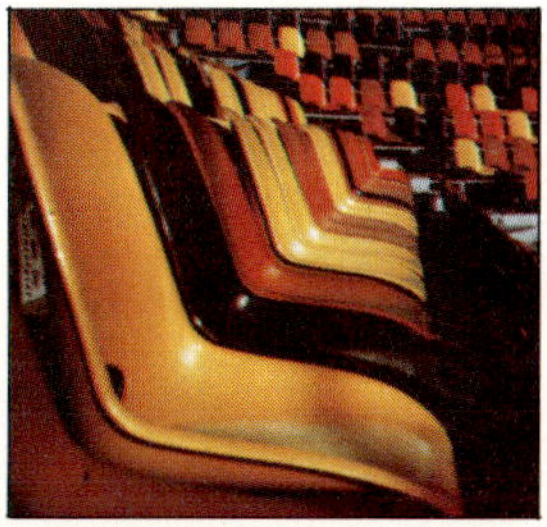

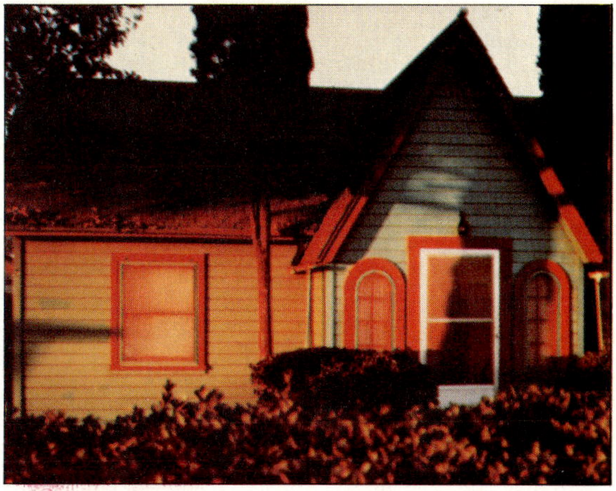

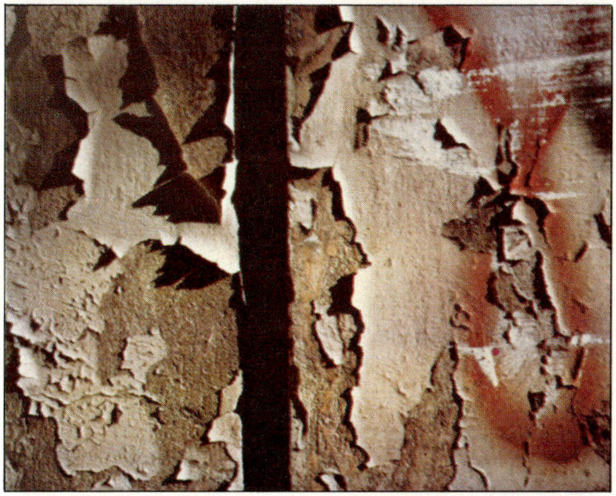

Texture and light
Oblique lighting will bring out texture and form in your subject because the shadows formed define the different surface levels. Exploit this effect in your pictures – look for side-lighting to bring out a delicate detail such as the peeling paintwork, left. Or find hard sidelight to emphasize the contrast between light and dark in a subject, and to bring out its form, below.

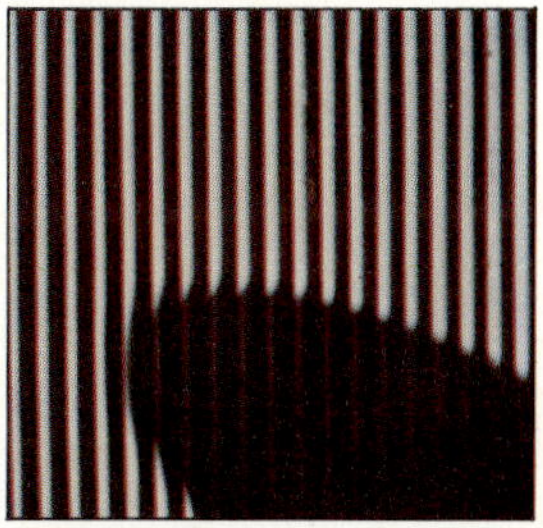

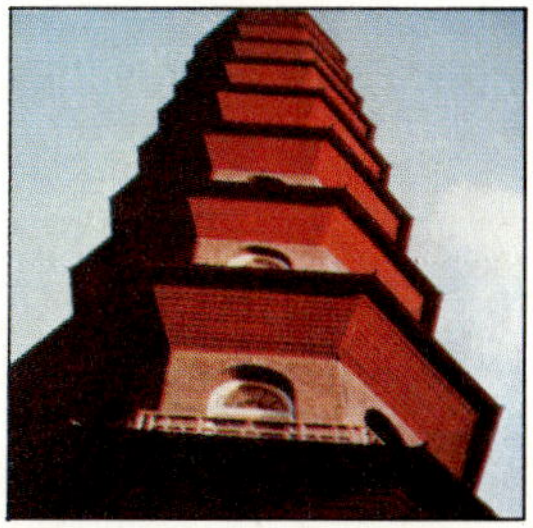

The direction of light
As the sun moves across the sky it strikes the earth from different angles. At noon, you must be content with direct overhead lighting, but at other times of day you can choose the light you want by moving around your subject.
Front-lighting flattens the form and texture of the house, right, but enhances color. Backlit, the palm trees, center, are thrown into dramatic silhouette. Texture and form are best revealed by side-lighting.

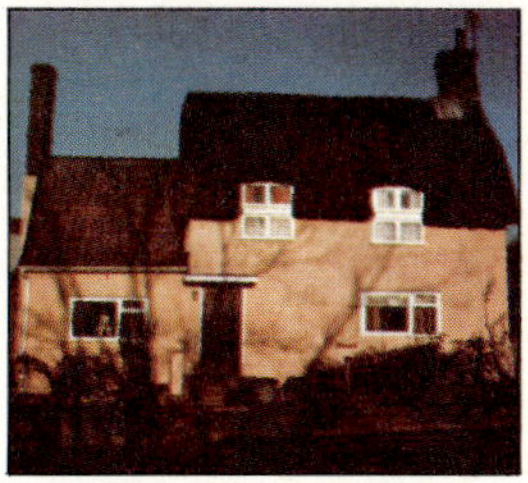

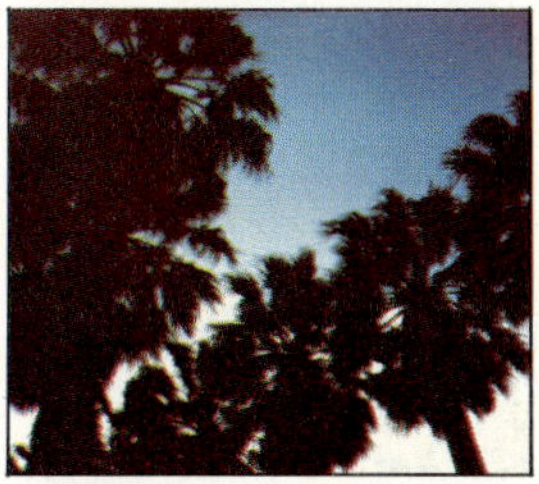

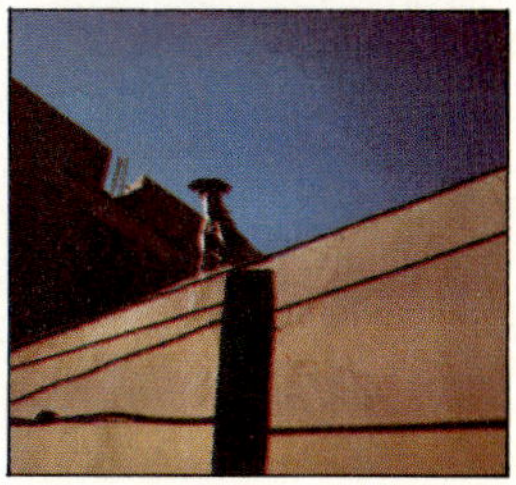

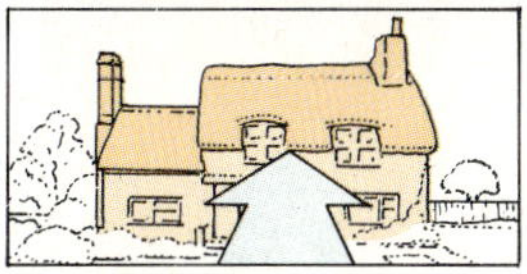

Front-lighting

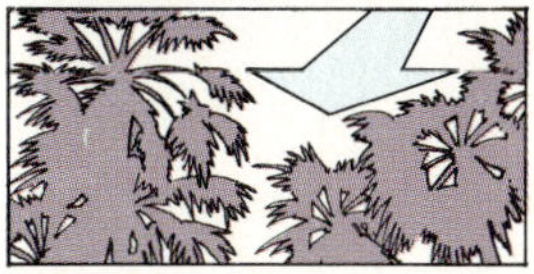

Back-lighting

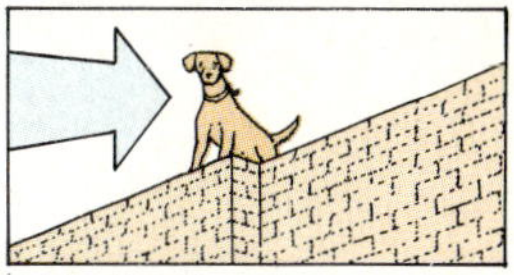

Side-lighting

Making use of flash

Flash enables you to take instant pictures anywhere, no matter how dim the lighting, as long as you keep within flash range (p.23). Use it indoors and outside to brighten colors and ensure sharp pictures. Its main drawback is that you cannot see its effect in advance. Try to predict where shadows will fall or reflections occur, and how fall-off will affect subject and background. Pastel colors or skin tones nearer than about 5 ft (1.4 m) may bleach out unless you diffuse the flash.

Flash and mirrors
Shooting in a mirror with flash gives unusual effects – side- or back-lighting from reflected light, front-lighting from the flash. Flash glare may enhance the shot, as below. If you want to avoid it, shoot at an angle, below right. (Don't aim the flash at the center of the mirror – your picture may be dark.)

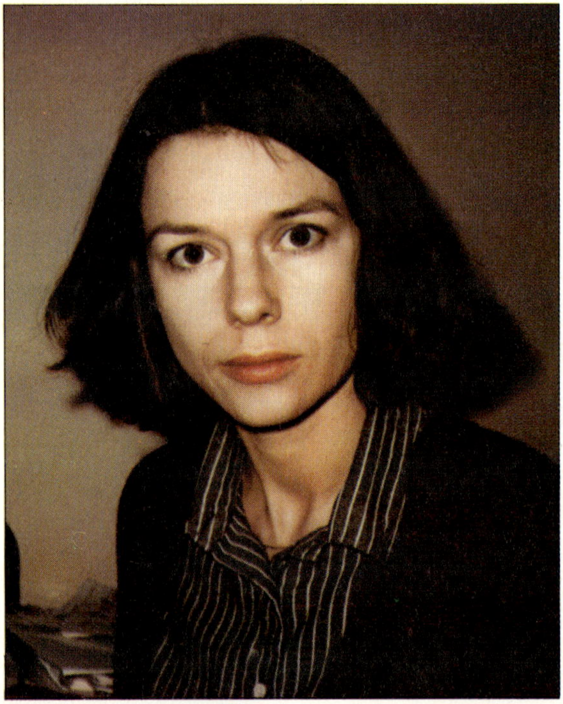

Flash and atmosphere
Direct flash can cast hard shadows and give a flat, lifeless result, below. Room lamps are more atmospheric, but give a strong orange cast, bottom. For a natural portrait, move closer and diffuse the flash (p.23), as left.

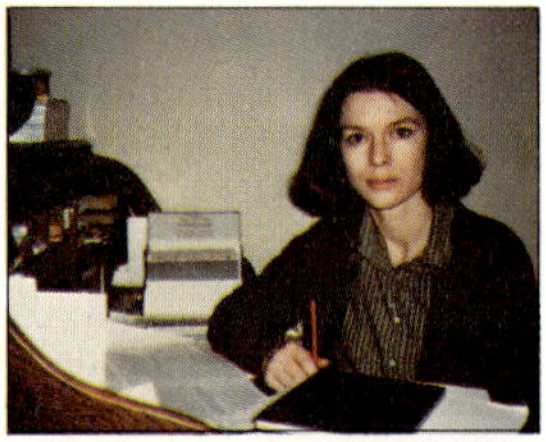

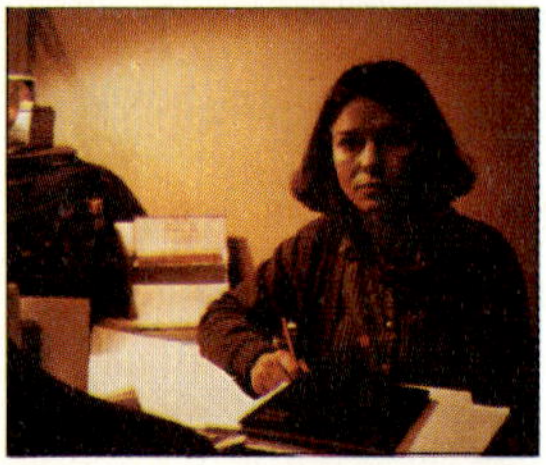

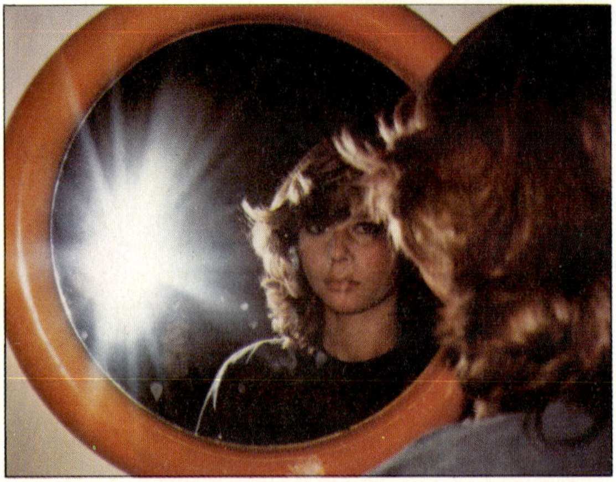

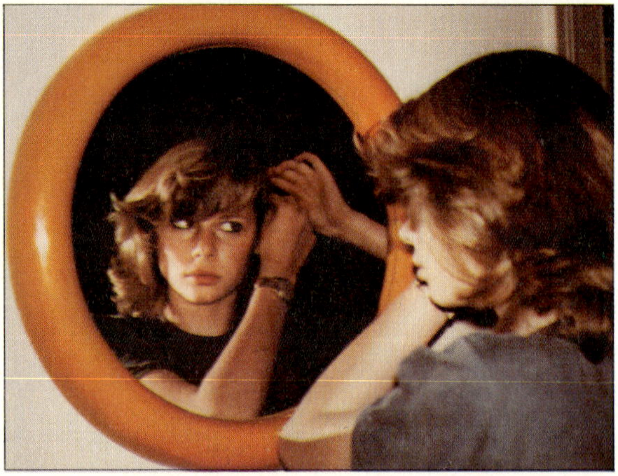

Edge fall-off
When using flash to photograph a group of people, try to arrange the group so that faces are well within the frame, as right. If people are too near the edges of the frame, as in the picture below, their faces may be unlit.

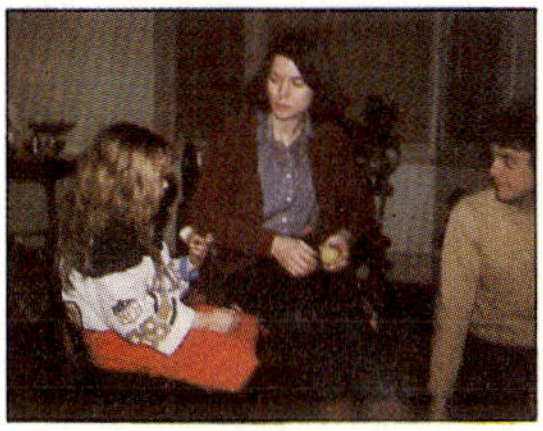

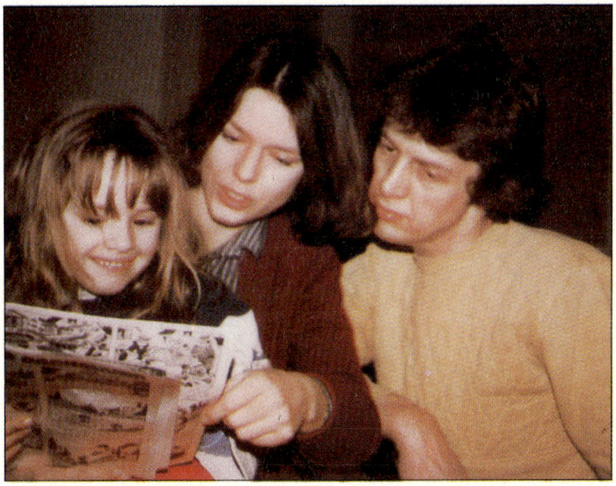

Distance fall-off
Place subjects roughly the same distance from the camera, as left, or they will be lit unevenly, as shown below.

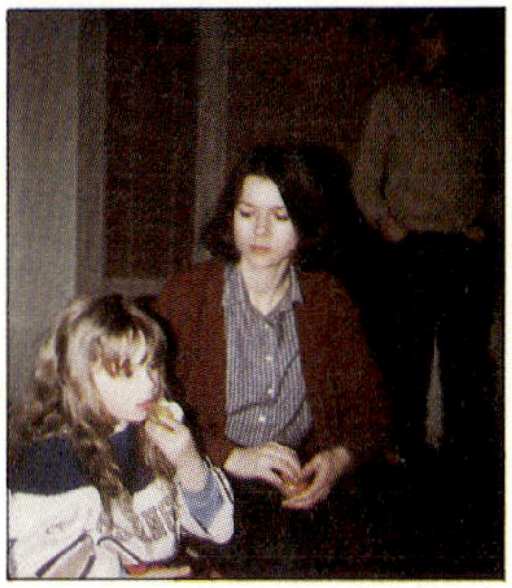

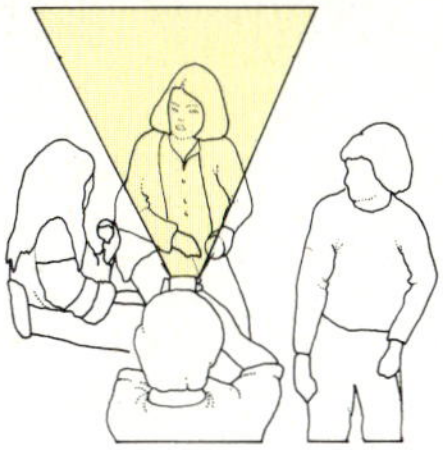

Understanding fall-off

When using flash, you must take special care to compose your shots well. Flash illumination falls off sharply with distance, so that subjects at the picture edges or too far away from the camera may receive too little light, as shown in the diagrams. Remember that the loss of light with distance is increased if you diffuse the flash – always set your L/D to lighten. And bear in mind that you can use fall-off to advantage when you want to darken the background (see below).

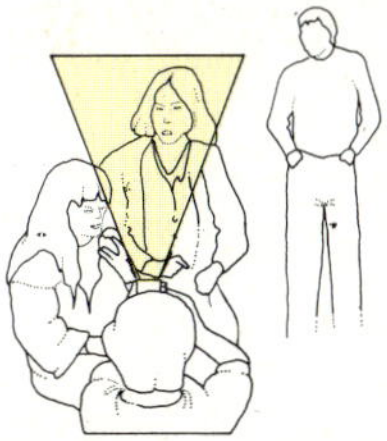

Background shadows
If the background is too close or too light, shooting from below or from the side will produce ugly shadows, especially if the camera is held so that the flash is below the lens. Use a high viewpoint so that shadows are hidden, as below.

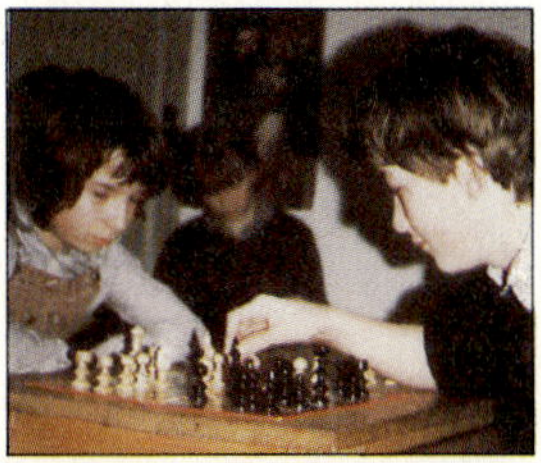

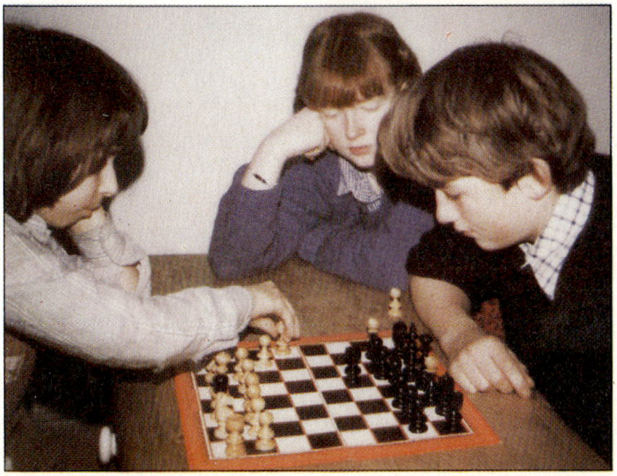

Color and detail
Use flash to record color in a detail, as right. If you want to black out a cluttered background to emphasize your subject, try moving the subject forward so that the background is out of range, and goes dark, below.

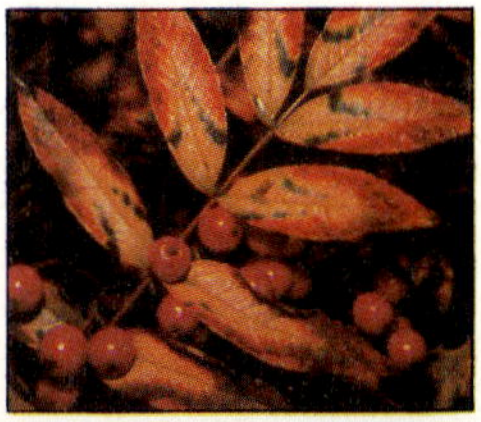

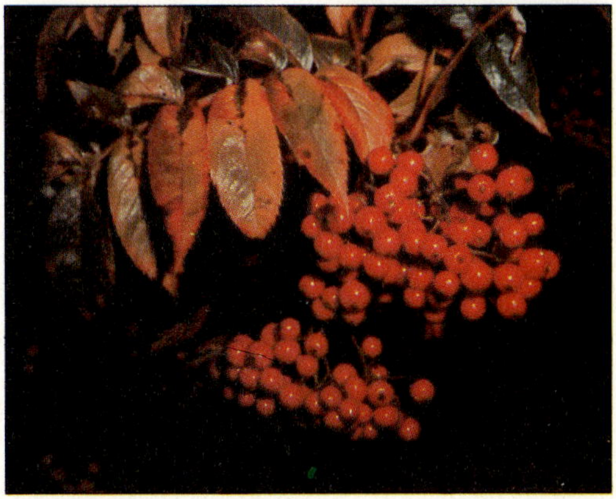

Getting good color results

Color is the single most powerful element in any picture; so you should control it carefully. Bright colors give strong results on instant film, while pale colors are more difficult to handle. Color results are affected by lighting quality (p.33) and by temperature (pp.62 and 69). Dull light or cold weather will distort or weaken colors, often with disappointing results. You will achieve great impact with color if you shoot a subject that consists of bold areas of contrasting color, in bright but even light. The photographer took the shot, right, in mid-afternoon, with the sun behind him so that the field was frontlit.

Light and color
You will get the richest color results on instant film in strong, even light. Color shot in bright light is known as "saturated" color. Dull light will give paler, less saturated color.

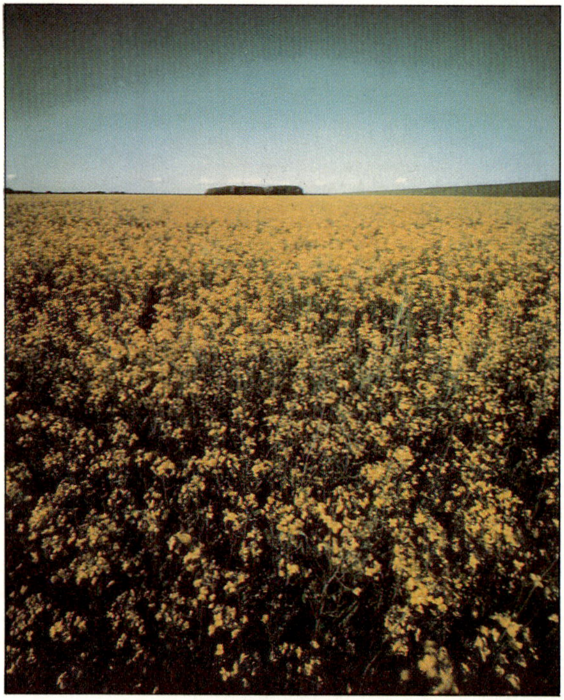

What makes color?
All colors are formed from different combinations of the three primary colors of light – red, green, and blue. Complementary or secondary colors are formed by combining two primaries.

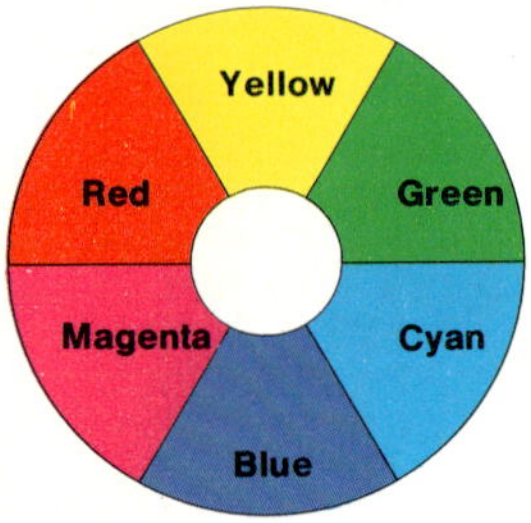

The color wheel
The primaries, and the complementary colors formed from them, can be shown as a circle of saturated, pure hues, above. The circle has a warm half (red, yellow and magenta) and a cool half. Warm and cool colors are said to provide contrast.

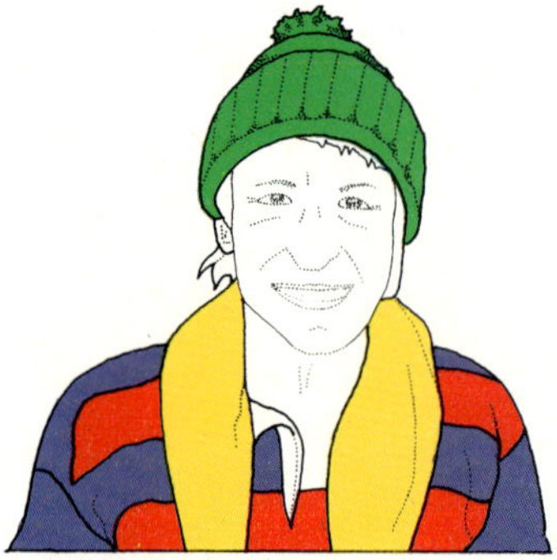

Primary colors
The diagram above shows the true colors of the subject, right.

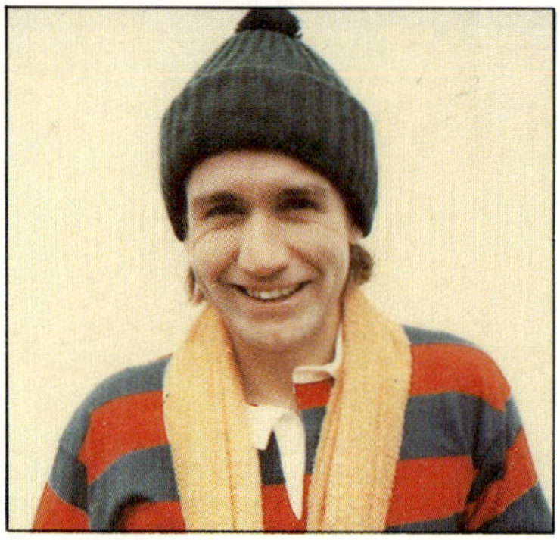

Bright light
All the colors in the subject are strong and clear (well saturated).

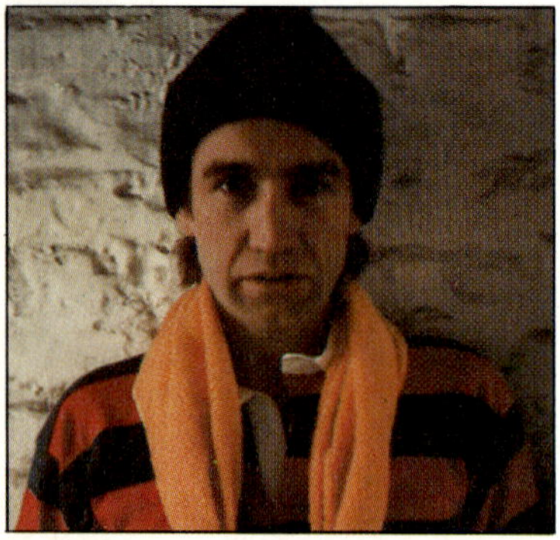

Dull light
Colors are softer, lacking impact, though red is still strong.

Adding color in dull light
Most colors will appear desaturated and flat in dull light, as shown far right. But red is so strong on instant film that it will stand out despite poor light, as right. When you are shooting outdoors in dull weather, choose colorful subjects, include red if you can, and frame tightly to exclude large areas of colorless background. To add color, look for bright "props" such as umbrellas, clothing, painted doors or shop fronts. If you cannot add color, try using flash to brighten the lighting. Or move in very close, to show detail and texture.

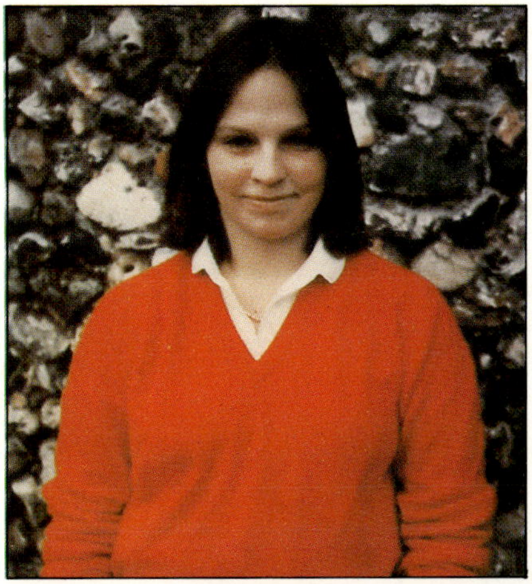

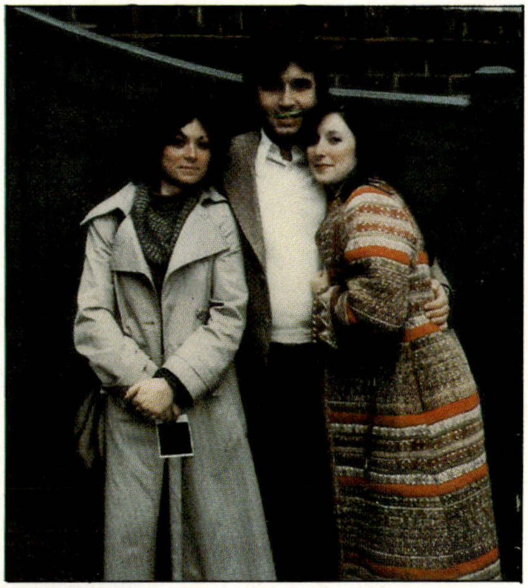

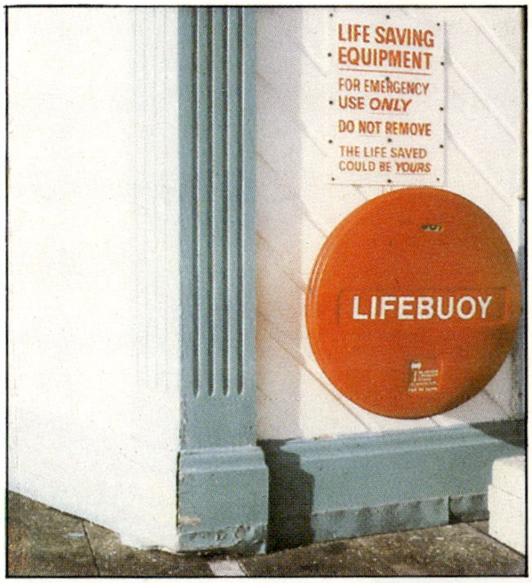

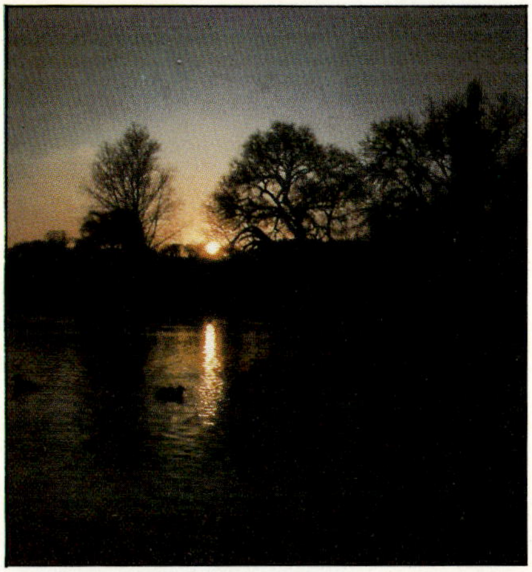

Color and contrast
In very bright light, or very uneven lighting, you will get "high contrast" – a wide difference in tone between highlit and shadowed areas of your subject. On instant picture film, this kind of lighting can cause problems – the highlights (brighter areas) may burn out, as far left, desaturating color. Moving the L/D control to darken will bring back color to the highlight area, but the rest of the picture will be darker too, as left. Decide what will suit your subject best before you shoot – both these pictures are effective.

Colors of light
When you take an indoor picture without using flash you will have to take into account the effects of available light. Available light can be artificial (room lights) or natural (daylight). These lights present different colors. Daylight indoors may have a soft, blue cast, particularly in winter, right. Artificial light, on the other hand, has different casts. Household bulbs give a warm, orange tone, far right. Whereas most fluorescent tubes would give a cold, greenish cast (p.75).

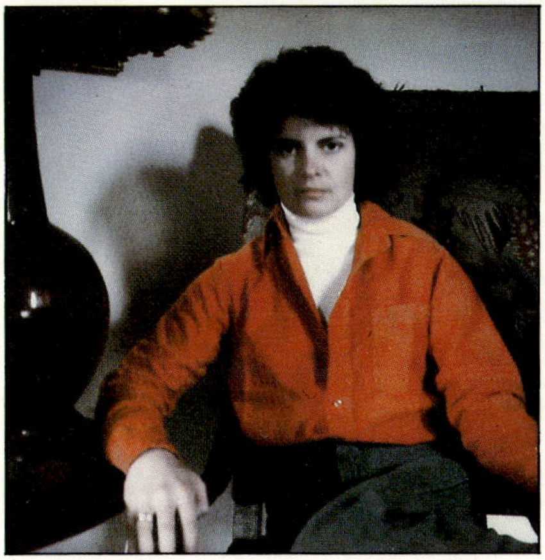

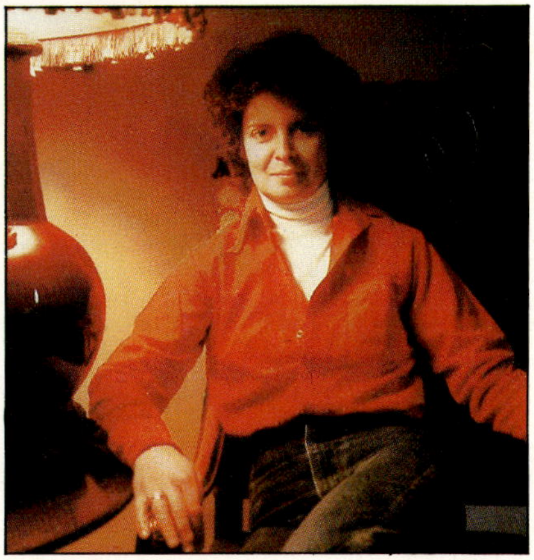

Putting color in the picture

In composing your instant pictures, take care how you use color. Subjects with rich, bright colors, particularly red or orange, will give a good result, even on a dull day. Try to avoid shooting pale or dull colors in weak, flat light – you will generally get a lifeless, monotone result. For effective muted color shots (facing page), look for misty weather, interesting textures, or the soft colors of dusk or dawn, rather than gray days.

Strong color
Strong color is vibrant and bold, below. It requires bright direct lighting to bring out its full brilliance. Keep your strong color pictures simple. If you include too many different colors the impact will be lost. Shooting a close-up detail in a single, bold color gives a rich, semi-abstract result, right.

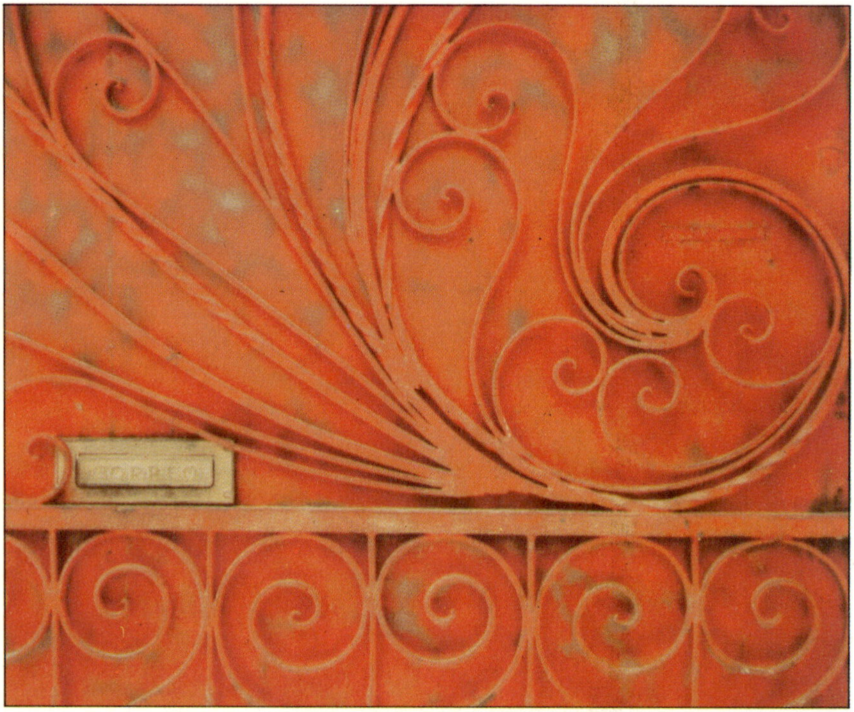

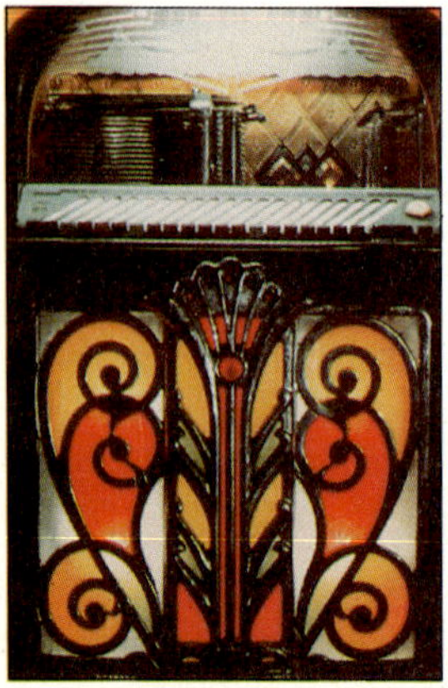

Color contrast
Contrasting colors are colors that are opposite each other on the color wheel (p.36) – blue and yellow, red and green or blue. Color contrast always makes a lively picture – look for a contrasting background, or frame details closely (p.29). The close-up shot of some colorful hanks of wool, right, has created a bold image that makes use of color for color's sake. With an SLR camera (pp.12–13) you can move in very close for maximum impact.

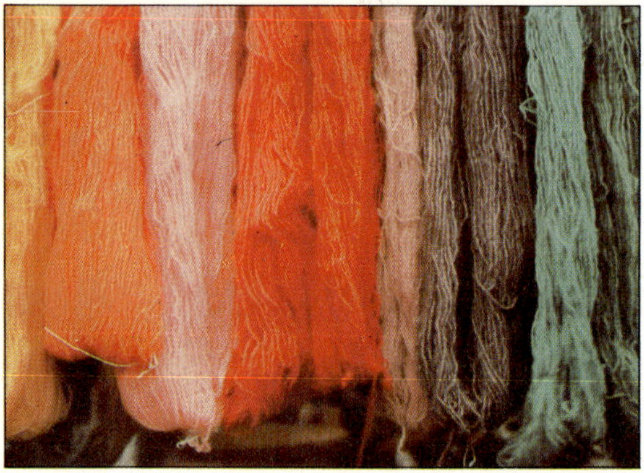

Isolated color
Even a relatively small area of strong color will dominate a picture, if it is set against a neutral or monochromatic background, right. Instant film has a strong red which you can exploit for isolated color shots. When the sky is overcast and dull, the sea gray and stormy, or city streets are colorless and dull, look out for the chance occurrence of isolated color. A child in a red coat, a colorful umbrella, even a red traffic light, will bring your picture to life. For maximum impact, place the spot of color off-center.

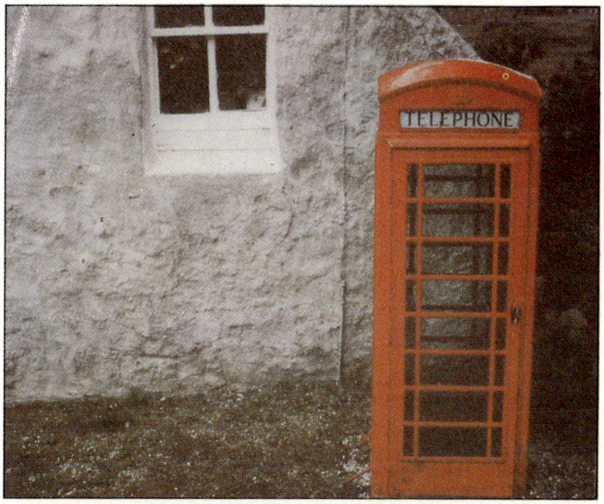

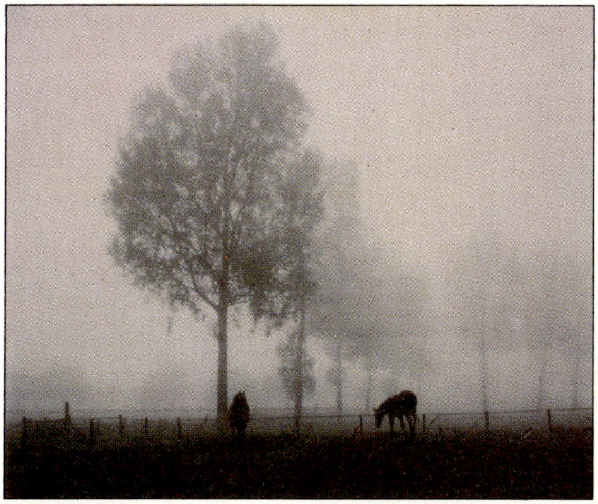

Muted color
Muted color can be romantic, bleak or dramatic. Look for its subtle tones and textures when light is softened and scattered by haze, rain or smoke, as above. Investigate the countryside, urban and industrial areas for atmospheric shots.

Colour harmony
You can convey a feeling of harmony by restricting your view to a range of tones of one color, right, or a variety of pastel shades, or all warm or all cool colors. Keep your composition simple and use repetitive lines and shapes to echo the harmony.

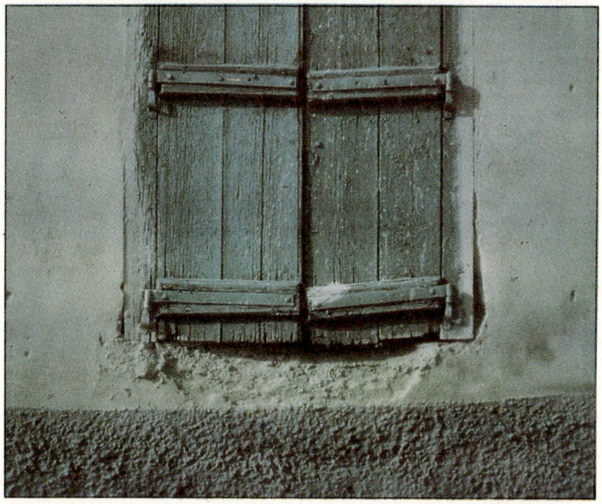

Using background to brighten color
A dark background will make subject colors appear more vivid. A simple way to achieve this effect is to take a flash picture (p.35) with the background some way behind your subject – the background will disappear into darkness. If you diffuse the flash this effect will be more dramatic. With close-up still life shots, like the flower head, far right, place the object on a piece of black velvet.

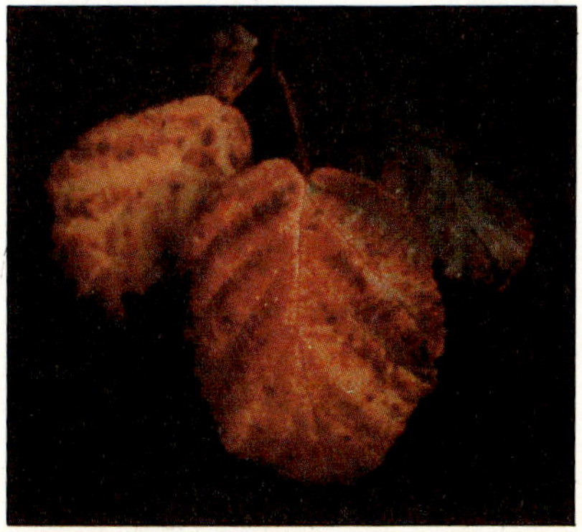

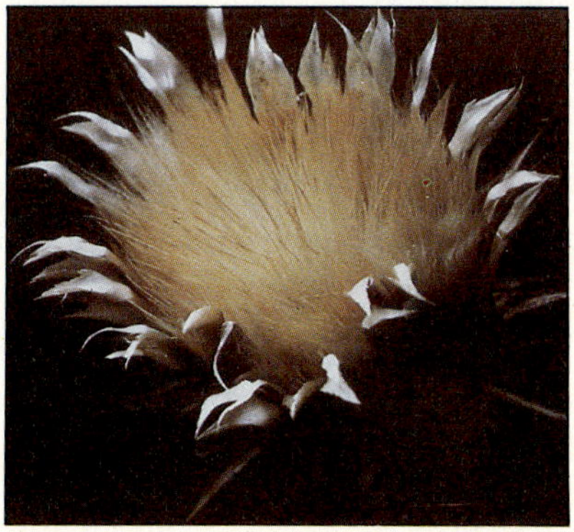

Using black and white film

Black and white can be graphic or abstract, where color is sensual and realistic. Use it to simplify lines and shapes, to bring out texture or provide an atmosphere. For additional examples of the creative use of black and white peel-apart instant picture film, see pp.42–3.

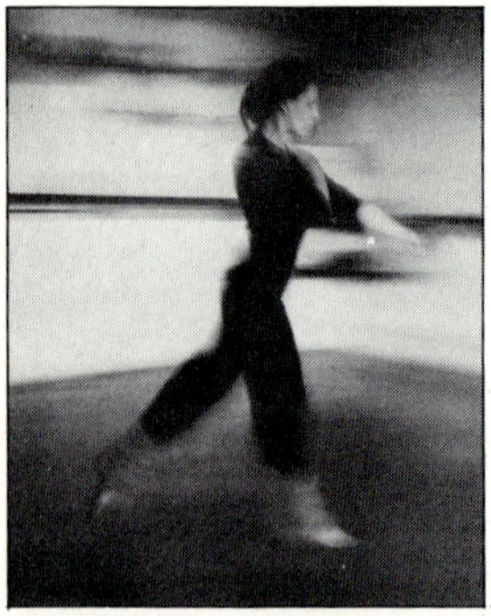

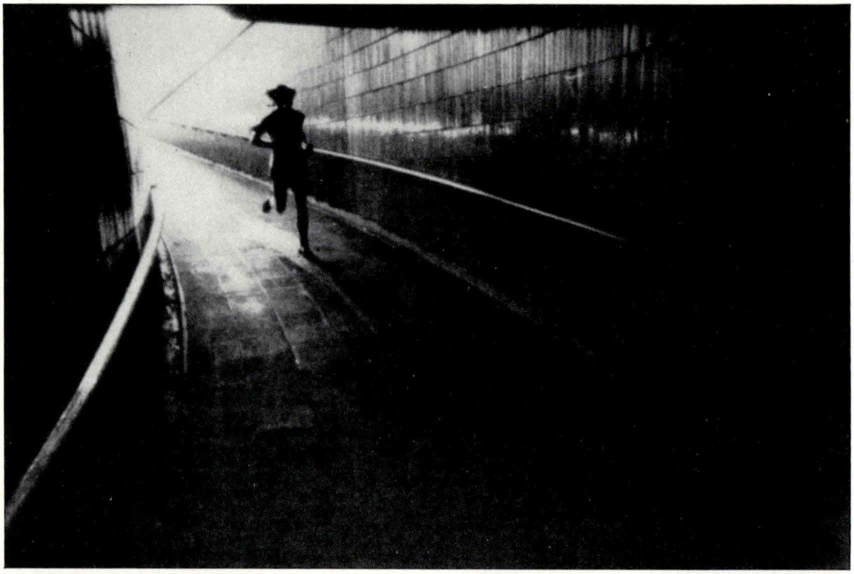

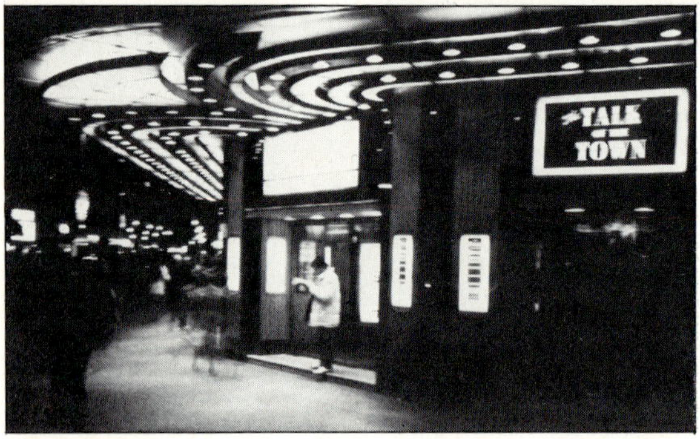

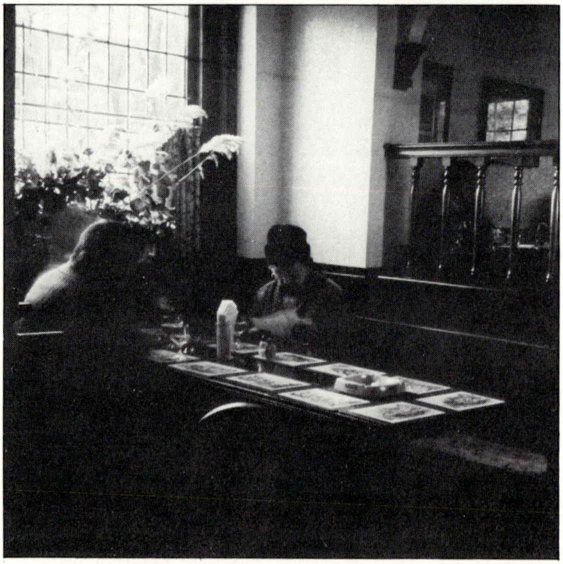

Advantages of black and white instant film
Black and white peel-apart film is available with a speed equivalent to 3000 ASA (instant color films have an ASA equivalent of 75). Fast film responds more quickly to light and is therefore ideal in low light situations – dim interiors, dusk, and night shots. Black and white films have two other advantages over color – cost is lower and you can get Pos/neg film (ASA 125) with a negative that you can use for making prints.

Timing the development
You must follow the instructions in your film pack carefully when developing peel-apart film, or you will spoil your print. Suit development time to the temperature and use a watch or timer to judge development accurately. If you underestimate you will get a pale, underdeveloped result, as right, and if you overestimate, your black and white instant picture will be too dark, far right.

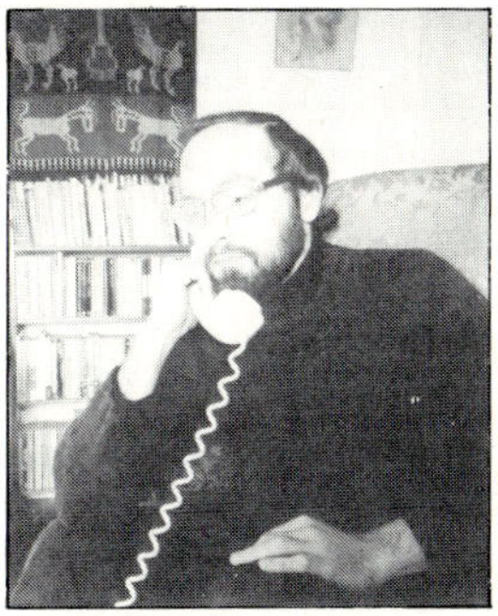
Underdeveloped

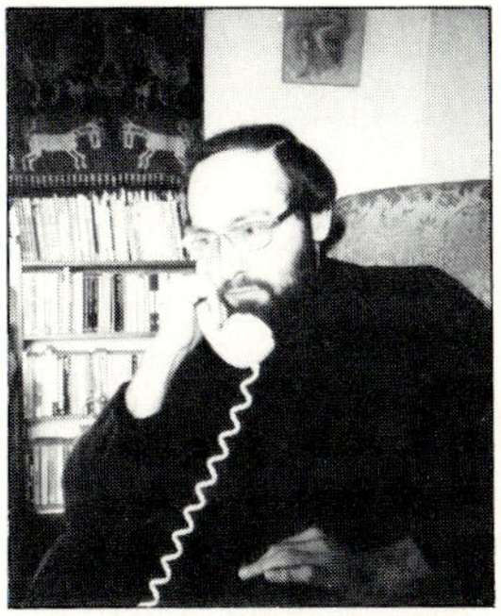
Correctly developed

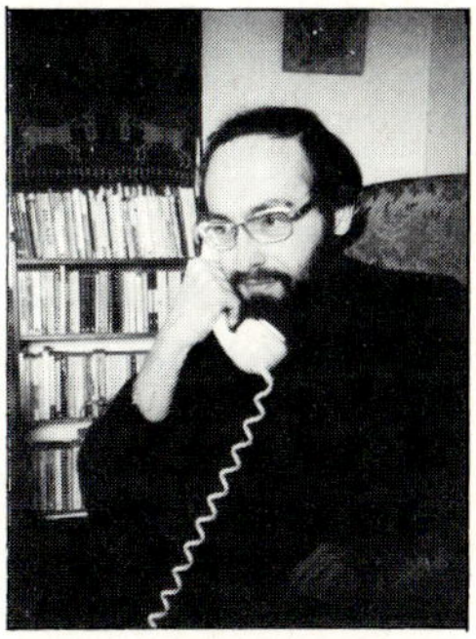
Overdeveloped

Positive/negative film

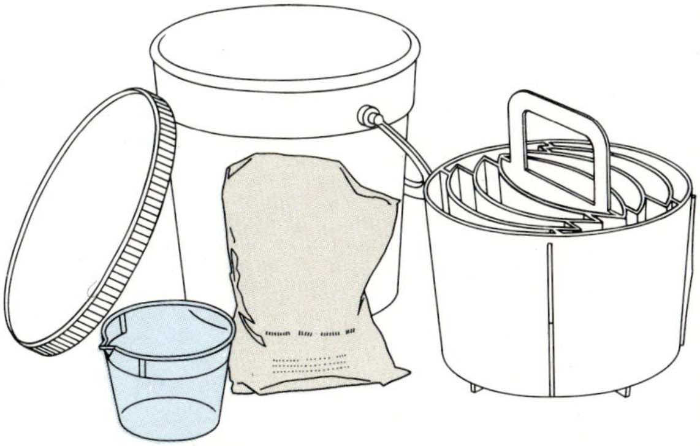

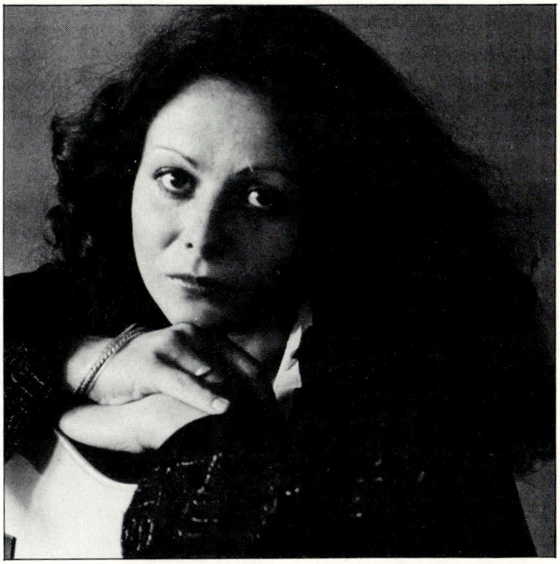

Using the negative
You can make your own prints, right, from a retainable negative. Once you have pulled the film out of the camera, you must clear negatives within 3 minutes. Prepare a solution from sodium sulfite powder and warm water in your field processing tank, above, before you go out shooting.

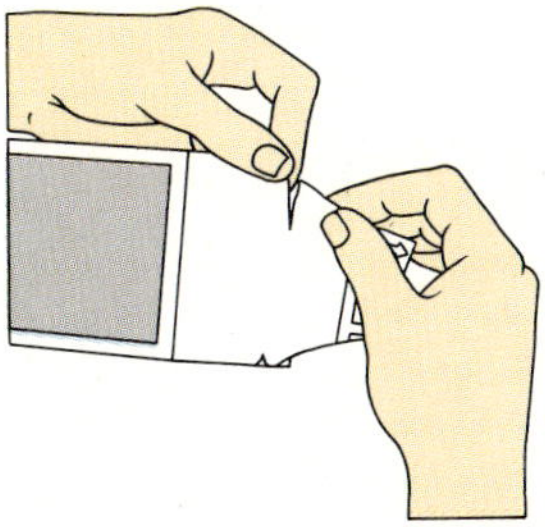
Hold the negative by its long top tab; carefully tear off and discard the paper film leader (above the pod of chemicals).

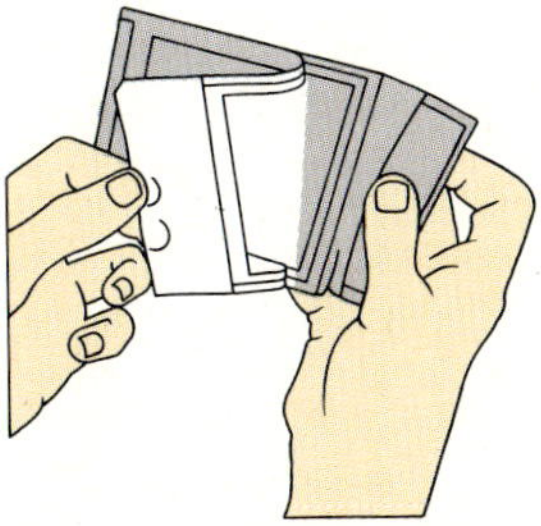
Hold the negative by the top tab; remove the masking paper, and discard it. Always put the negative in the tank immediately.

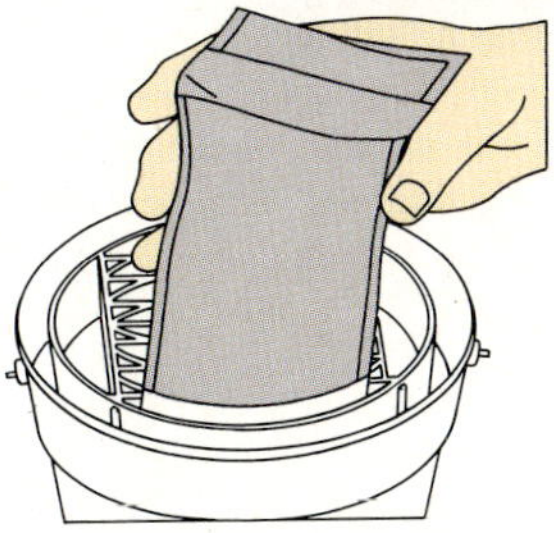
Agitate the negative for 30–60 seconds. Remove the tabs and backcoat material. Store in solution for up to 72 hours.

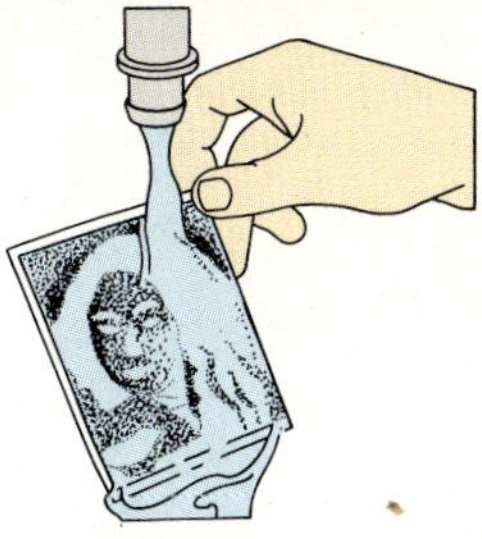
Wash the negative in running water (see film leaflet for time), dip it in wetting agent, and hang it up to dry.

Working in black and white

The most useful quality of black and white is its ability to simplify a complex subject. A scene that is overwhelmed by a variety of colors will look more powerful when shot in black and white – the conflicting colors will be reduced to patterns and shapes. When you are looking for potential black and white subjects, try to see them in terms of tone – the range and interplay of light and dark – rather than color. Look for the effects of light direction and quality (pp.32–3) too, as these are even more important when color is absent. You can shoot in any kind of lighting, even under room lamps (where color shots may show unattractive casts).

Texture, shape and form
Use the subtle range of tones in black and white to reveal texture, as in this picture of bleached wood grain, right. Soft, oblique lighting enhances texture. Or use tonal contrast to dramatize shape, as below.

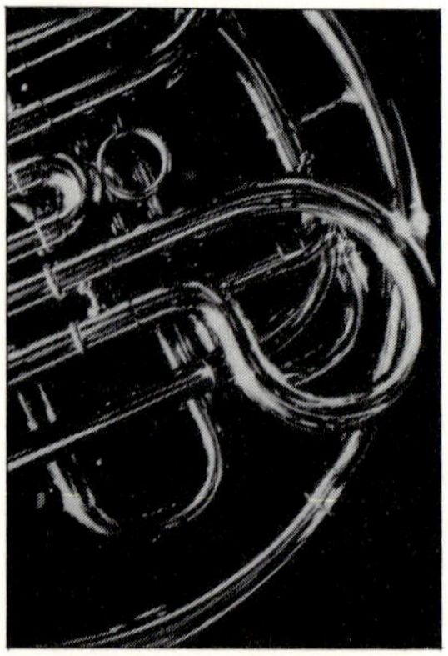

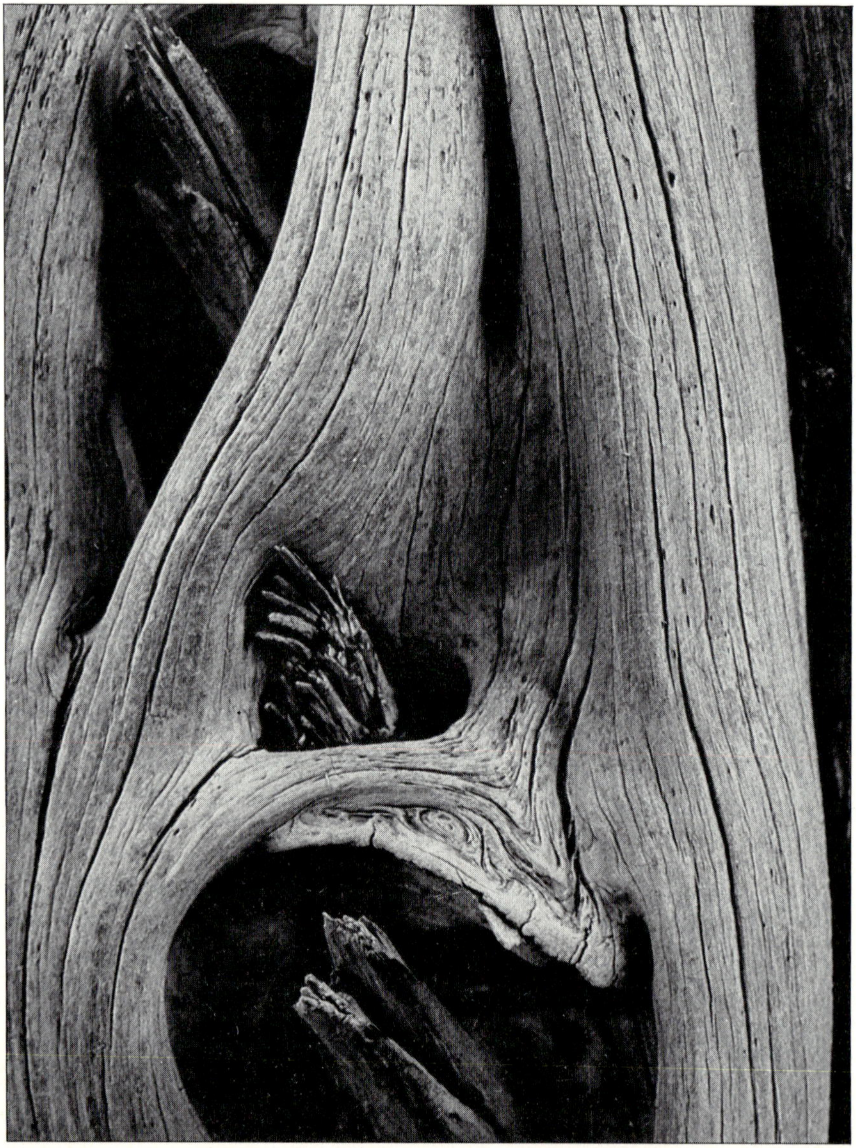

Taking a landscape
When you are choosing a landscape subject, look for clear outlines and shapes, picked out in planes of different tone – the curves of hills or trees, patterns of fields and fencing, or the symmetry of buildings. Try to offset the main shapes with areas of fine detail or texture. Simple subjects are often the strongest – as with the houses, right. Notice how the large area of delicate grasses in the foreground softens the scene, and provides a textural contrast to the solid shapes behind.

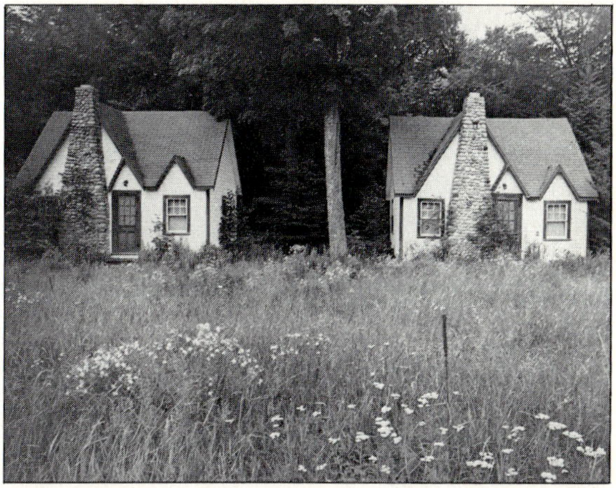

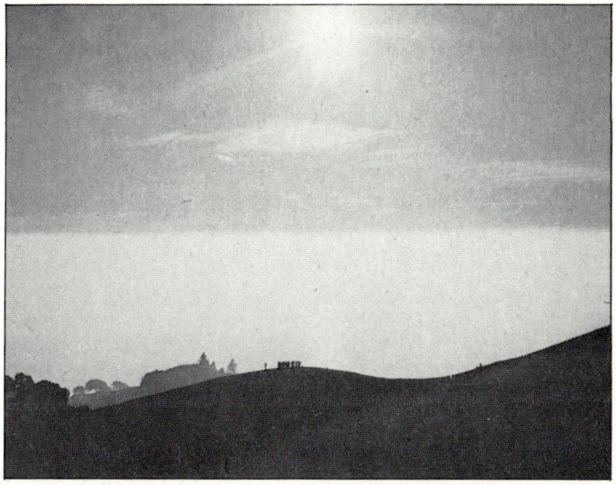

Tone and depth
Use black and white to capture the subtle variations of tone in an evening landscape, above. The different layers of tone will give an impressive sense of distance and space to your picture, and a tranquil mood.

Taking a portrait
Black and white film is often a good choice for an indoor portrait. Its high sensitivity (p.40) allows you to shoot by available light, as with the group right, to obtain a soft, natural effect that would be destroyed by flash.

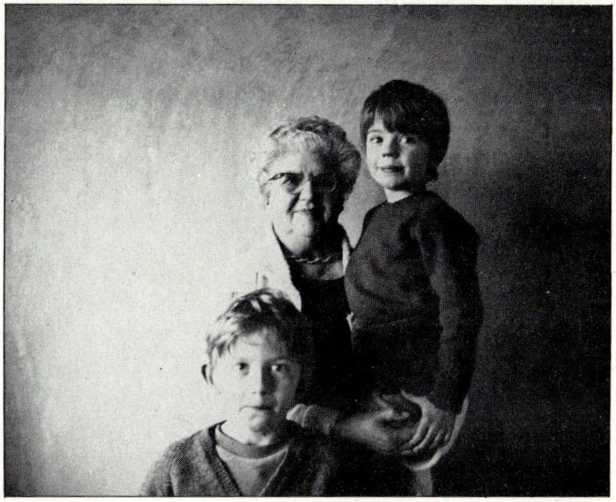

Black and white tricks
You can take double exposures with peel-apart film. Select a simple background, like the tree trunk right, set the L/D control to lighten, and press the shutter. Then move the L/D to normal, and shoot your main subject. Now remove the film and develop it (p.26). To get the effect, far right, use Pos/neg film (p.41), and have the negative printed on harsh contrast printing paper. (Your photo dealer or a professional photo lab will have this.)

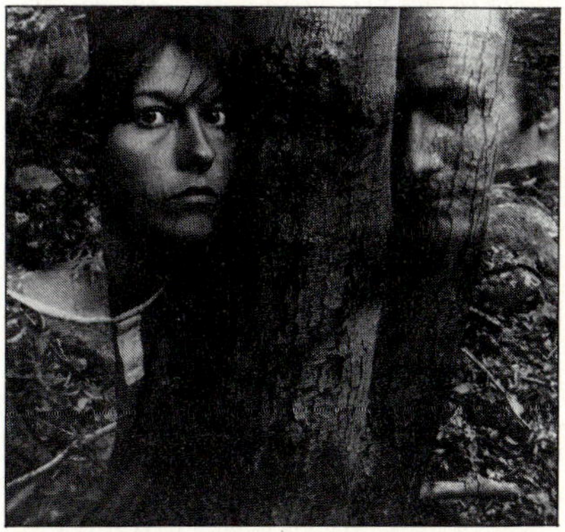

Double exposure

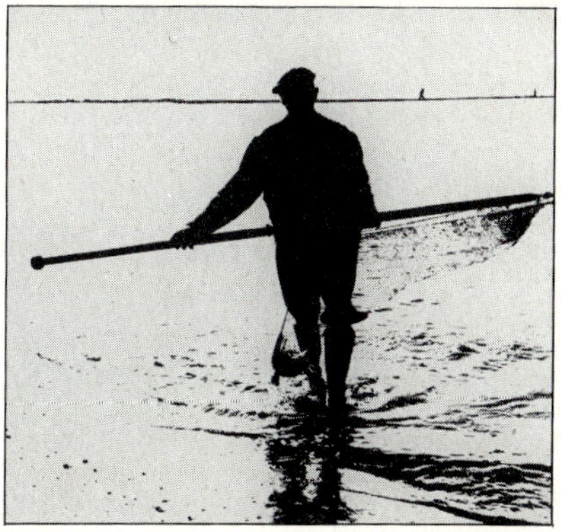

"Pen and ink" effect

Taking pictures at night

The results you can get at night depend on your instant camera. Several models allow long exposures of one second or more. Use a tripod or find a support (p.17), and you can take a wide range of night subjects. Some simpler cameras will not take pictures in very low light; these restrict your night shots to very brightly lit subjects, taken close up. Try shooting light sources for their own sake. Neon signs are good subjects – make use of wet, reflective sidewalks to light up the dark foreground, right. Automobile lights, below, will trace patterns of light across the frame during a long exposure. Be prepared to try several shots – instant film reacts unpredictably to long exposures.

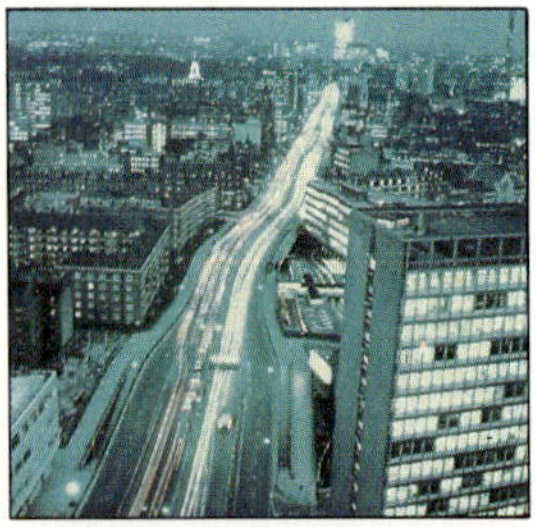

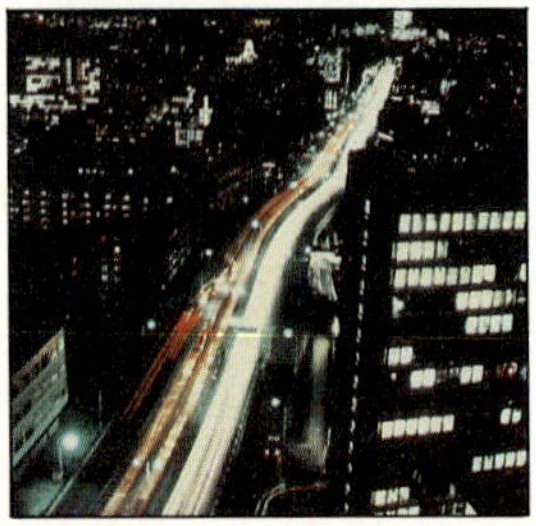

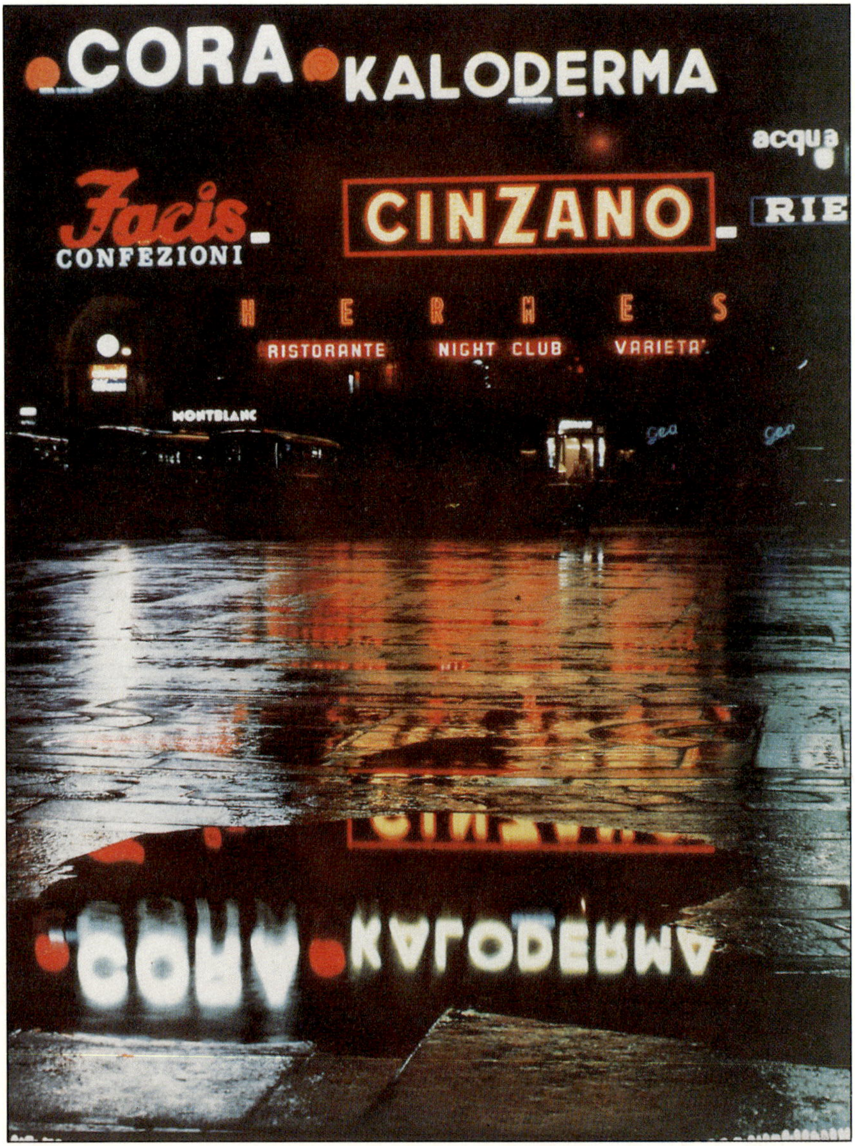

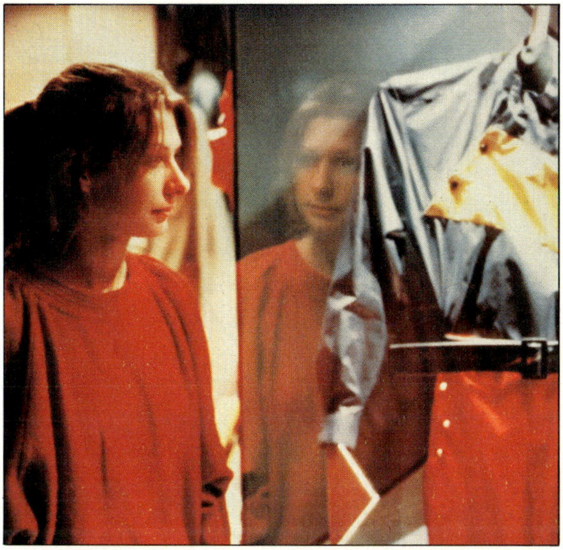

Using window lights
You can take any subject at night, without using a tripod, if it is lit brightly enough. Store windows, below, and cinema or theater entrances provide a bright, even spill of light. To photograph a person at night, stand your subject close to the light source so that the face is well lit, as in the picture left.

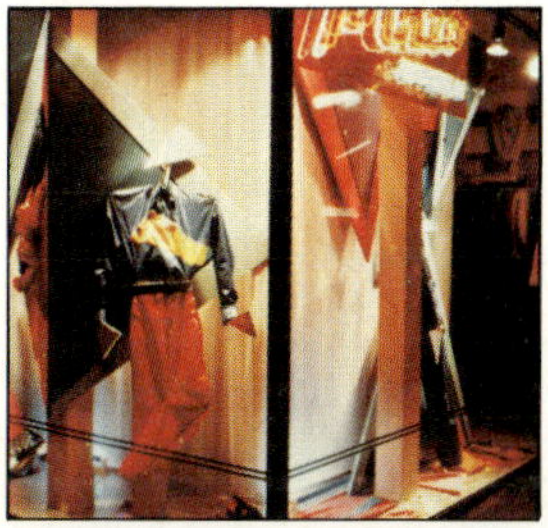

Shooting a silhouette
City streets provide night subjects that are well lit – either artificially, below, or by the last light of dusk. You may have to take a time exposure if the light level is too low in order to record some form and detail. Here the tree is silhouetted against the bright building, and rimmed with the light spilling from behind it.

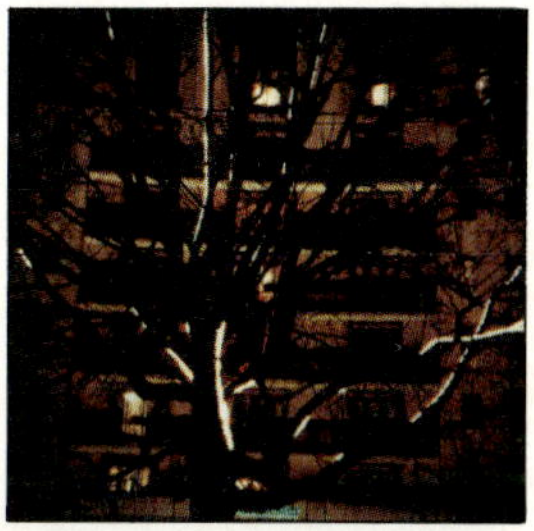

Taking a time exposure
There are two ways to give a long exposure. You can let the eye control it automatically, and adjust results with the L/D.
Or you can control it yourself – even though the camera is automatic. If you cover the eye with black tape, the shutter will stay open for as long or as short a time as the button is held down, or until you uncover the eye. (If the picture doesn't emerge, press the shutter again.) Try a couple of shots to find the best result. With either method, you must use a tripod or support (p.17). Use a cable release/remote shutter button and ask your subject to stay still, for a sharp result.

Controlling results
Suit your method to the light and subject. For the portrait below, exposure was automatic, but the L/D was moved all the way to lighten to show detail. For the moody, romantic shot right, the eye was covered and exposure was timed. It took several shots to achieve this result.

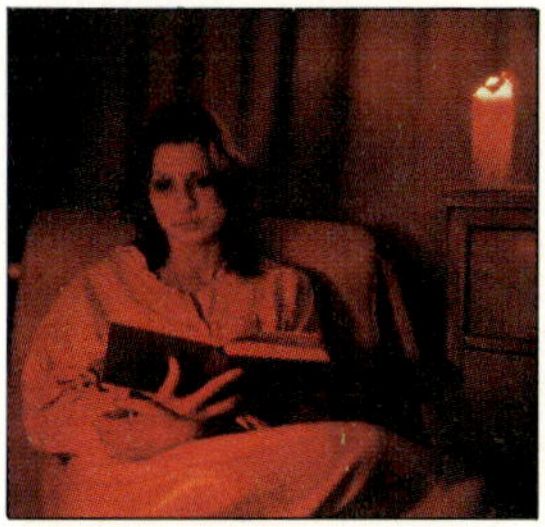

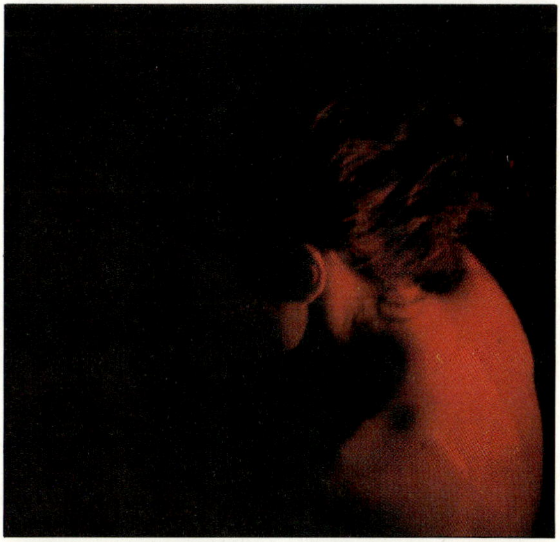

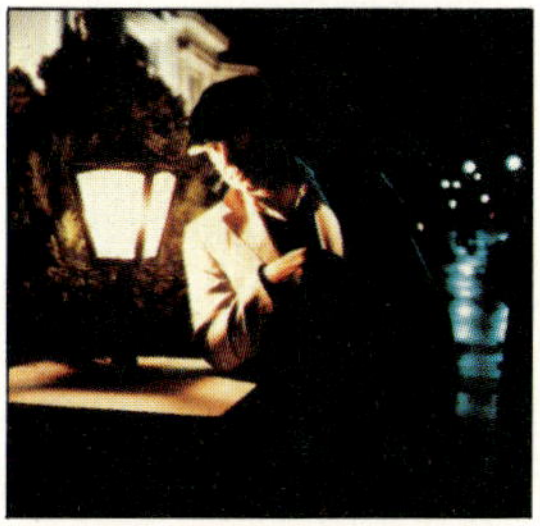

Effects of artificial light
Instant picture film is designed for daylight or flash illumination – various color shifts occur in artificial light. Some street lamps produce a blue cast, fluorescent light a yellow-green cast and tungsten lamps give a red tone. These effects can give dramatic night pictures.

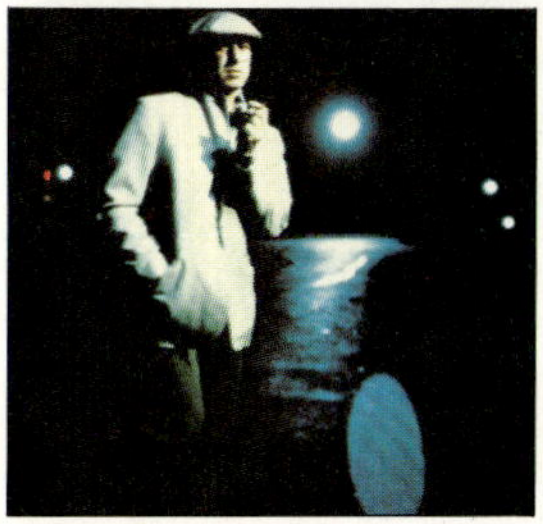

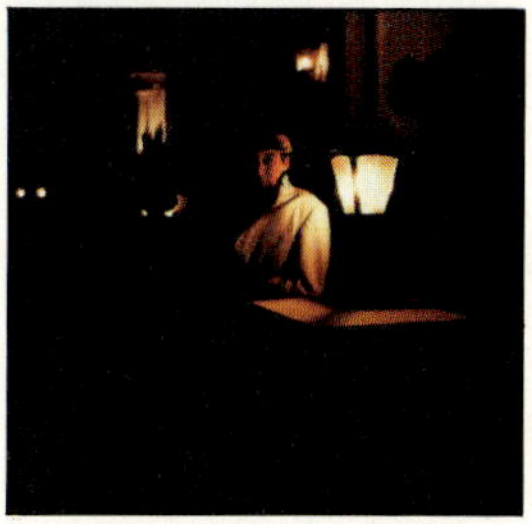

Handling moving subjects

When shooting moving subjects, you can either try to freeze the action, or allow it to blur. Unless you can get close enough to use flash, freezing motion means using a fast shutter speed. This is not easy, as instant cameras are all automatic, and will choose a fast shutter speed only in very bright light. Even then, speeds will not be very high, as instant color film is less sensitive to light than conventional films, and so requires longer exposures. You will find it easier to freeze action if you shoot it head-on, or choose the climax or peak of an action, or pan your camera.
In dim light, your camera will select a slow shutter speed and any movement will blur. Some degree of blur can help to convey an impression of motion. But don't attempt to shoot fast sports on instant film.

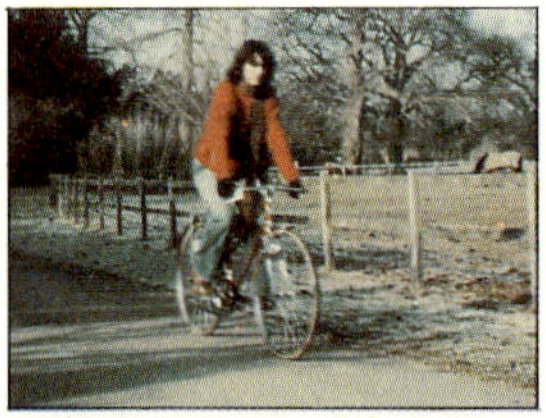

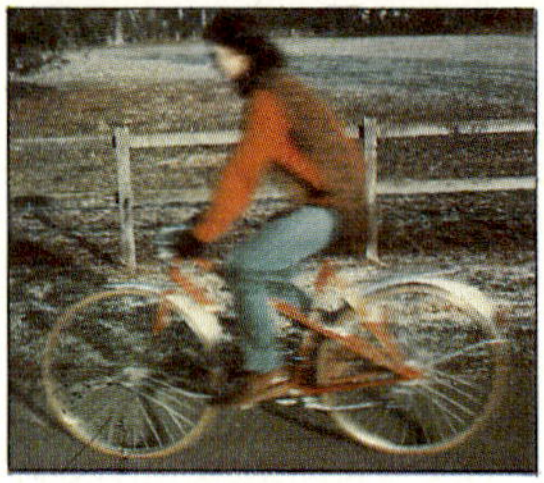

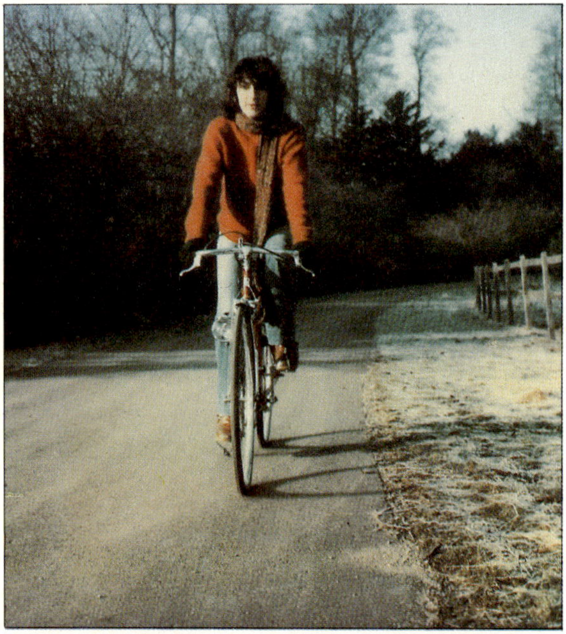

Shoot head-on
It is easier to freeze action moving directly toward the camera, right, or obliquely, top. Subjects moving across the frame are likely to blur, above.

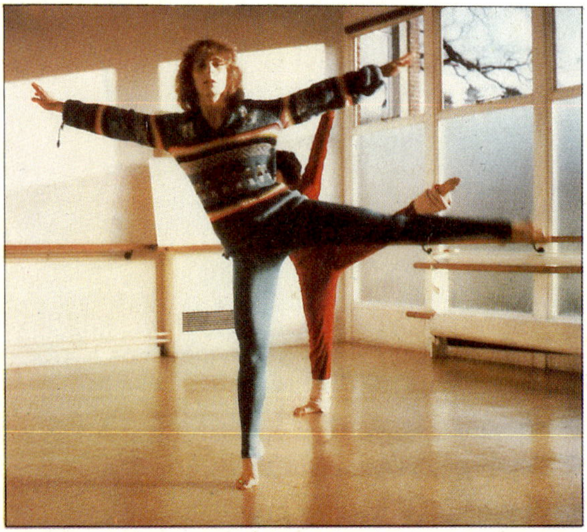

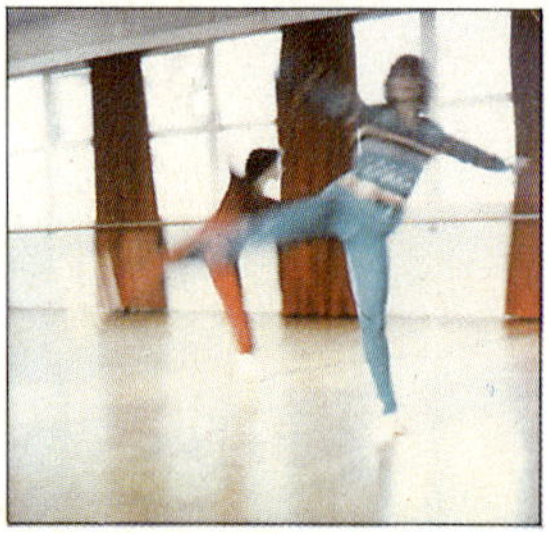

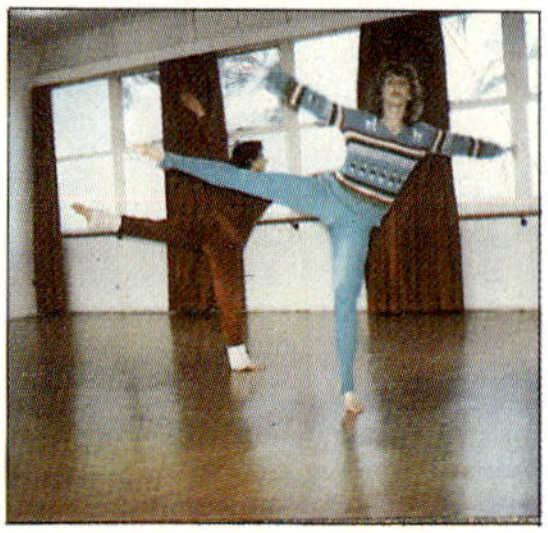

Peak of action
Action often slows down or halts at its peak – the climax of a dancer's movement, for instance, as left. Such moments make expressive shots, and are easier to freeze. Plan your viewpoint in advance so that you catch the action against a fairly clear background, and prefocus on the point where you expect the peak moment to occur. If you miss the peak, you will get blur, above center. To be sure of a sharp result, you should use flash, as in the picture above right.

Capturing atmosphere
Use lighting to enhance the mood of the action – look for strong light to bring out color or soft light to suit graceful movement. If you take a picture without flash in artificial light, such as tungsten (p.72), you will get a soft, warm effect. A dark background, far right, will complement warm colors. Try to capture the peak of the action to express the dancer's grace and pose, right. Or let her actions blur, far right, to convey an impression of motion.

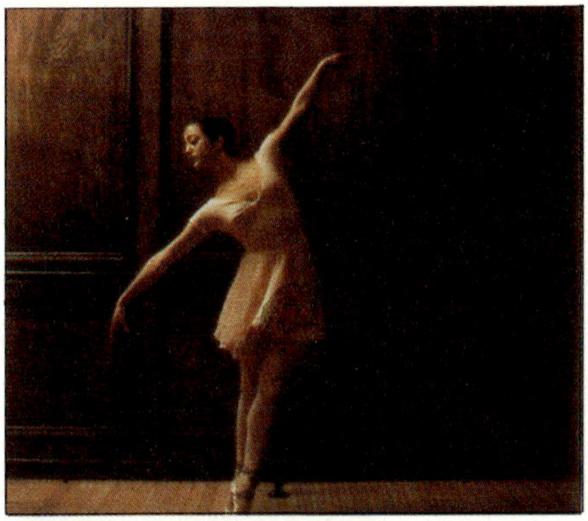

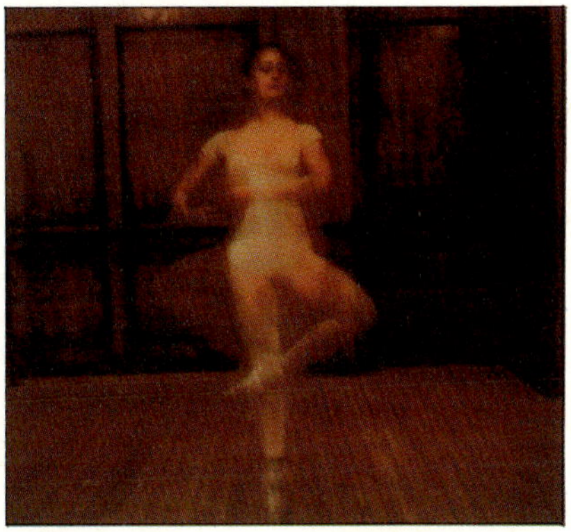

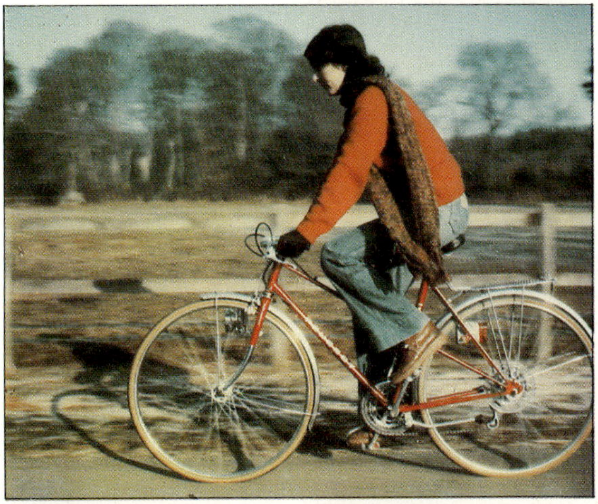

Panning for fast action
Panning helps to freeze a moving subject when you shoot broadside on, left. To "pan" the camera, first focus on a point where the subject will pass. Frame the subject, and swing your whole body smoothly to keep it in the viewfinder (see the diagram), pressing the shutter as it passes the point you have selected. The background blur is more dramatic with fast subjects than with slow ones. You can suggest speed by overpanning, as in the picture right – start your pan behind the subject and pan smoothly past it.

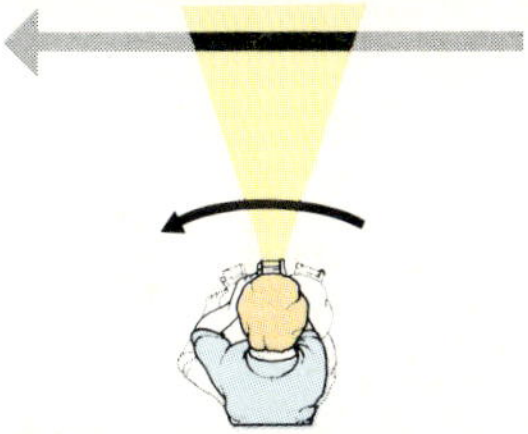

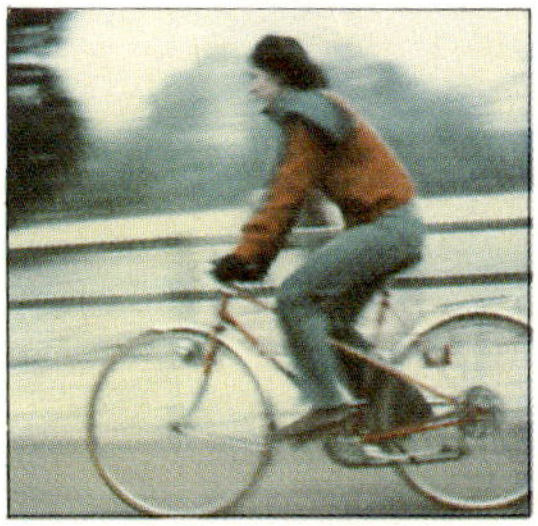

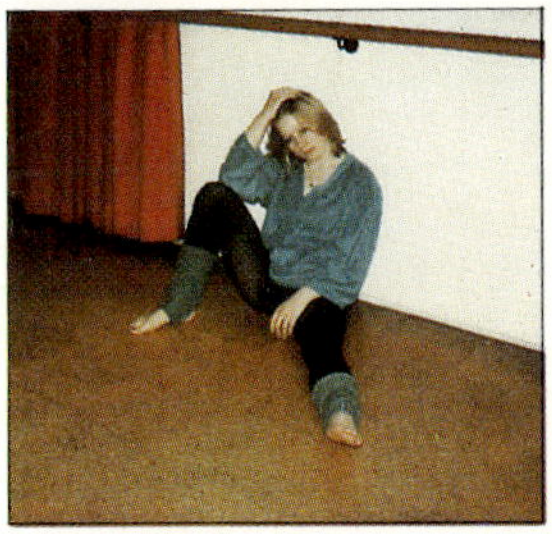

Varying the mood
Remember to take some photographs after the action is over, too. The shot above, showing a quiet moment at the end of the day, portrays a very different mood from the pictures of the dancers on the facing page.

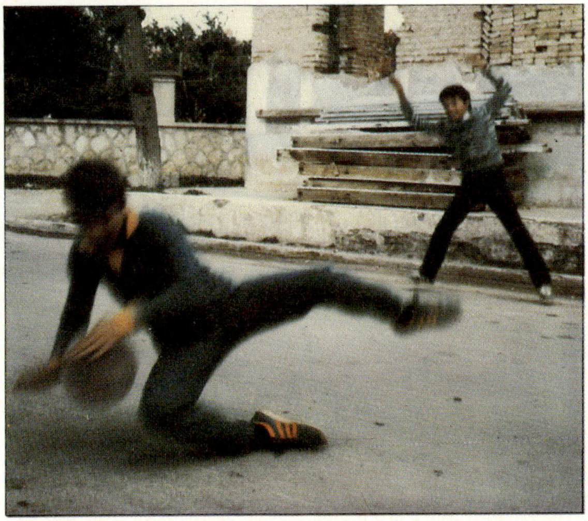

Capturing excitement
Look for lively expressions and exciting groupings when photographing moving subjects. Anticipate movements that will occur and be ready to press your shutter immediately. Don't let the speed of events overwhelm you – make sure the background is uncluttered before you press the shutter, and don't forget to focus (p.19). There is no need to freeze the action every time – sometimes blur will add to the sense of action, as in the shot left. Look around for children playing – from skateboarding to ball games – they make ideal subjects for action shots.

The family at home

The instant pictures you take of your family at home are likely to be among your most successful – you are working with people and surroundings that you know well and instant picture cameras will make photography fun for your subjects too. Try to show relationships between people and shoot when they are reacting to each other, or to a point of interest, not to the camera. Don't allow your familiarity with your home to blind you to distracting colors and details in the background.

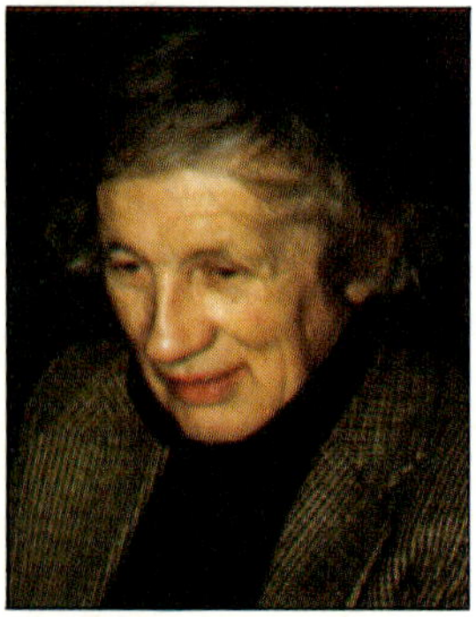

Taking pictures of older people
Don't restrict your instant photography to shots of the children – grandparents make excellent subjects too. Whenever possible, take portraits by soft natural light, indoors or outdoors, as right. If light is very low, use diffused flash (p.23), as above. Soft lighting is flattering, and reveals the fine detail and character in a face.

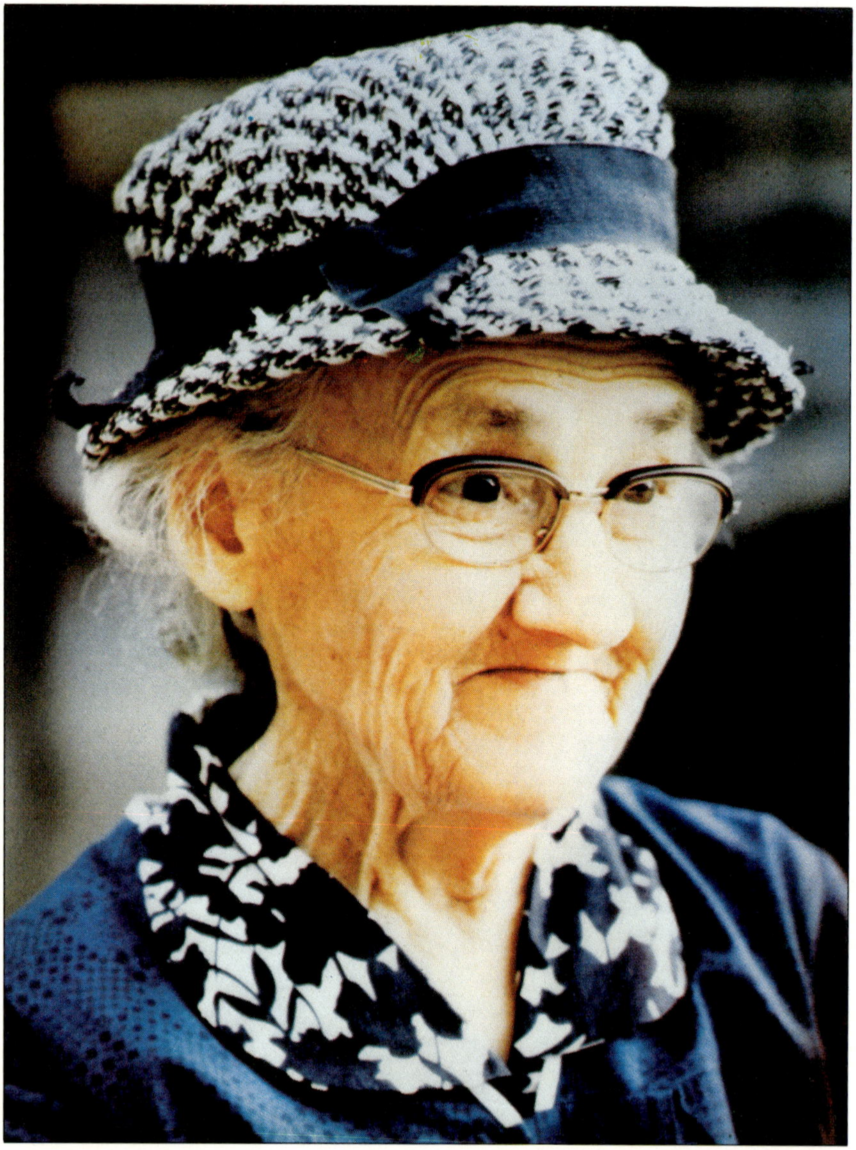

Family groups
Lighting and color contribute greatly to the mood of a picture. Soft light enhances an intimate mood, right. Concentrate on faces – get as close as you can (p.79), and make use of natural light.
In all these pictures the subjects' heads are well arranged – they are looking toward each other, or in the same direction. Your picture will be weaker if they are looking in opposite directions, below.

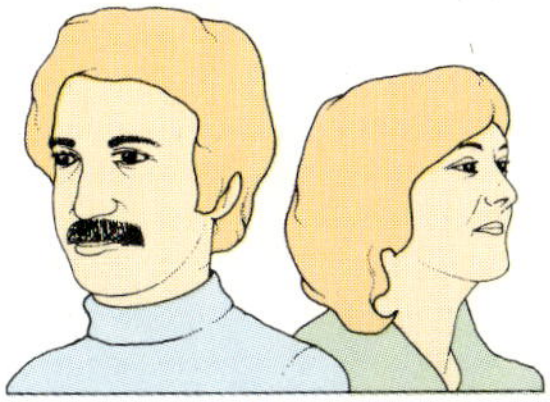

Wrong head positions

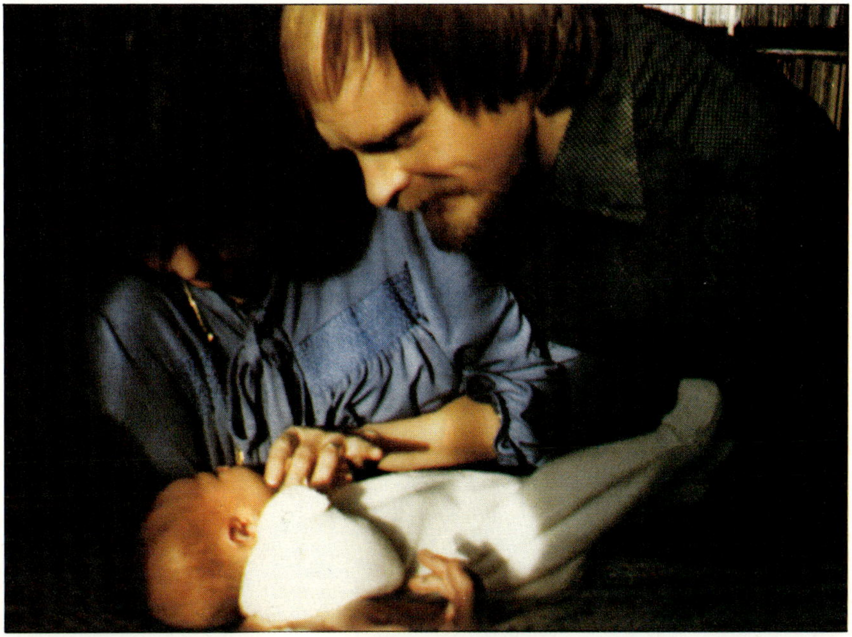

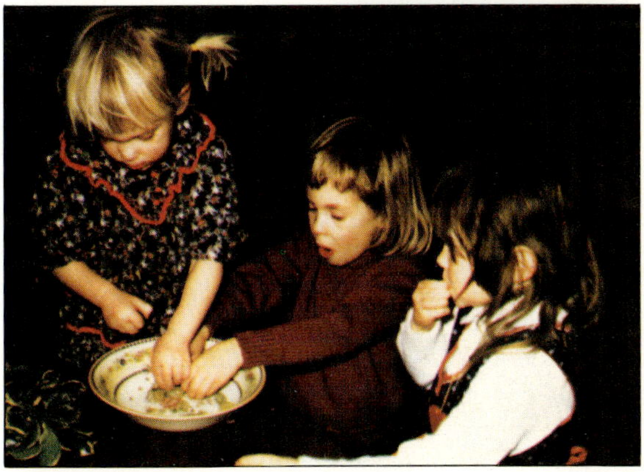

Shooting while unobserved
You will achieve the most natural, unselfconscious instant pictures of your family when they are unaware of the camera. Shoot while they are taking part in an absorbing activity, as above, or engaged in lively conversation. Choose your viewpoint so that all the faces are clearly visible, and the background is uncluttered. Children look most natural when photographed from their own eye level, as in the picture above. Timing is as important as any technical skill when taking pictures of people in groups. Wait until everyone's attention is centered on one point of interest, and faces and gestures are animated, as right. Then shoot quickly.

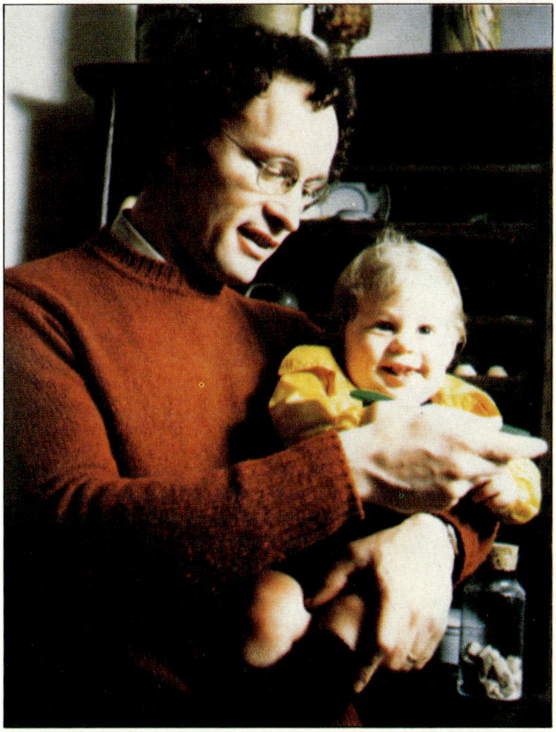

Photographing babies

During their first year, babies grow and change fast – learning to smile, reach out, sit up, move around, feed and play. An instant picture camera enables you to make a visual record of your baby's development from the start. Whenever possible, use natural lighting indoors and soft, even light outside. If flash is necessary (pp.22–3), diffuse it – direct flash is too harsh. Do not pose your baby or dress her up specially for the occasion. Get down to her level, move in as close as you can (p.79) and photograph her among her toys in familiar surroundings. A baby is often too small to fill the frame. Choose a brightly colored prop to fill out the picture, as right. Or use a dark background for dramatic indoor shots, below. Take care in natural light that shadows do not fall across faces. Try photographing a baby in his mother's arms, looking over her shoulder, as below right.

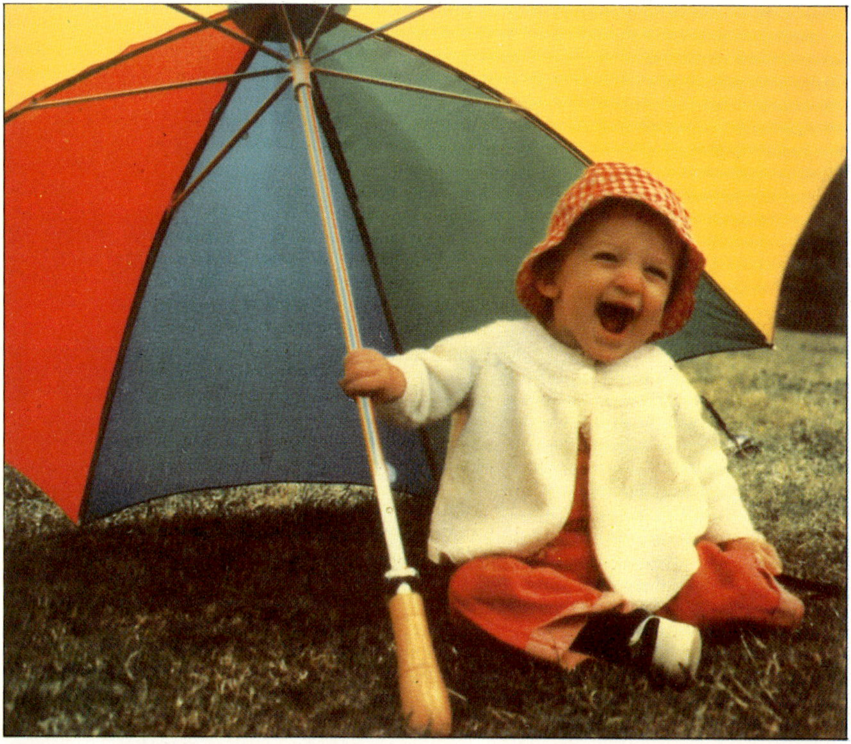

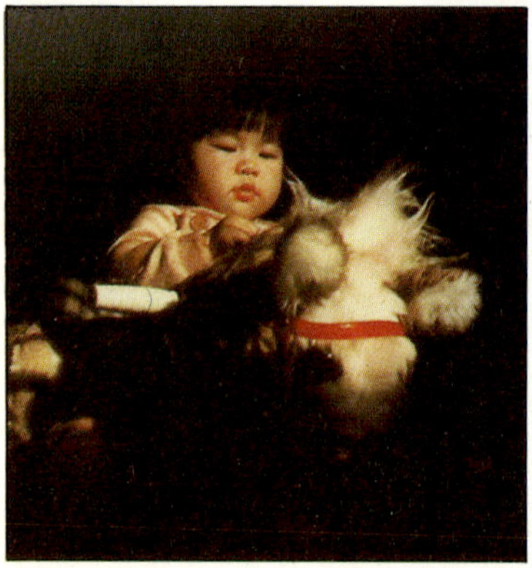

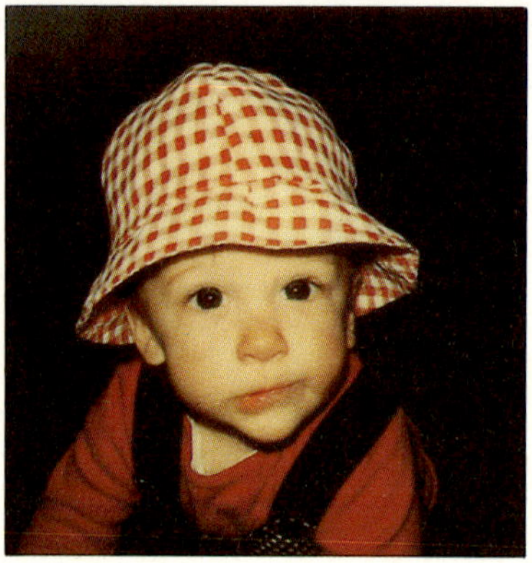

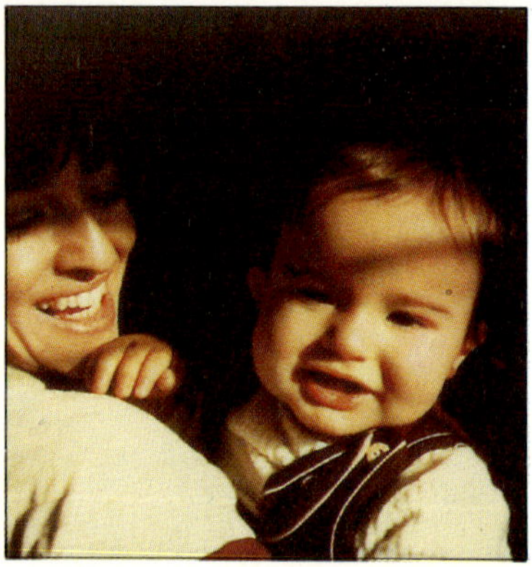

Propping up your baby
Until a baby is strong enough to sit up on his own, you will have to find some means to support him, right. Place soft-toned cushions or a pillow behind him, below, or place a baby chair inside a larger chair, as in the picture right.

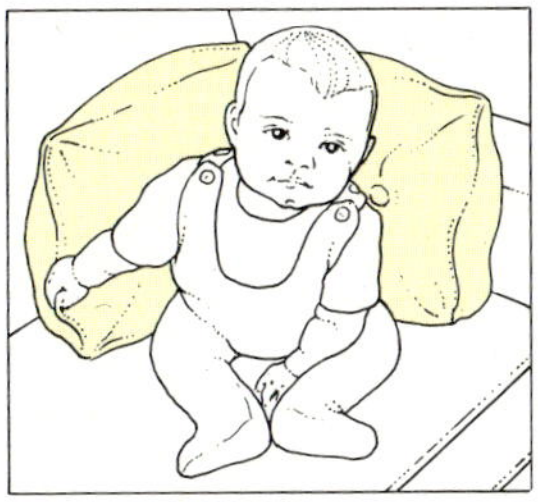

Making use of pillows

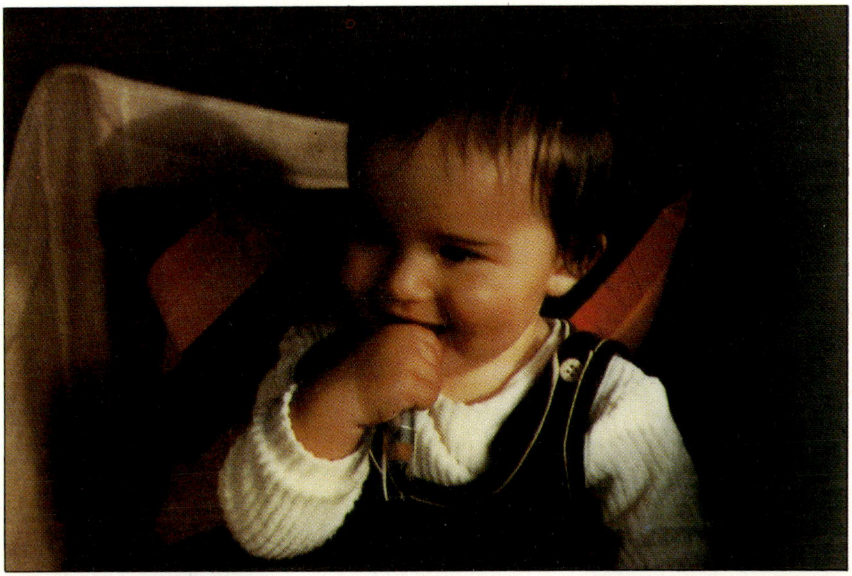

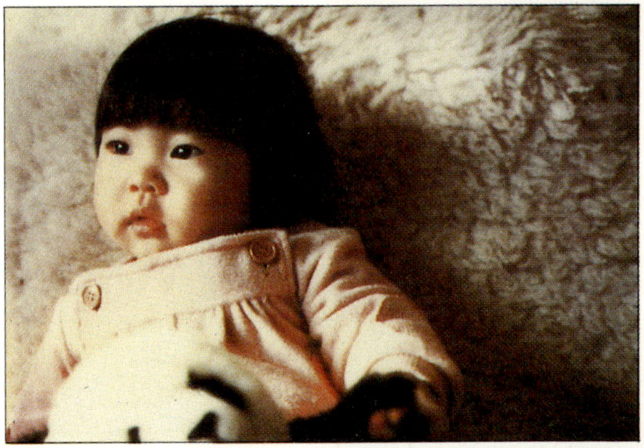

Expressive moments
Babies make delightfully unself-conscious subjects. Make the most of their range of expressions, right, by having your camera ready at all times, and taking shots in sequence. Catch them as they wake up, before they begin to move too rapidly, and shoot in natural light.

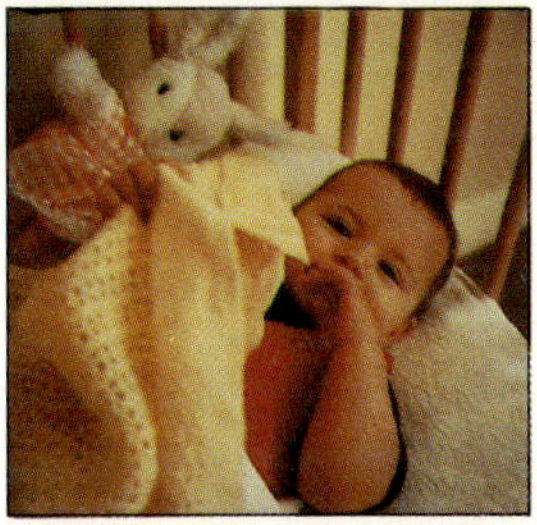

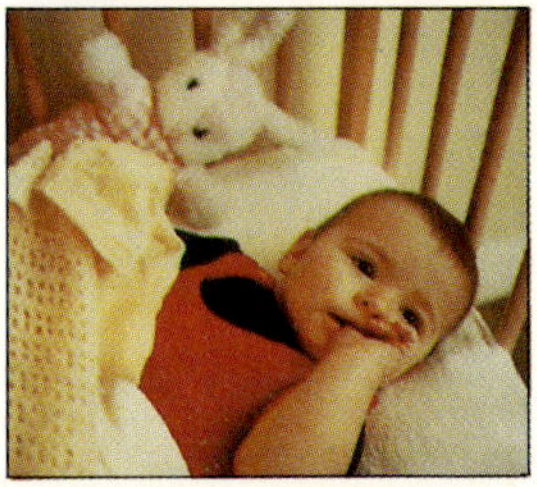

Available light shots
Indoor pictures in available light will give the most natural result. Make use of strong shafts of sunlight to highlight the baby's face. Your camera will select a slow shutter speed (p.20), so use a tripod or find a support (p.17). Leave the L/D control in the center position, as above, if you want to see most of the baby's features when your subject is lit by bright light from a window. Move the L/D control to darken for a moody shot, right.

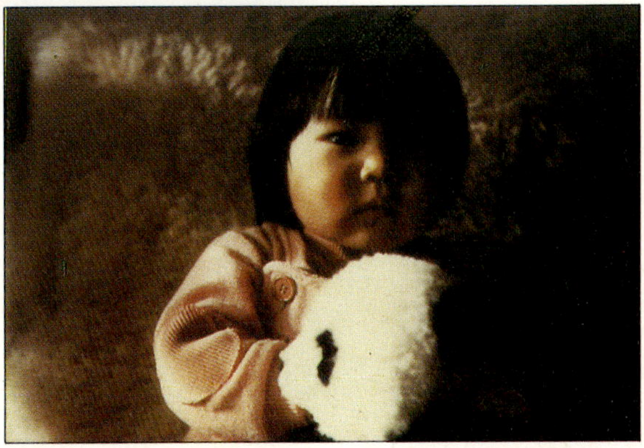

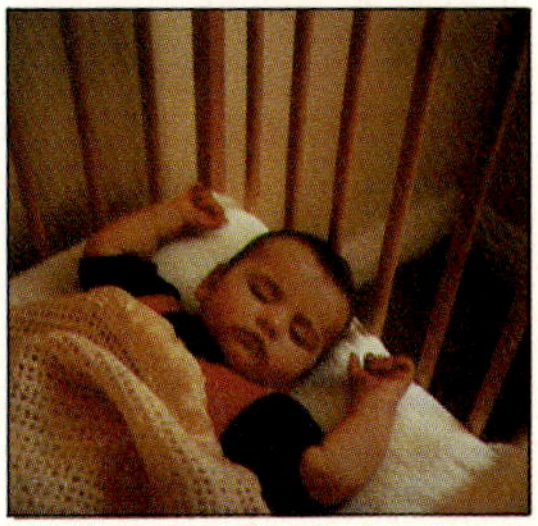

Photographing children

Children can be lively and excited one moment, quiet and pensive the next. Make the most of their ever-changing moods and expressions by having your instant camera available at all times. Children enjoy the magic of instant pictures – the novelty often arouses a response that makes a lively shot. Try to use natural light wherever possible. If you use flash you should diffuse it (p.23). Take advantage of bright clothes and toys in order to get plenty of color into your shots.

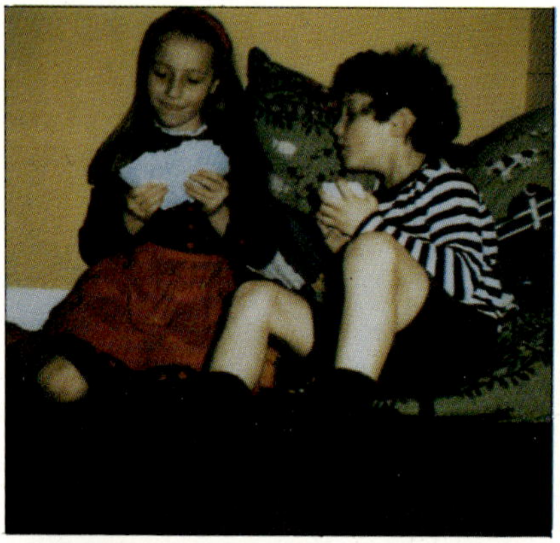

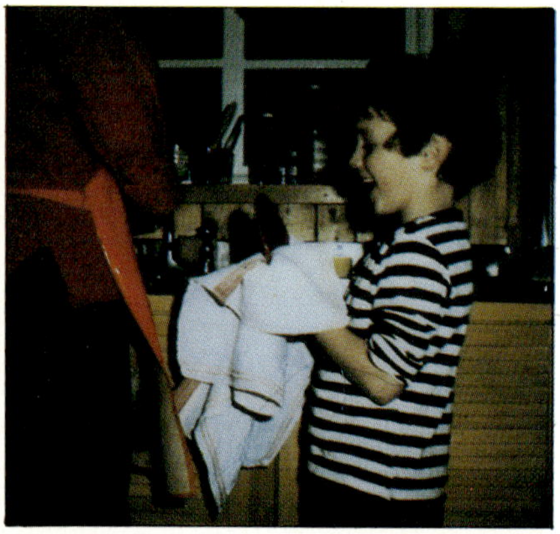

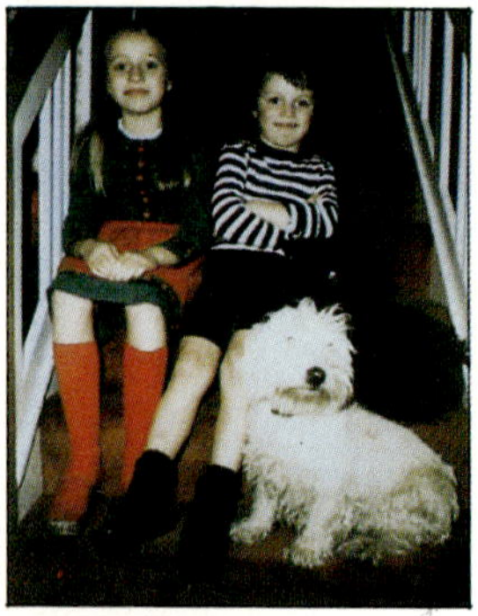

Avoiding self-consciousness
The picture, above, is spoiled by self-consciousness. You can avoid results like this by giving children something to do, top right. You will get your best shots when the subjects are unaware of the camera. Children look most natural when they are photographed from their own eye level. If a child is shy of the camera, put her at ease by turning the occasion into a game, right.

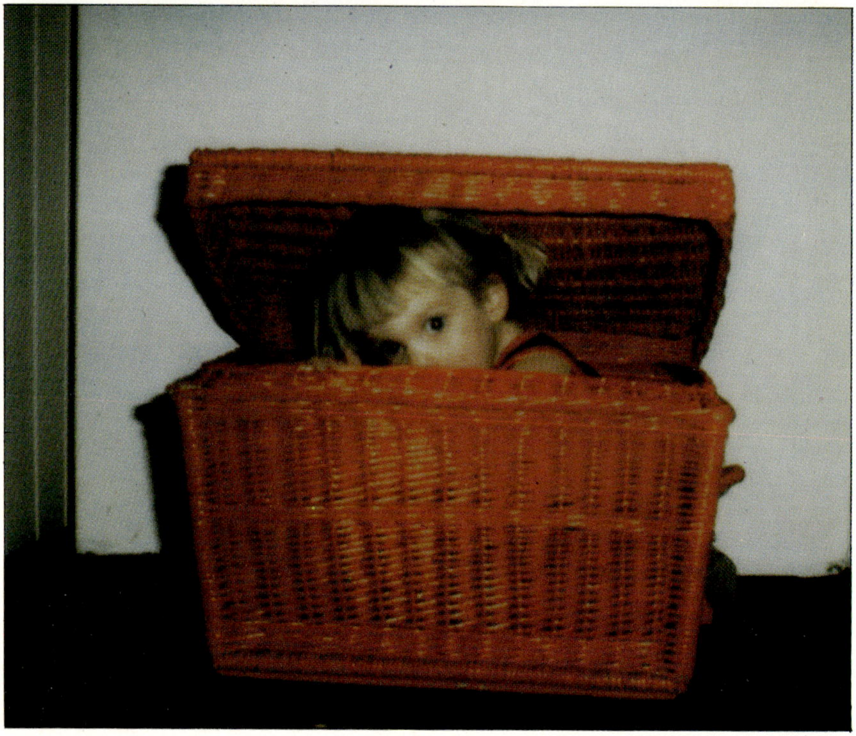

Using light and color
You can strengthen the mood of your shots by using color and lighting sensitively. A colorful frame, right, emphasizes the bright, sunny mood of the picture of the small boy, caught in a mischievous moment. The dreamy, slightly wistful mood of the girl, below, is enhanced by soft, natural lighting and harmonious tones.

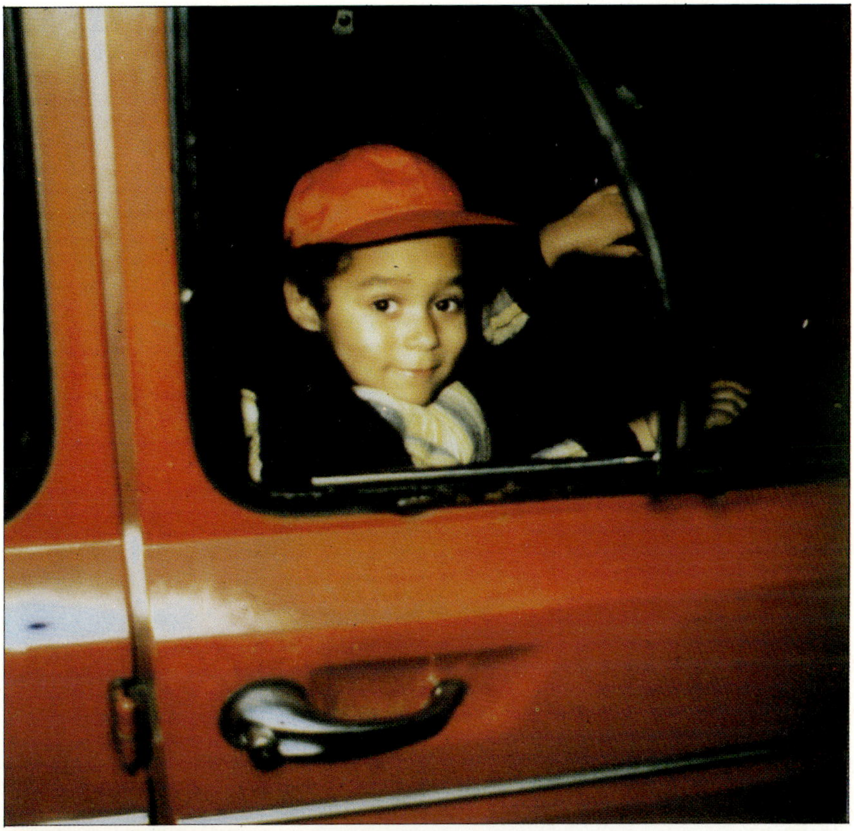

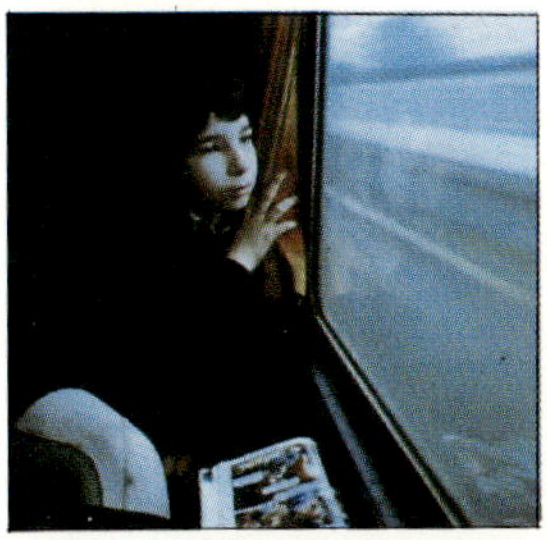

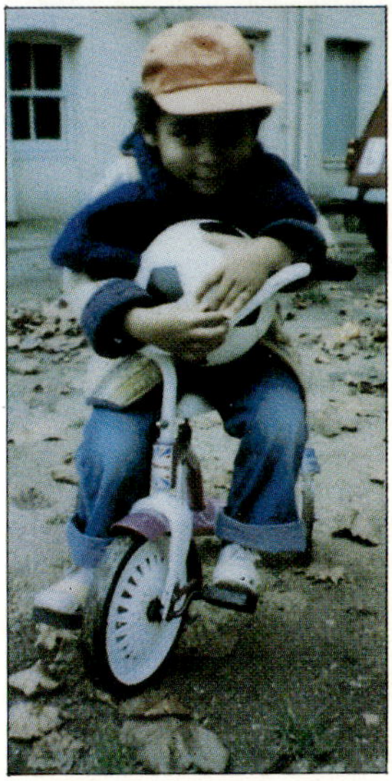

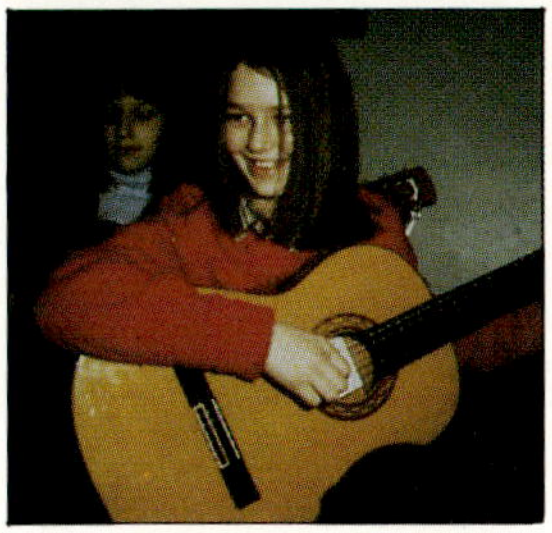

Capturing children at play
Children involved in play, indoors or outdoors, will soon forget the camera, enabling you to shoot freely. Be patient and wait until expressions are lively, left and above. Then shoot fast before the moment is lost. Choose an unusual viewpoint for a dynamic shot, right.

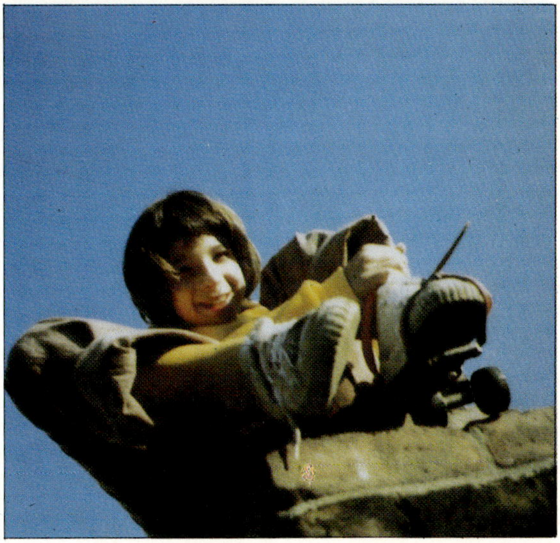

Taking portraits outdoors

Taking good outdoor portraits is not easy. For an attractive result you must choose the right lighting for your subject, see facing page. Take your flash out with you – you may have to use it to "fill-in" any ugly shadows. You can use any kind of bar or cube for fill-in flash, but not all types of gun – some will not fire in bright outdoor light so check your manual before shooting. Before taking a picture, look around your viewfinder to make sure that the background does not dominate, and check your framing for parallax (p.18). If you are shooting someone outside a window, through the glass, you cannot use autofocus – you must switch to manual and focus yourself.

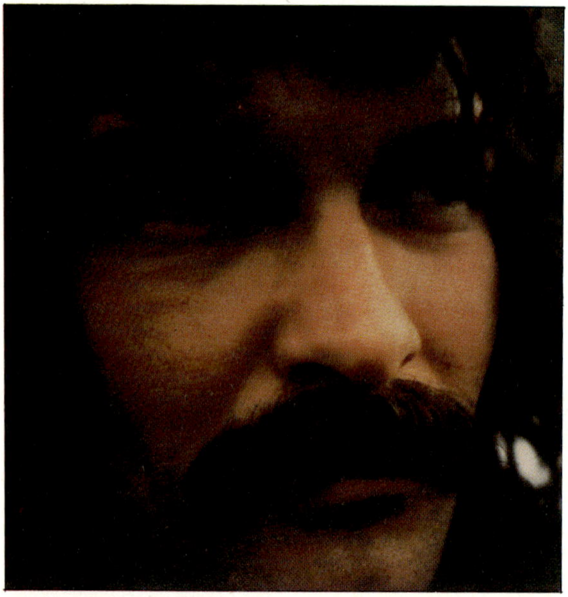

Focusing on a face
Take a face close-up for good detail, left. Focus very carefully, making sure that the eyes are sharp. With a split screen (p. 19), place the circle over the upper part of the bridge of the nose. Remember to keep within your camera's range (p.79), when you try to fill the frame. Don't get the subject to look straight into the lens or you will get a stiff, awkward-looking result. Choose a slightly oblique view which shows the most attractive side of the face. Take care that eyes are not lost in shadow. If you have a telephoto lens (p.90), use it for a more flattering result – it avoids the problems of distortion (an exaggerated nose, for example).

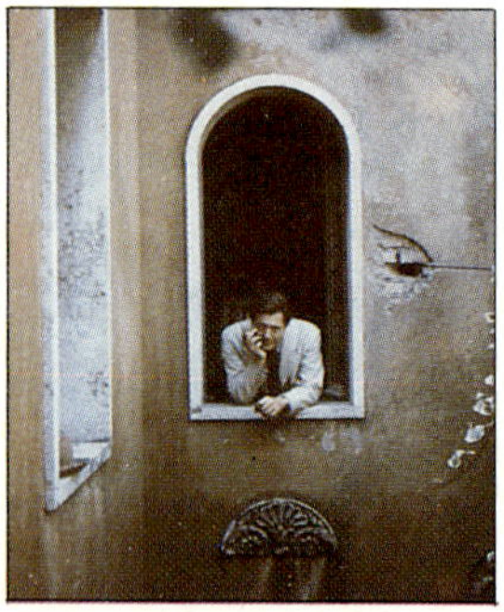

Finding a frame outdoors
Windows and doors provide interesting frames for outdoor portraits. Change your view of the subject by asking him to move around in the frame. Make sure that your subject's pose is casual, not formal.

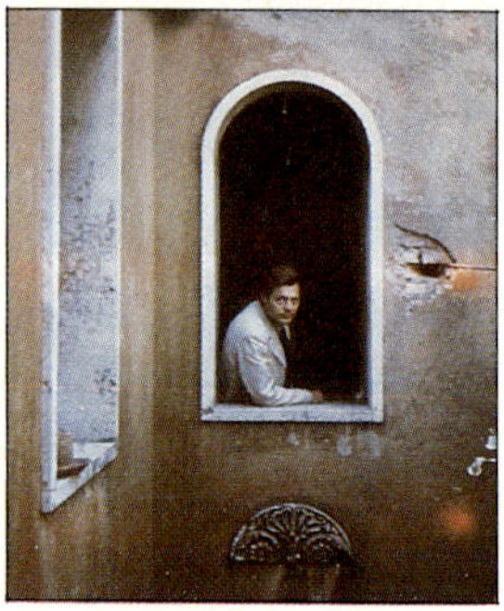

Relating subject to setting
Include the subject's surroundings in an informal portrait for a natural-looking shot. Shoot the subject engaged in an activity, and use lighting and framing to enhance mood, right.

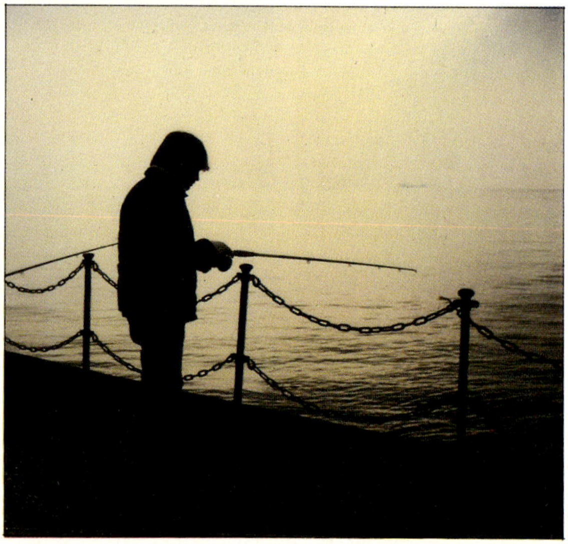

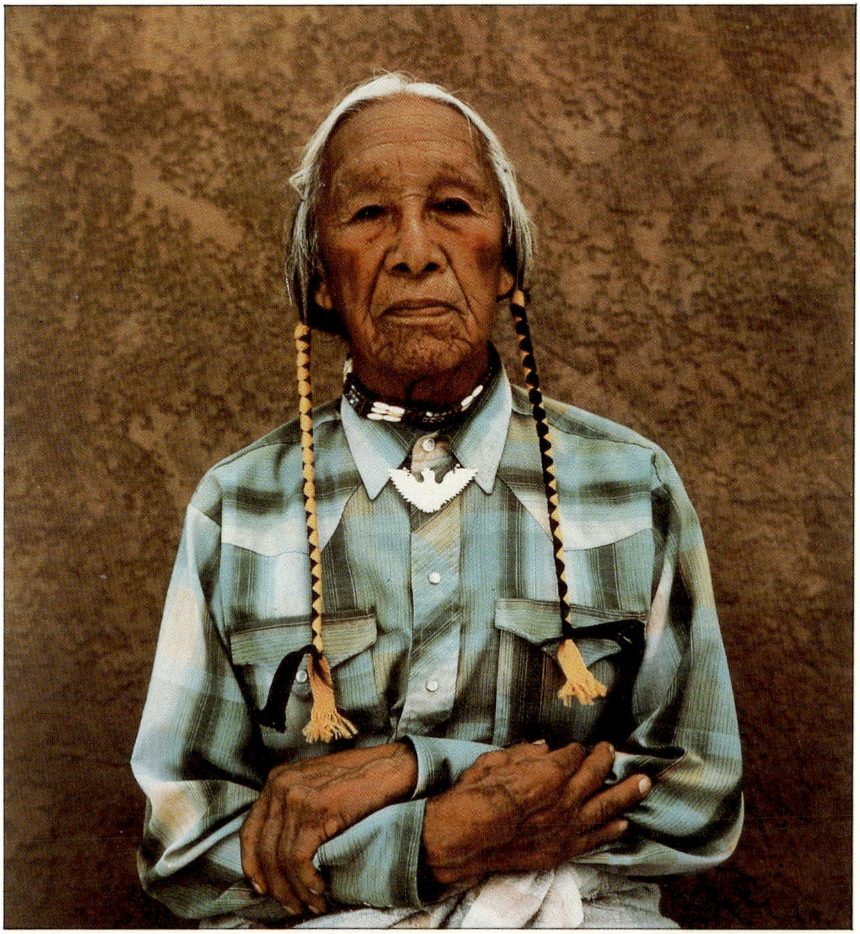

Choosing the right light
Bright, hazy sunshine or bright shade generally provide the best lighting conditions for outdoor portraits. The soft light produces good facial modeling. It reveals skin color and texture, and there are no ugly shadows obscuring the subject. And in hazy light or shade as left the subject can look comfortably toward the camera, without squinting, no matter where the sun is.

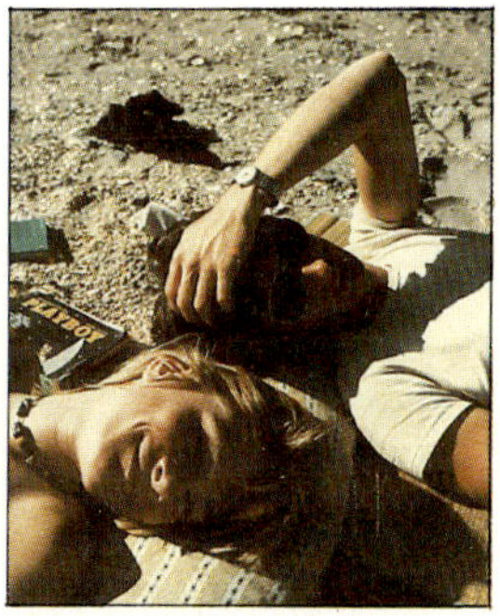

Problems of shadow
Strong overhead sunlight can make people squint and cast ugly shadows on their faces, as in the shot above. To correct this, use fill-in flash and set the L/D toward darken.

Light and shadow
Bright light often causes contrast problems, see above right. Arrange your subject so that the sun highlights attractive features, and the shadow does not spoil the picture. Shadow and light together on a face look ugly – it is better to keep your subject's face completely in shadow. In the shot right, shadow cast by overhead sun emphasizes the dramatic dress of the subject. Bright light from behind highlights blonde hair, far right. Set the L/D to lighten, to show detail in the face.

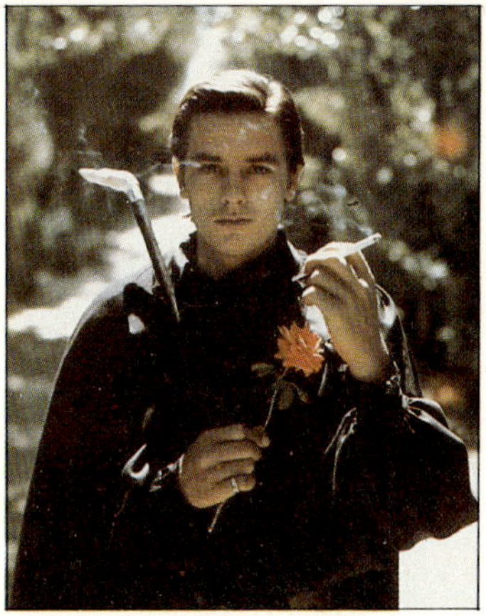

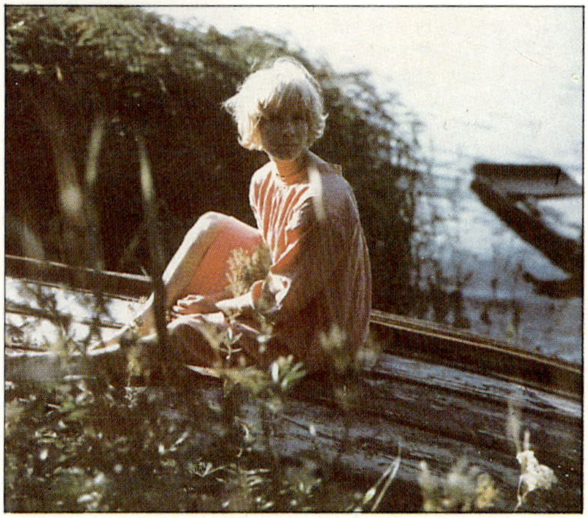

Taking portraits indoors

Instant photography is an exciting medium for portraiture – your sitters will feel more involved in the picture-taking process as soon as they see your first shot. Taking good instant portraits indoors is not always easy, but with time, care and patience you will get excellent results. If you follow the guidelines given here, you will avoid the commonest pitfalls. By day, place your subject about 3 ft (1 m) from a window against a complementary background. Use a white wall or white card (see facing page), to reflect some light back on to the shadowed side of the subject's face. If the light is too low, use diffused flash (p.23) instead of the reflector. When it is dark, use diffused flash alone, and place your subject near a light wall (for a light background) or more than 6 ft away from any wall (for a dark background). Choose a fairly close viewpoint, say 3–4 ft (1–1.2 m) with an SLR or 4–5 ft (1.2–1.5 m) with a direct vision model, so that your subject dominates the frame. Always check that the background is clear.

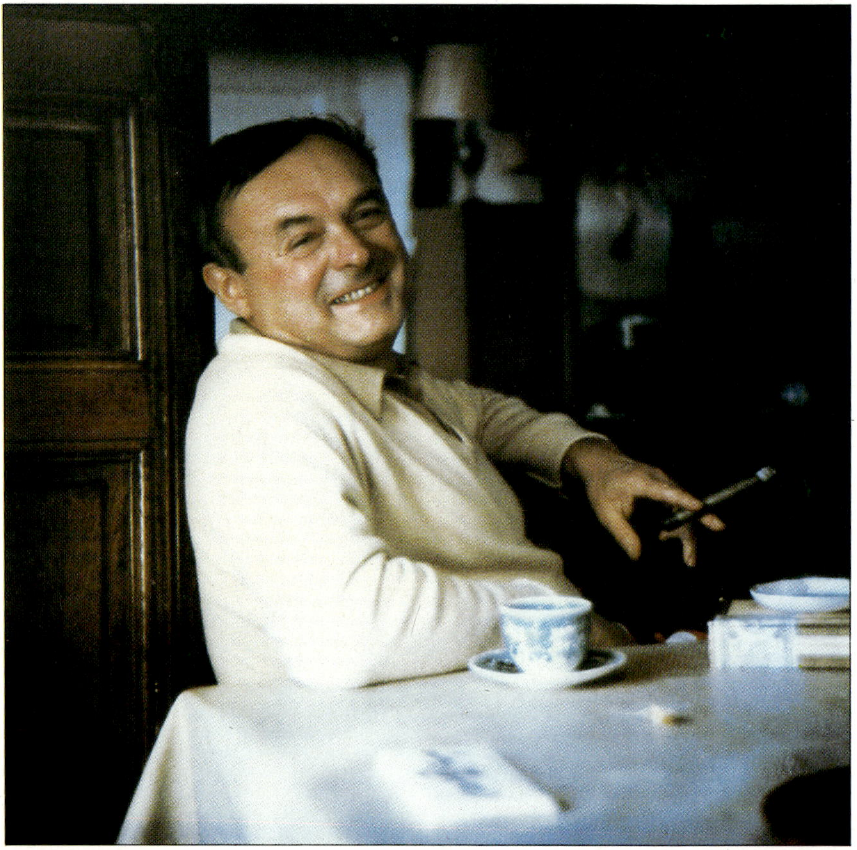

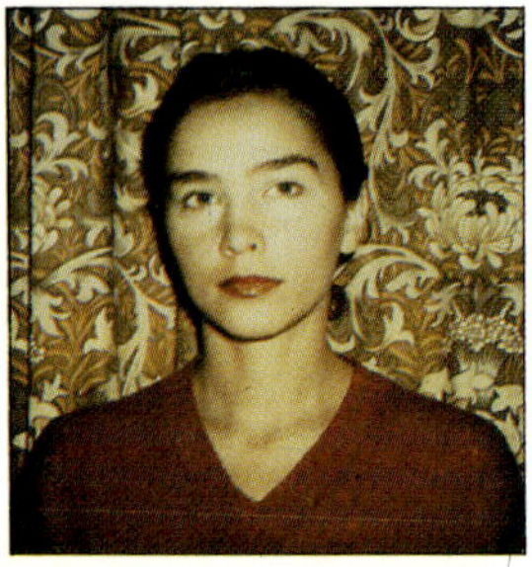

Capturing personality
Never ask your subject to stand still and look into the lens – the result will be stiff and unflattering, left. Get her to relax so that she forgets the camera. Include hands if they help reveal character, right. Or shoot while the sitter is absorbed in an activity, far right, so that her expression is natural.

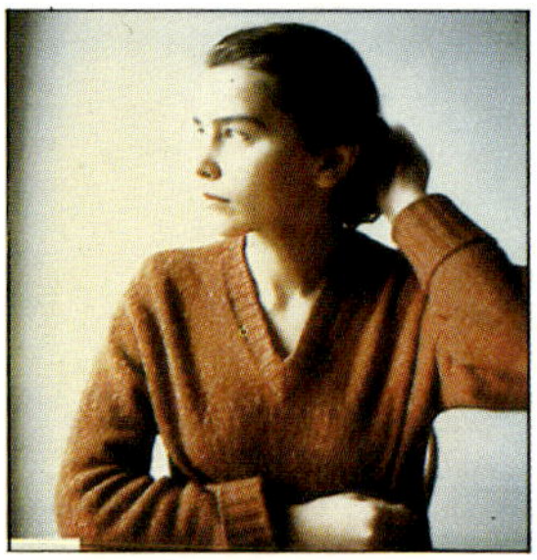

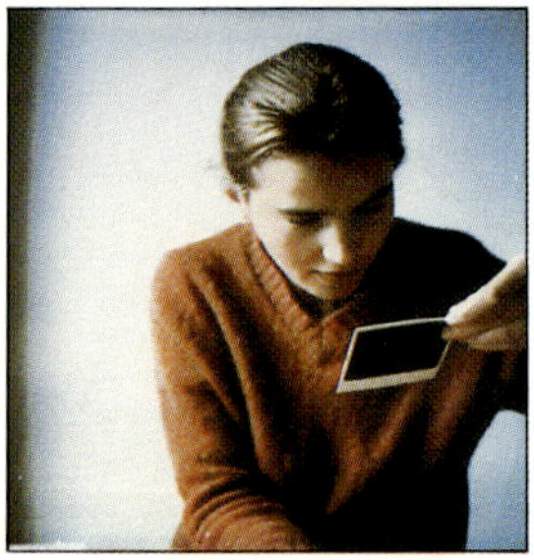

Problems of natural light
In the shot, center, light falling through the window casts hard shadows on one side of the face. If you move the L/D control toward darken, right, or toward lighten, far right, you will only darken or lighten the whole picture. Use a reflector to avoid this problem.

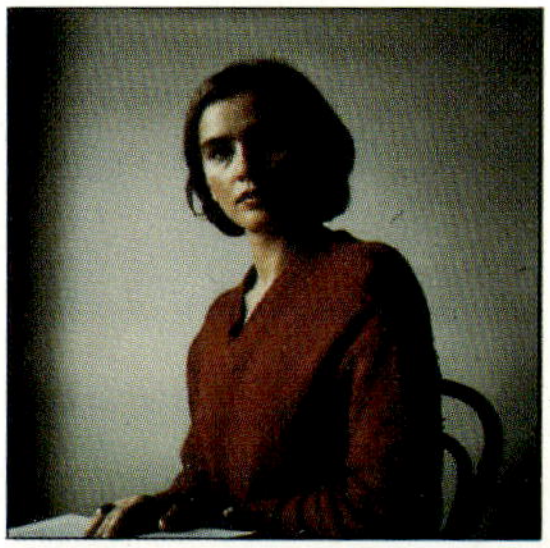

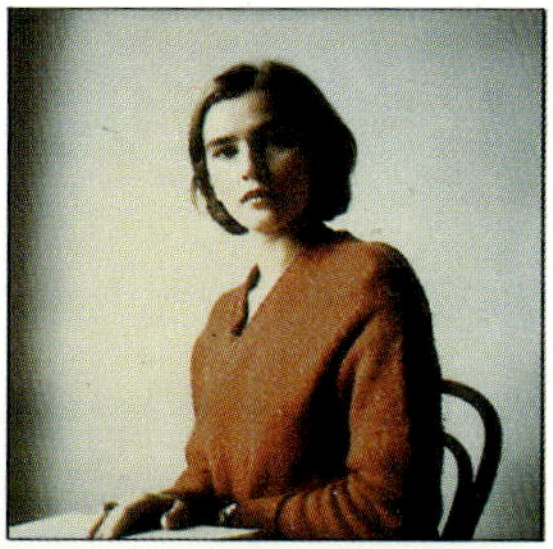

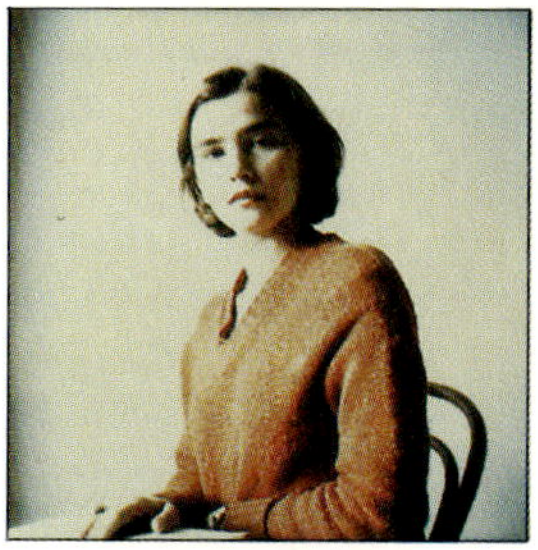

Techniques for portraiture
To avoid hard shadows on your subject's face you should place a reflector opposite the subject, as in the diagram far right, to reflect more light on to the face. The result, right, is a softer, more evenly lit picture showing greater detail. You should study your subject from different sides – few people have such regular features that they look good from any angle. If you want to capture an animated expression, talk to your sitter, to obtain a response, as you shoot.

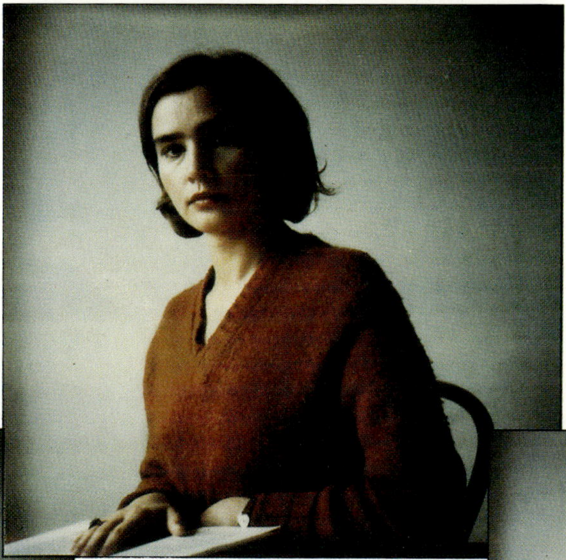

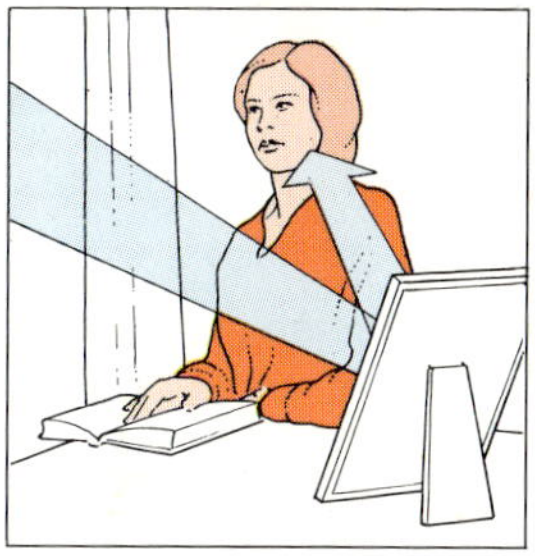

Using a reflector
Place a reflective surface, such as white card, about 3 ft (1 m) from the window opposite your subject to reflect light on to the face.

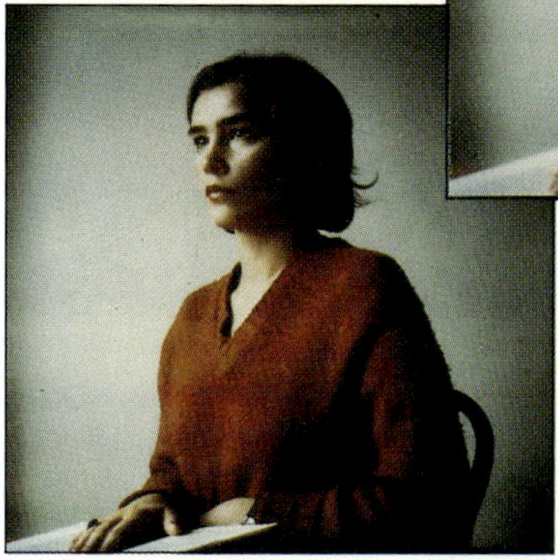

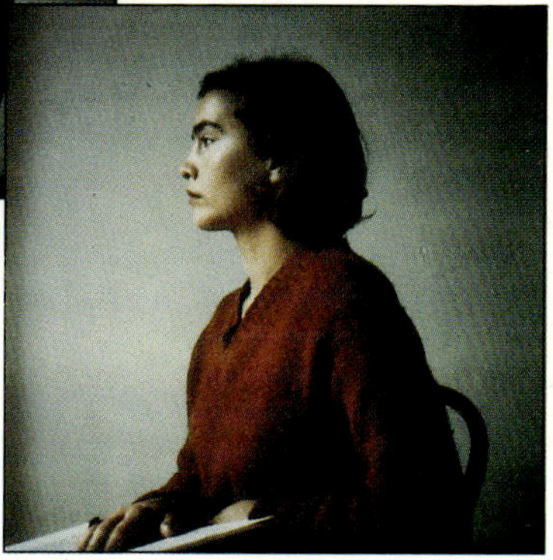

Choosing a viewpoint
Look at your subject from all sides: try a full face position, above, a three-quarter view, left, and a profile, right, and decide which view you prefer before taking your picture.

Flash problems
Direct flash will give hard shadows and dark areas in your picture, particularly if you have chosen a pale background, so you must diffuse the flash (p.23). But a diffused flash result may be too dark overall, as shown right.

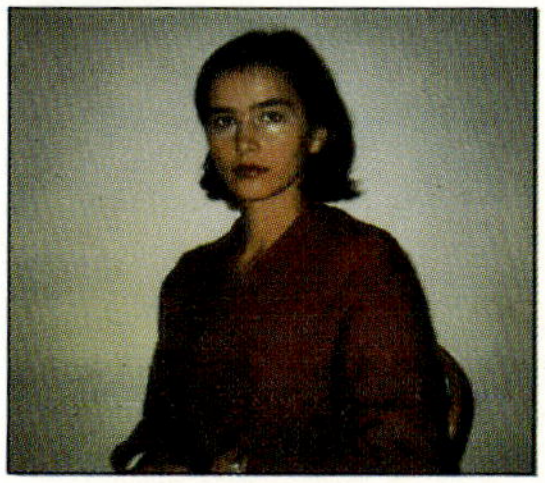

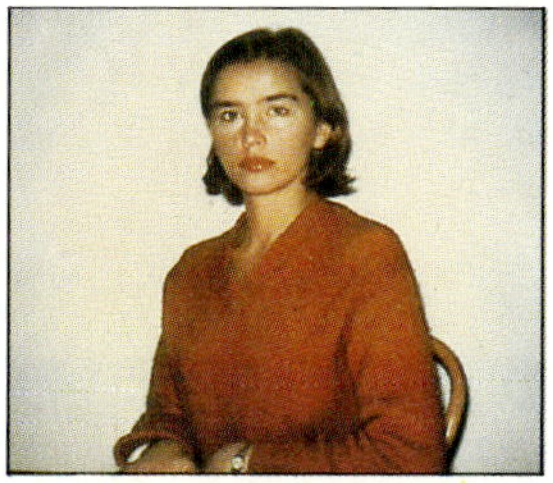

Correcting flash problems
For a good result, left:
- Move the L/D toward lighten as well as diffusing the flash.
- Check that you are within range (p.23).
- Face the subject squarely or you will get flash "fall-off" (p.35).

Photographing informal gatherings

At gatherings or parties, your instant camera and pictures will be much in demand! But this may not make it easy to get good pictures – the secret of good party shots lies in capturing spontaneity, humor, and atmosphere. Wait until interest has subsided, and you can shoot freely. Getting a clear view can be a problem too – your shots are often obscured at the last moment by people's hands or backs. To prevent this, try a high viewpoint, as below, for a large crowd. Or use a low view, right, to clear the background and dramatize a lively piece of action. If you get cluttered shots, you can mask them (p.85). Indoors, with moving people, you will have to use flash (pp.34–5).

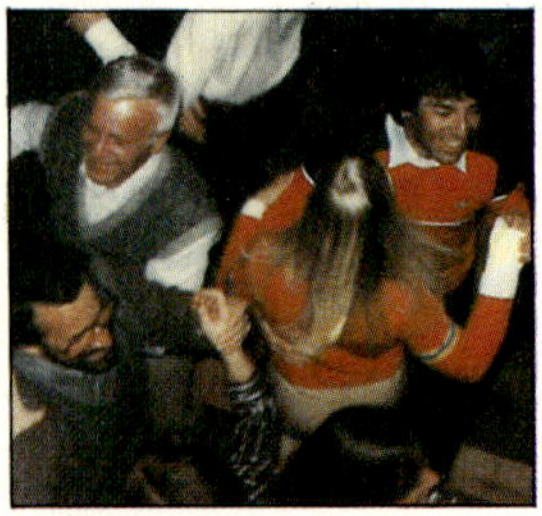

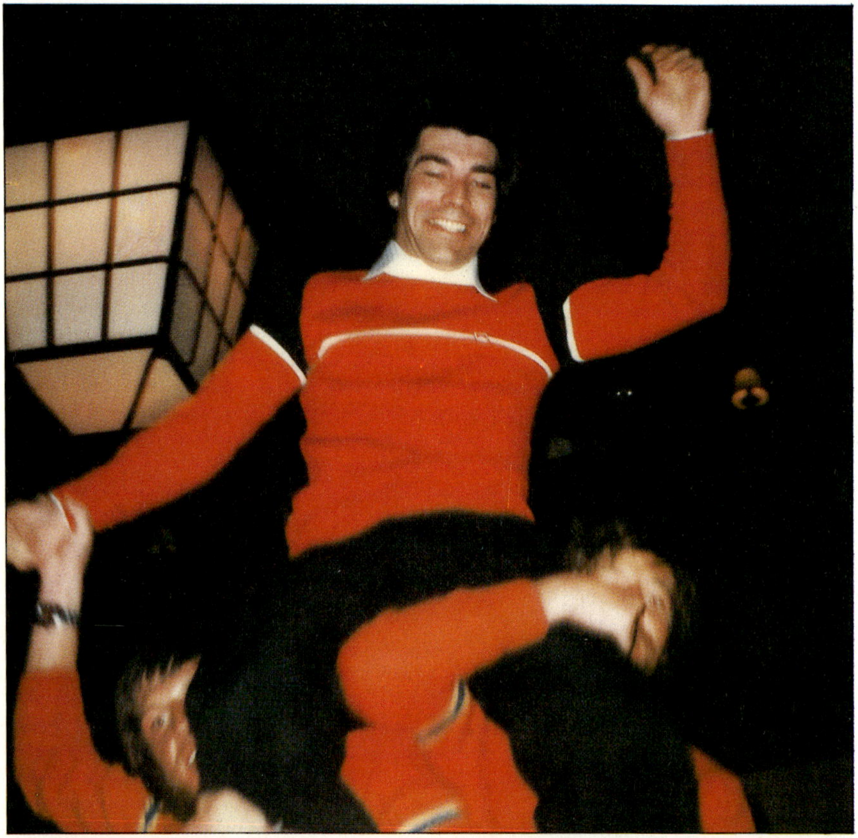

Friendly groups and candids
You can ask friends to co-operate for a well-framed group shot, right, without losing much spontaneity. But for shots of individuals or couples, find a viewpoint where you can catch candid reactions unobserved, far right. Make sure that heads are turned toward each other, not away, and faces are visible.

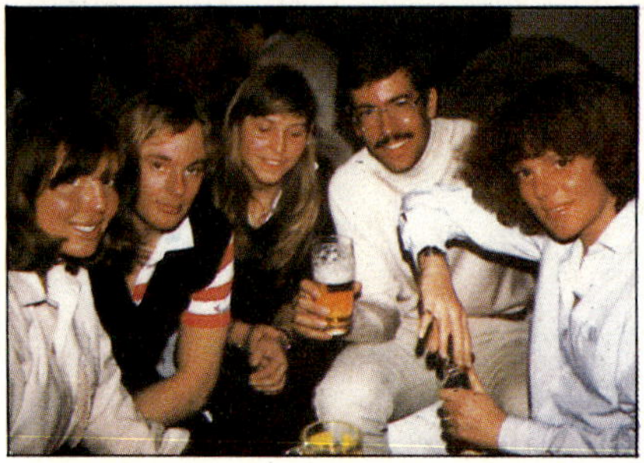

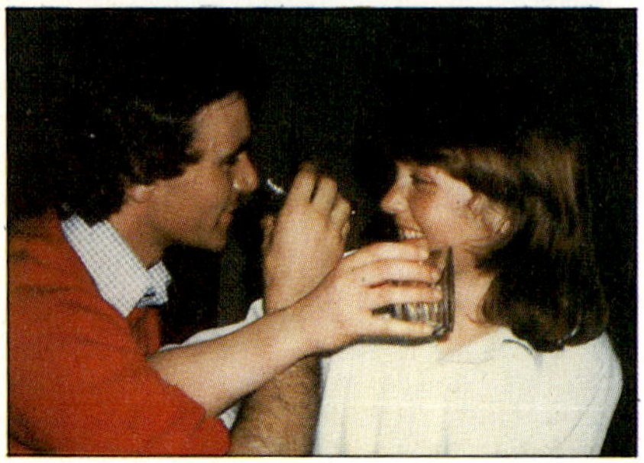

Outdoor gatherings
Follow the advice on outdoor portraits (pp.54–5). And plan your shots to cover the event – overall pictures of the setting, candids, group shots, and humorous action. Frame tightly to exclude distracting elements, and arrange people in a pleasing pattern, below, or around a center of interest, right. If you cannot arrange a shot, look for viewpoints that avoid muddled composition – high to contain a large group, low to clear backgrounds.

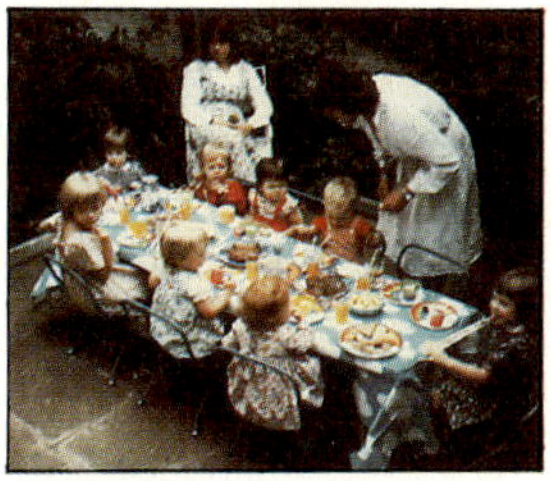

People around a table
A high view, above, takes in the whole scene, and reveals scale. A low one, right, shows faces and expressions. Shoot along the table, or obliquely, not across it.

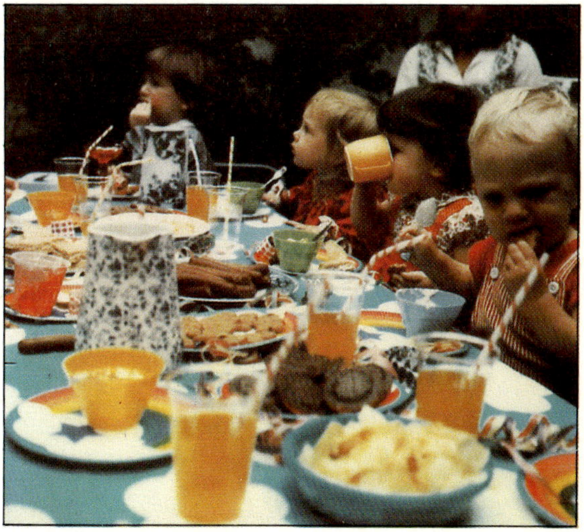

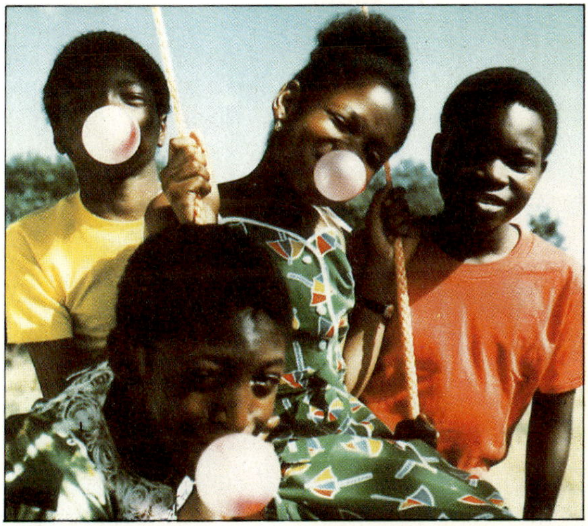

Capturing humor and atmosphere
The shot of the children blowing bubbles, left, shows perfect timing. If there is a lot happening, look through the viewfinder waiting for the action to take place – otherwise you will miss it. Children don't stay still for long, so you must be prepared to shoot fast. Notice how framing and choice of viewpoint has shown the heads at different levels, with faces clearly visible. Use lighting to enhance atmosphere – the bubble picture uses bright light to give good color and convey a happy mood. The shot of the shadows, left, shows an effective way of recording the end of a day out.

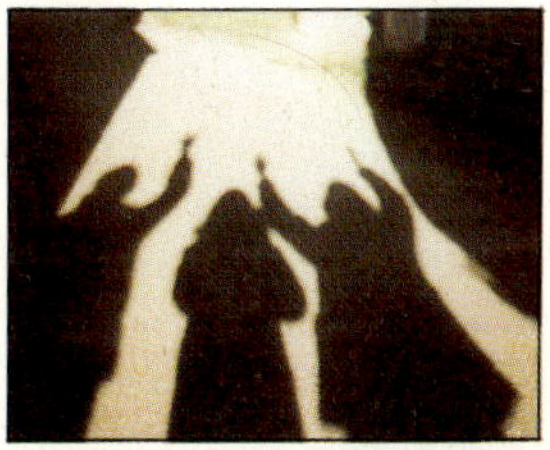

Arranging small groups
Make sure that everybody can be seen – particularly small children. If necessary, hoist them on an adult's shoulder, far right. Arrange people in a compact, attractive pattern, with heads at different levels, or use a device to link the group, like the man's arms, right. Check that there are no gaps in the group or ugly shadows on faces. Before pressing the shutter, attract everyone's attention and try to make people smile. A self-timer (p.86) enables you to include yourself.

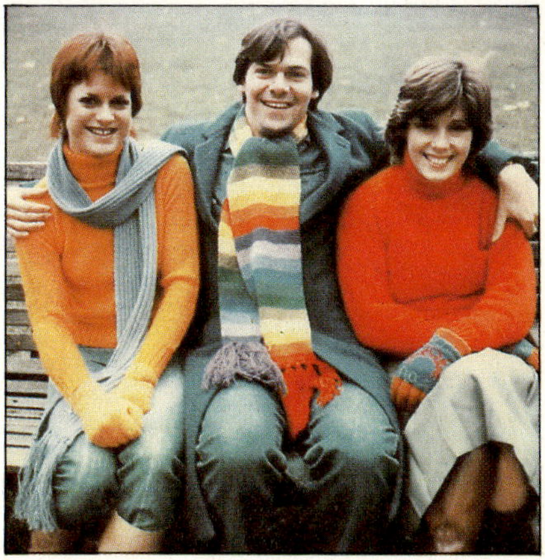

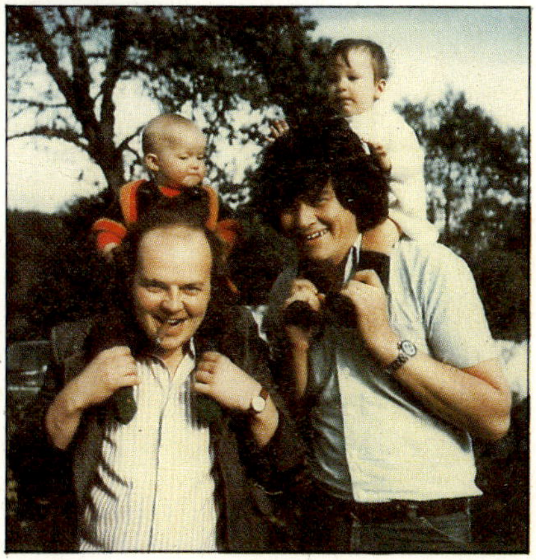

Taking pictures at weddings

A wedding is a one-time event so make sure your camera is working properly and take plenty of film. Concentrate on capturing the mood of the occasion, using natural light wherever possible. Leave the traditional poses to the professional. For a romantic full-length shot of the bride and groom, photograph them away from the crowd, outside in soft daylight. If you want to record the ceremony, right, ask permission to set up your tripod in the aisle, below. Don't use flash.

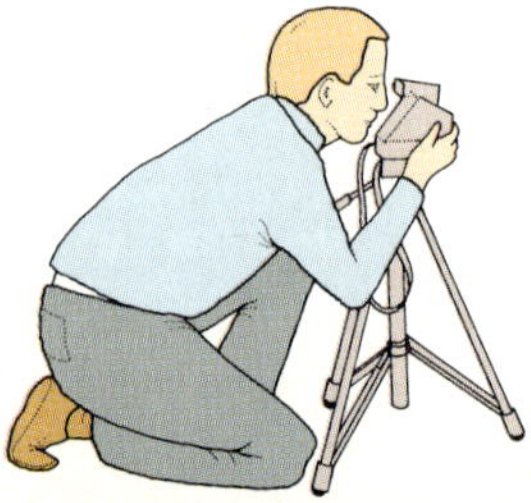

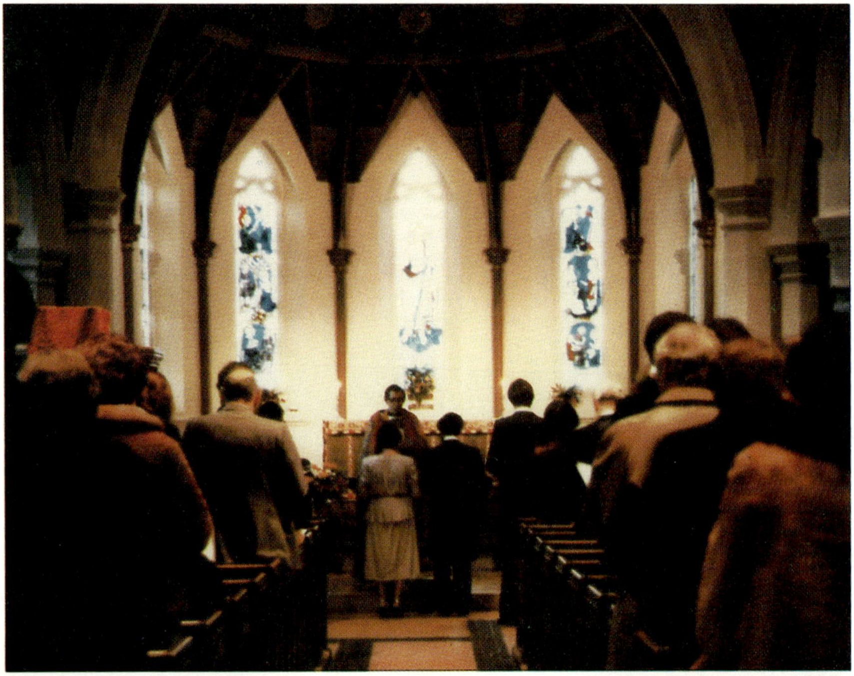

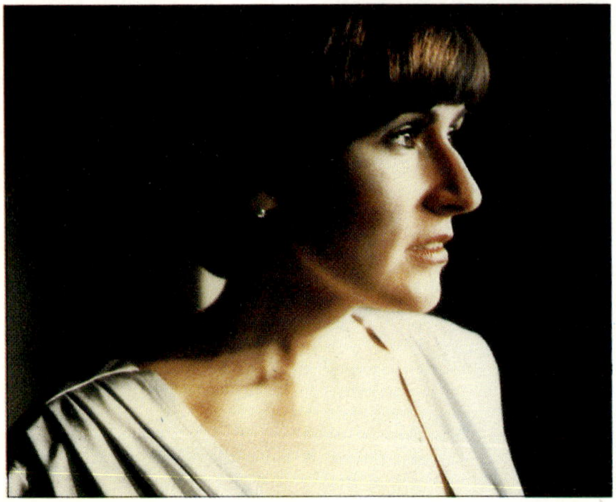

Covering the event

After the ceremony look out for the informal details and incidents that make every wedding unique. Don't attempt to take large groups – restrict yourself to candid shots of individuals or pairs, and move in close to colorful details, as right.

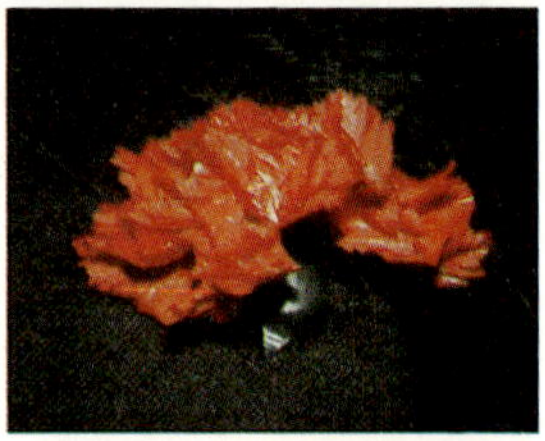

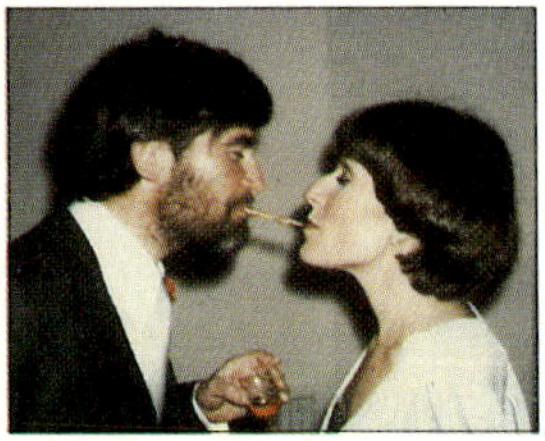

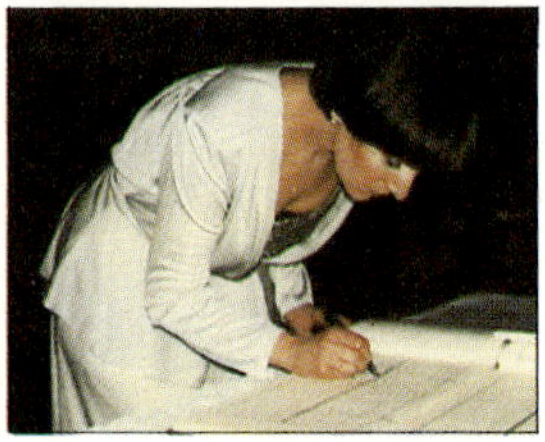

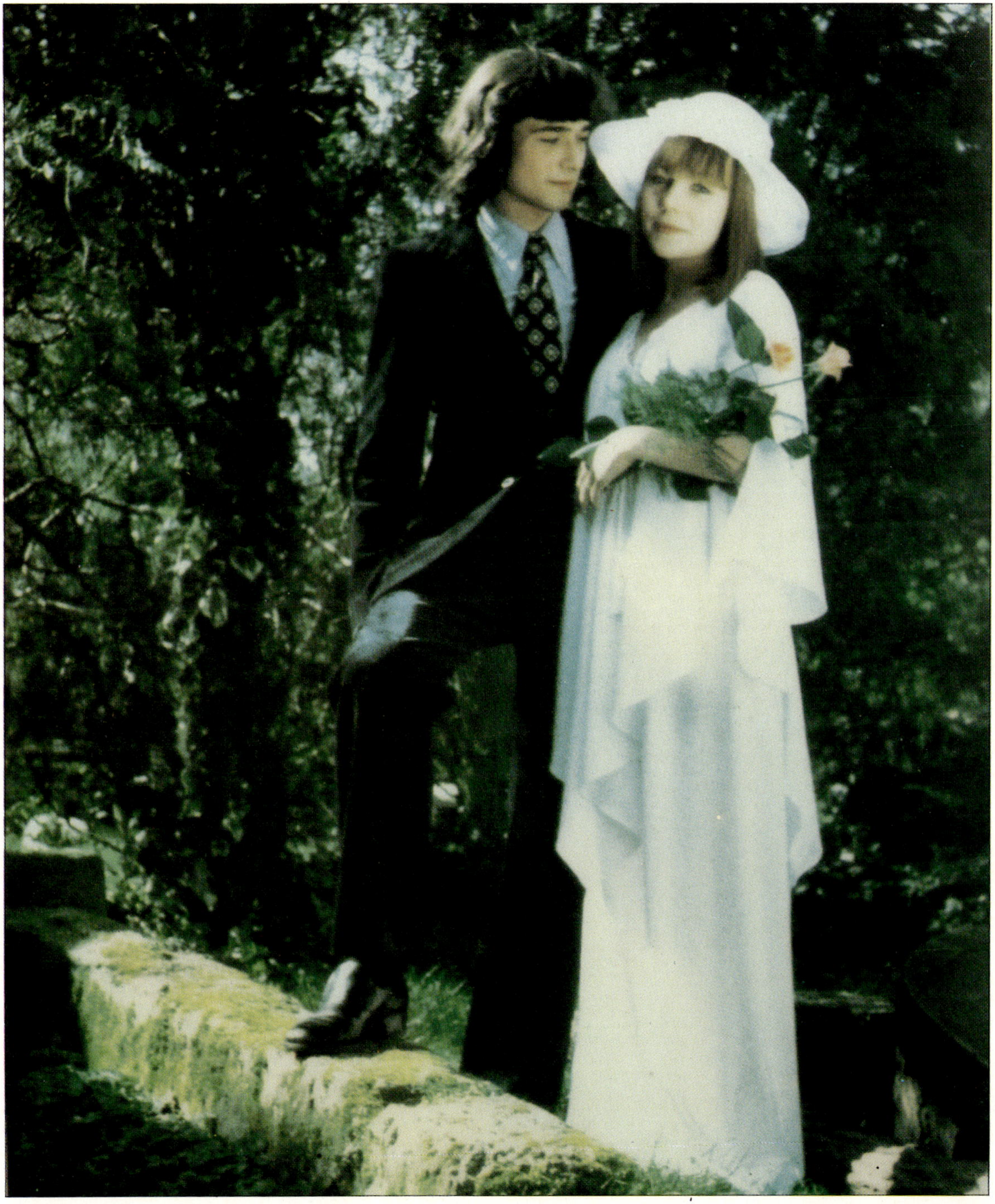

Shooting on vacation

The beach, and elements of sand, sea, sun and sky, make exciting picture material on vacation. To cope with glare off sand and bright water at midday, use a lens shade, or shade the lens and eye with your hand. Better still, wait till later in the day, when the light is softer. If the temperature rises above 90°F (32°C), set the L/D toward lighten, and keep developing prints cool or they may be too dark. Make sure you equip yourself with such useful items as:

- Plenty of film
- Flash equipment
- Spare batteries
- Camera case and strap
- Plastic equipment bag
- Puffer brush
- Self-timer
- Lens shade
- Close-up and tele lenses

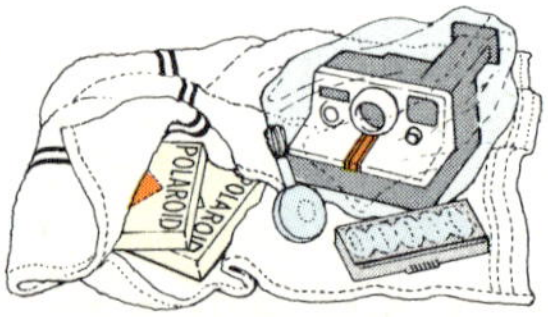

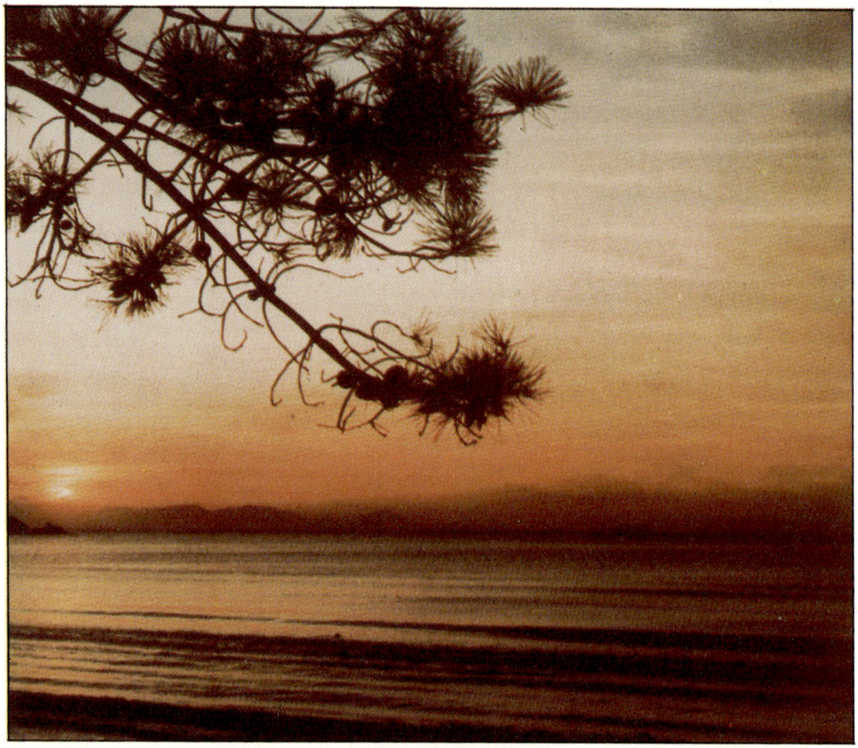

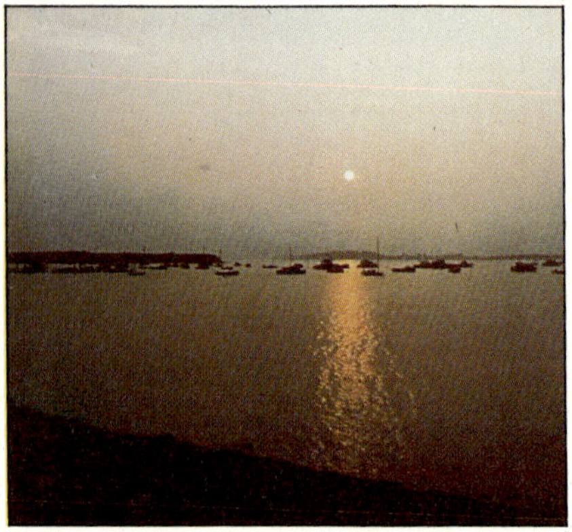

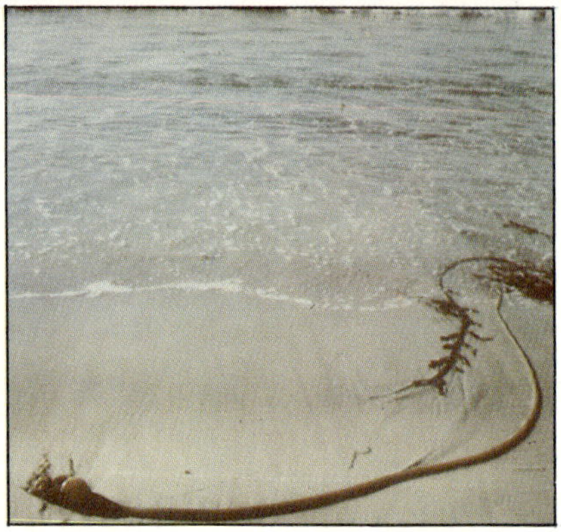

Shooting the sea
Daytime beach shots are often boring or cluttered. Instead, wait for a dramatic sky about one hour before the sun sets, above, move the L/D control to darken, and shoot. As sand often appears gray and dull on instant film, look for pattern and texture, left. Low oblique light will bring out the textured surface of water. The sea can appear rich and moody when colored by the light of the setting sun, as in the shot far left.

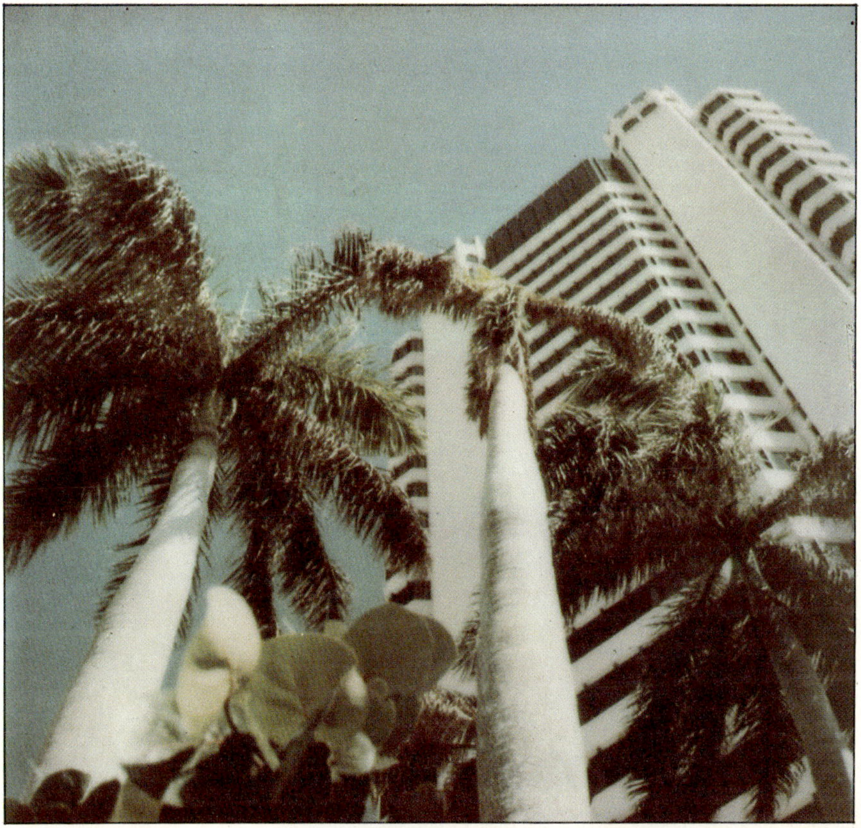

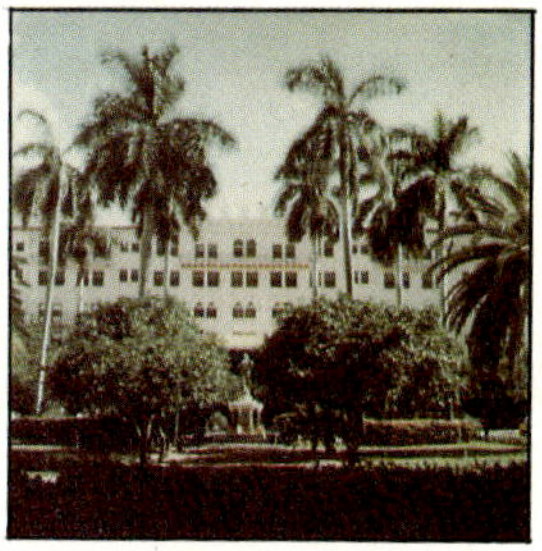

Places you visit
Don't take an ordinary view of the front of your hotel, above; it won't show the character of the place. Find an unusual viewpoint that includes the part that you stayed in, and try to emphasize the architectural features of the building. In the shot left, the low viewpoint highlights the form of the building and conveys an exotic atmosphere.

Vacation portraits
Take care when photographing people in bright, midday sun – you will get ugly, hard-edged shadows in your portraits, below. Look for softer lighting later in the day for a warmer result. Take pictures of the family enjoying new pursuits – sailing for example.

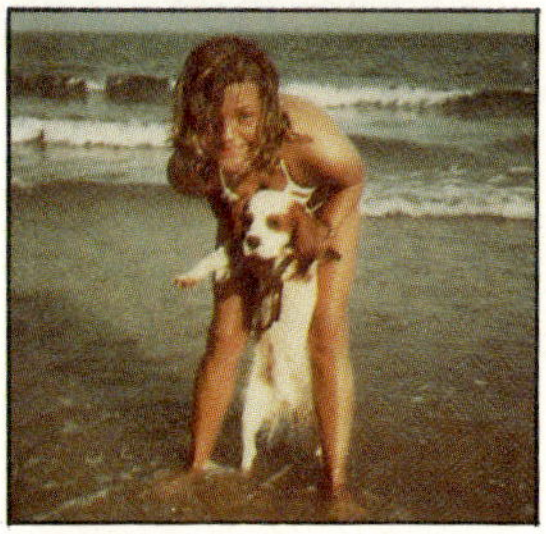

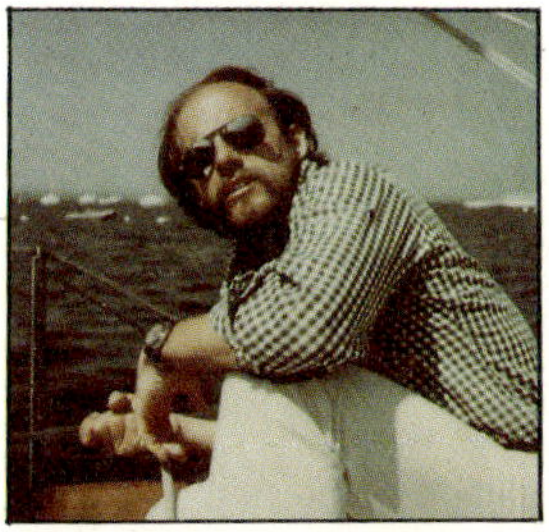

Beach shots
Frame tightly or choose an unusual viewpoint, right, to exclude large areas of sand. When shooting subjects that are in the sea, as above, kneel down on the shoreline and keep the camera low. Exclude the sky from your picture as far as possible, to reduce glare.

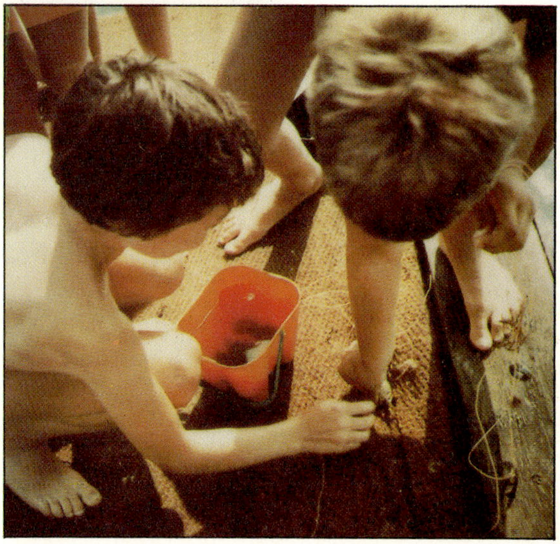

Recording your travels

A holiday in a foreign country is the perfect time to take instant pictures. You will see colors, shapes, textures, objects and people with completely fresh eyes and a whole new range of picture-making material will present itself. Try to take a wide range of different shots which will convey the atmosphere and "feel" of the place to family and friends at home. You can mail them your own instant pictures instead of purchased postcards. The dusk shot of the island castle, below, conveys a Mediterranean evening mood and a high viewpoint, right, reveals the dramatic setting of a Greek temple.

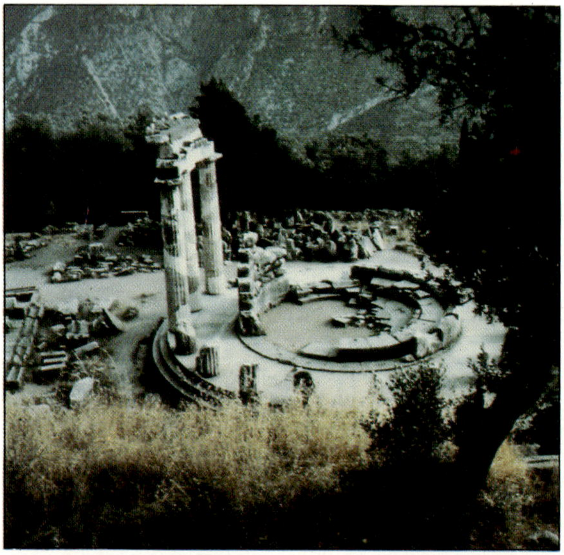

Foreground frames
Use the foreground to create depth or emphasis in your pictures. A foreground frame, below, draws the eye into the picture. As well as natural frames, like the trees below, look for architectural features such as an archway or a window to frame your shot. Set the L/D control to darken.

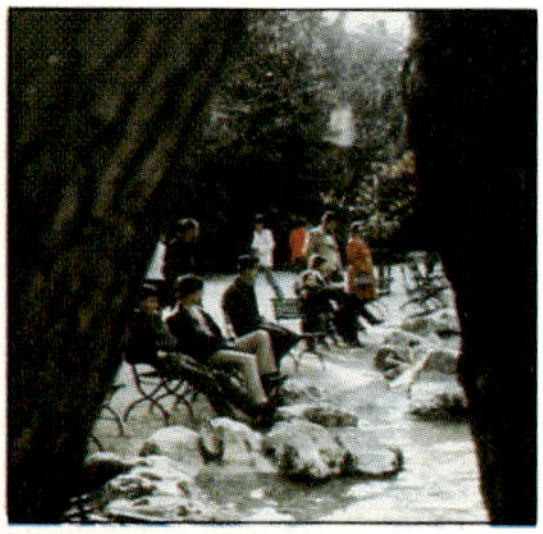

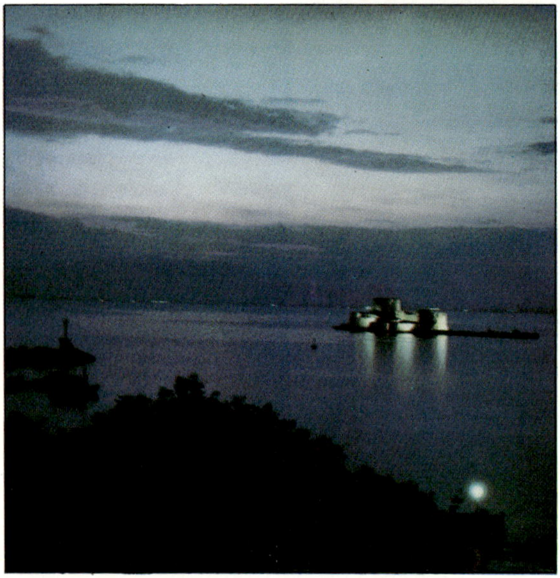

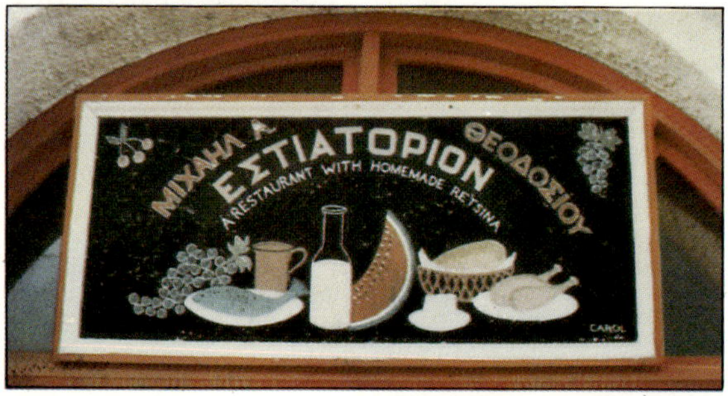

Finding details
Look around for details that are rich in color, texture and shape. A shot of the busy taverna would have been muddled, so the photographer selected the colorful sign, above. Make use of muted color to convey historic atmosphere, as in the shot of the wall painting, right.

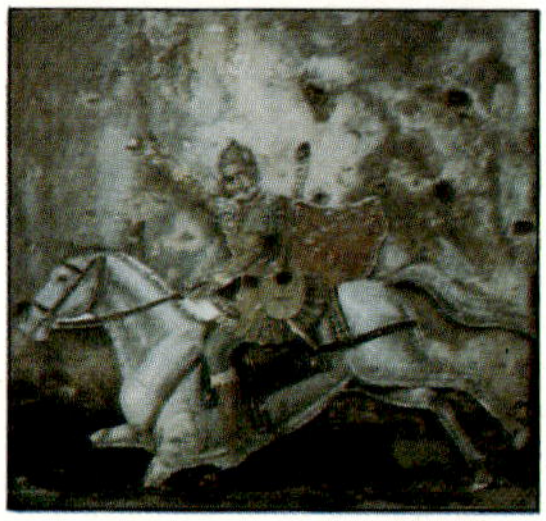

Local people
Your collection of pictures will come alive if you include some portraits and candid shots of local characters. Good portraits depend on an open, friendly approach and a respect for people's privacy. Be prepared to give some shots away.

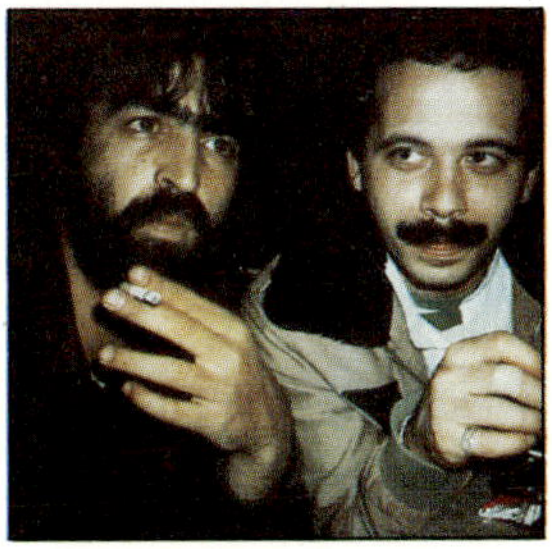

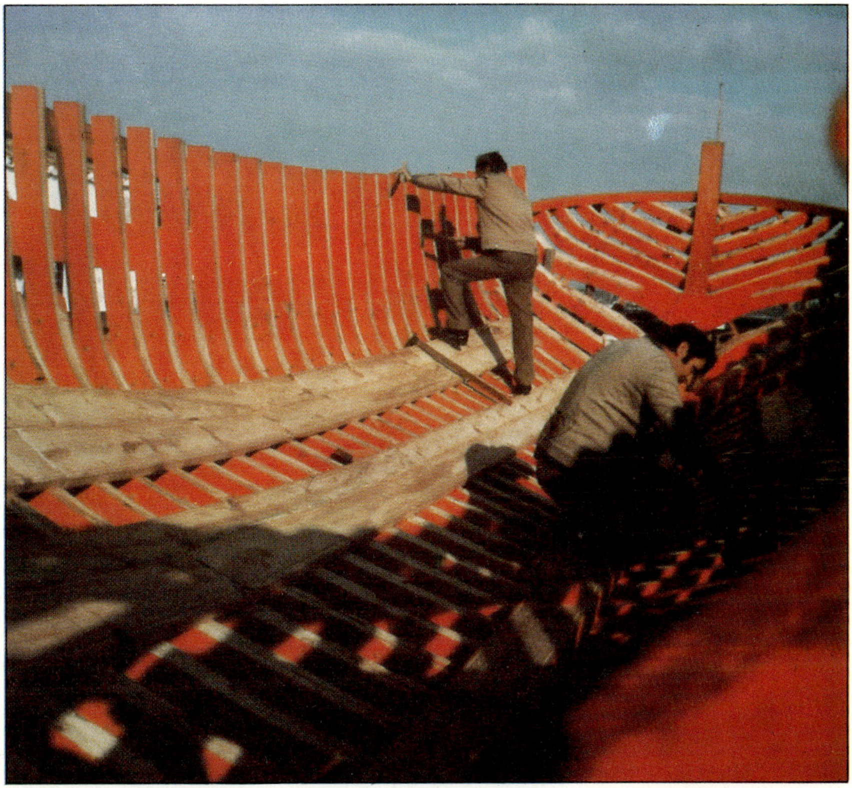

Take portraits close up of the friends that you make in your travels. And look out for people in their own environment absorbed in their work. The fishermen, right, busy building a boat, provide the perfect chance for a candid shot. The photographer used the pattern and color of the boat to strengthen the image.

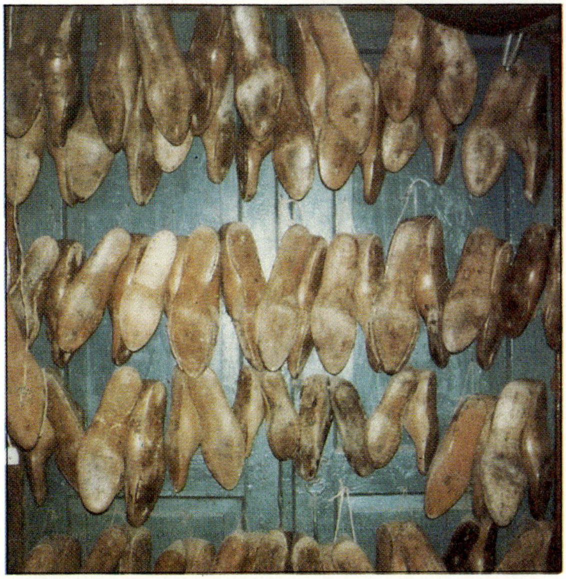

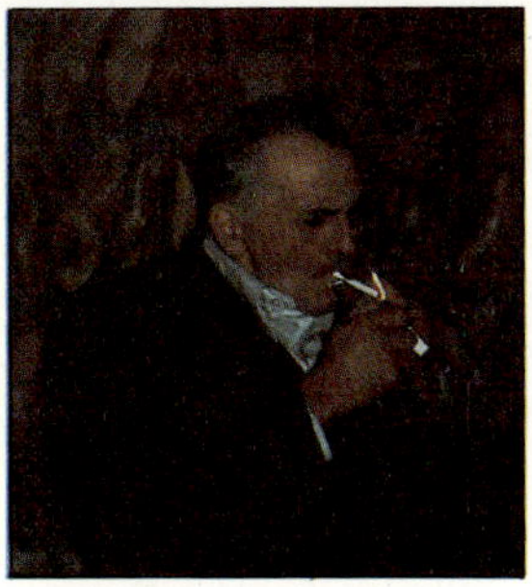

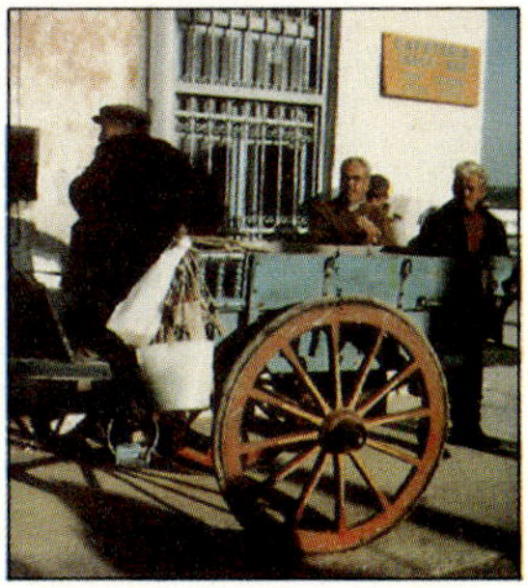

Street color
When you are walking around the streets, watch out for interesting stores displaying local arts and crafts. Photograph a craftsman with his wares in available light, above, or move in close and use diffused flash, left, to fill the frame with color and detail. Shoot street scenes which recall the customs and atmosphere of a place, like the shot, above right, of a group of Greek men chatting on a street corner. Their picturesque horse-drawn cart adds some foreground interest.

Taking pictures of landscapes

Changes in the weather play tricks with light and color outdoors – learn to exploit these effects and you will take effective landscape shots. When a storm creates dramatic light changes in the sky, right, take the sky itself as your subject. For a good result, move the L/D control all the way to darken. After the storm, look out for landscapes bathed in glowing light against dark clouds, and for rainbows, below left. In mist, haze or rain, create a mysterious or romantic mood with dim, muted colors. Include something in the foreground, like the horse, below right, for a stronger picture. Light may be low in these conditions; use a tripod and cable release (p.90) if necessary.

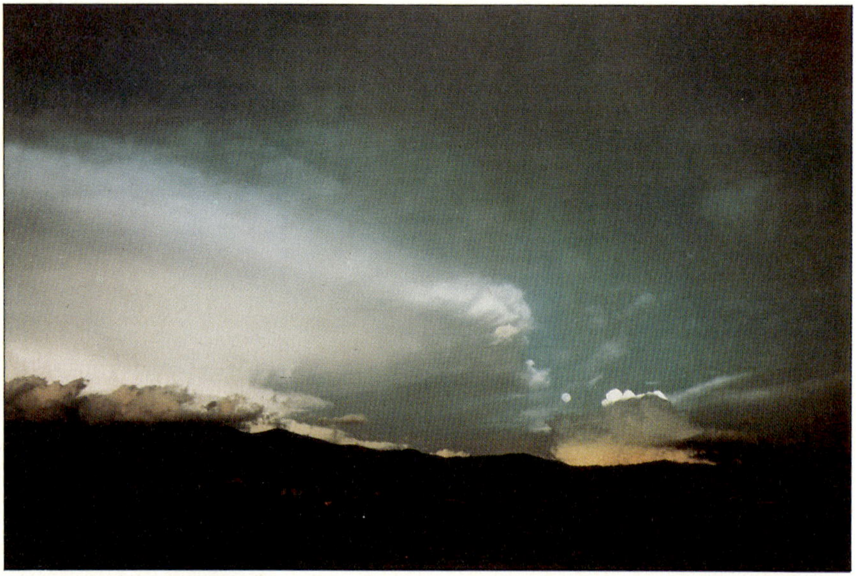

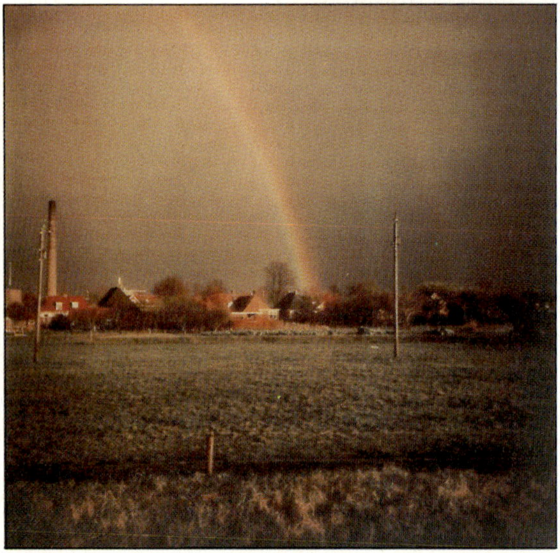

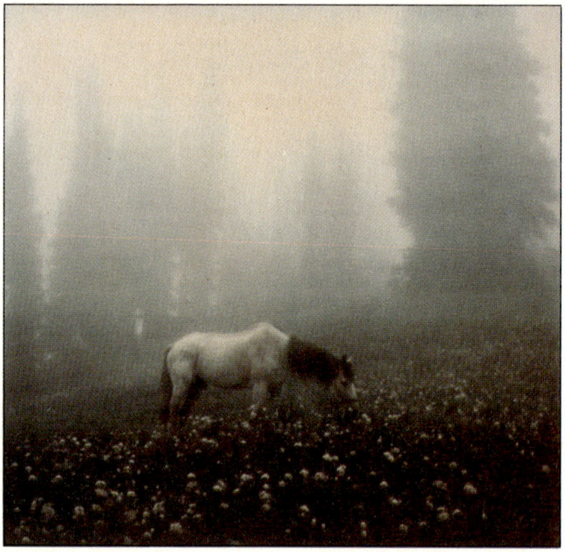

Depth and viewpoint
Outdoor shots are often disappointing, because they lack the illusion of depth. Try to link the foreground and background – the pier below leads the eye back to the autumn trees. A gate used as a frame or a person at the side of the picture looking in would work just as well. To highlight a coppery tree, shoot into the sun, taking care with exposure (p.21).

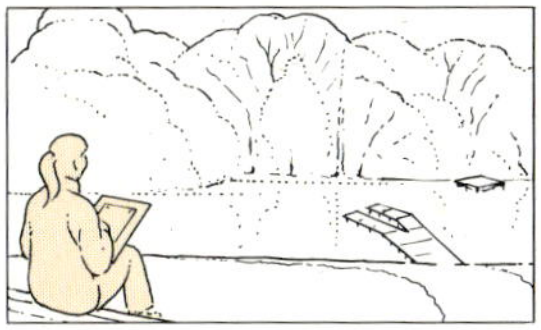

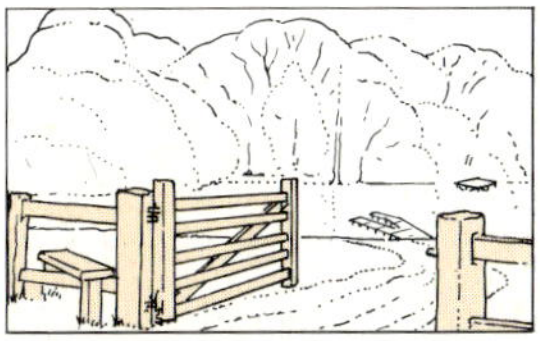

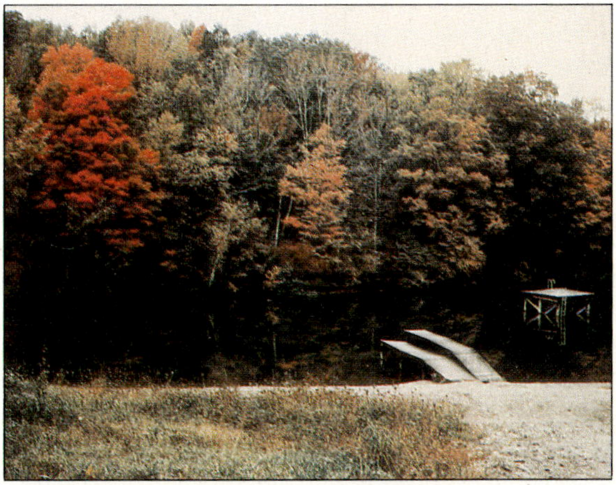

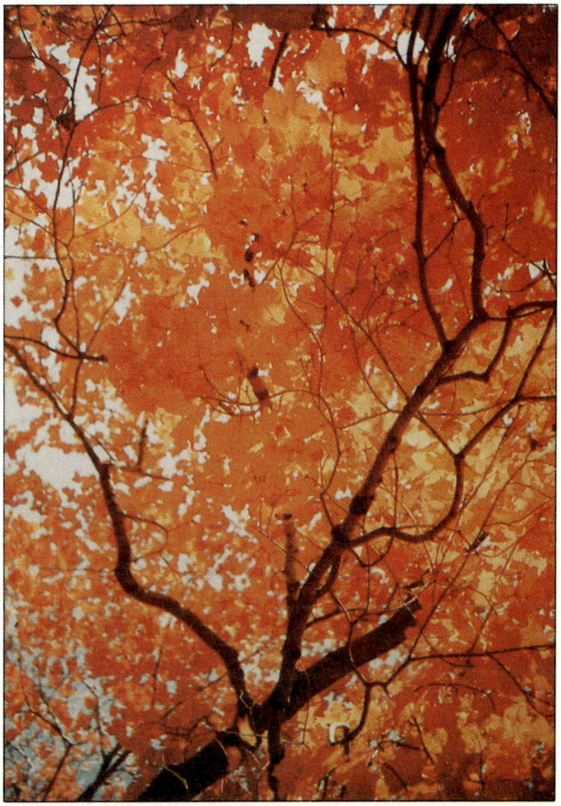

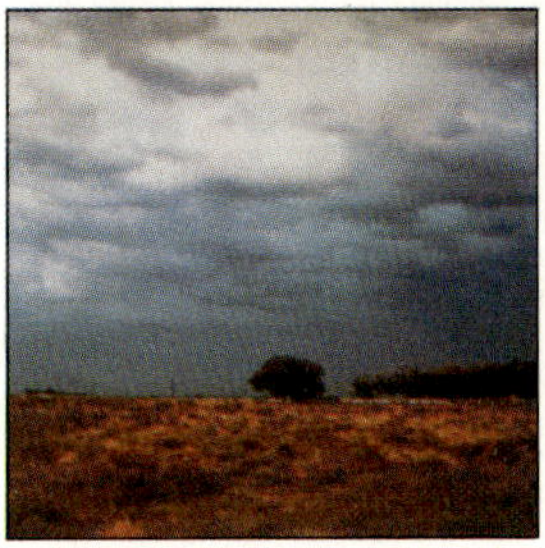

Using the horizon
Look out for light and color and select a viewpoint that enhances both. A low horizon, above, allows the pattern of light and color in the sky to dominate the scene. A high horizon is also effective: the twilight shot, right, uses a dark foreground to emphasize the isolation of the building.

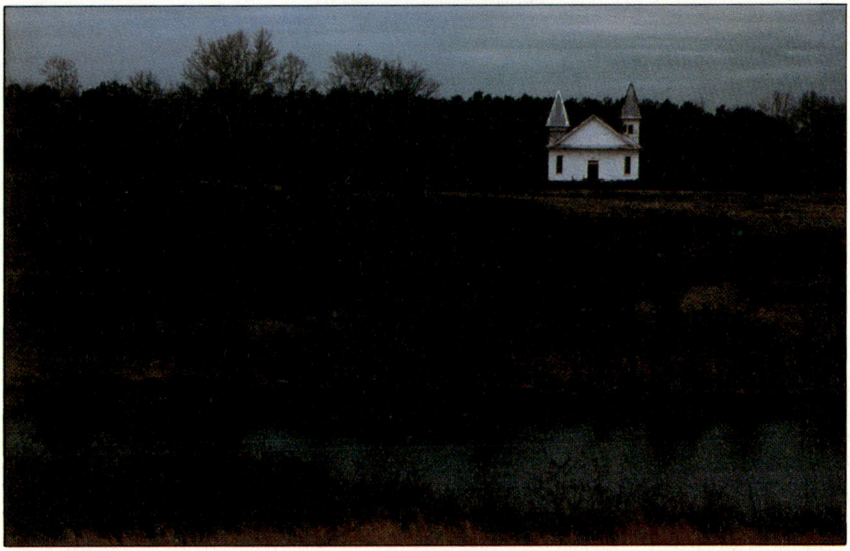

Taking snow scenes

Winter subjects offer a wealth of spectacular and colorful picture ideas. In general, stick to close-up and mid-distance shots – distance and scale are hard to convey in snow unless you include a point of reference, such as a building in the foreground. Look for bright colors to offset the cold mood of winter, or wait for warm evening light. To relieve bare expanses of snow, make use of light, see facing page, to enhance patterns and textures formed by fields, trees and fencing – or shoot through a frame. Protect your camera by keeping it in a waterproof case, and carry it by its neckstrap inside your coat. Take care to keep the developing print warm, or the colors in your picture will be affected, see box, facing page.

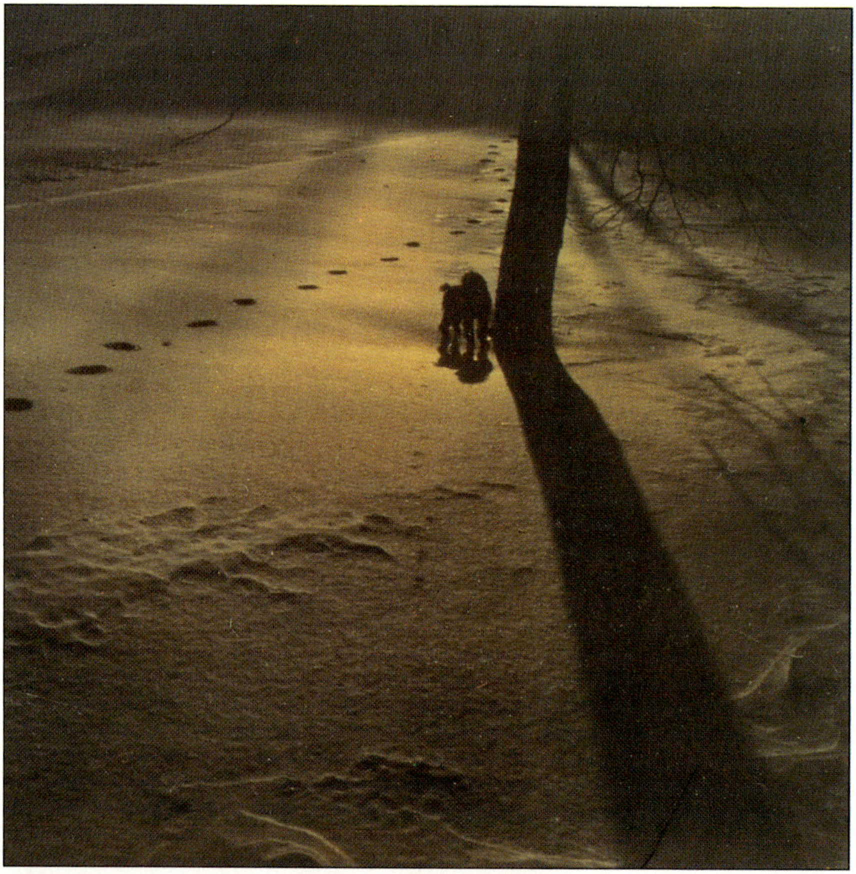

Moonlight on snow
If your camera takes long exposures, you can take winter pictures at night (pp.44–5). Moonlight on snow produces an eerie yellow cast, right, which you can use for effect.

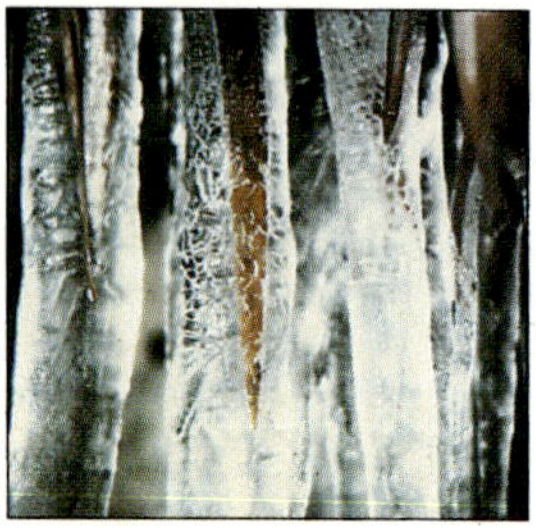

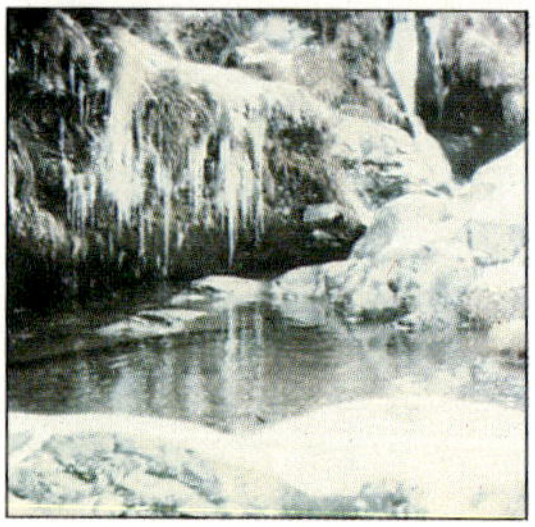

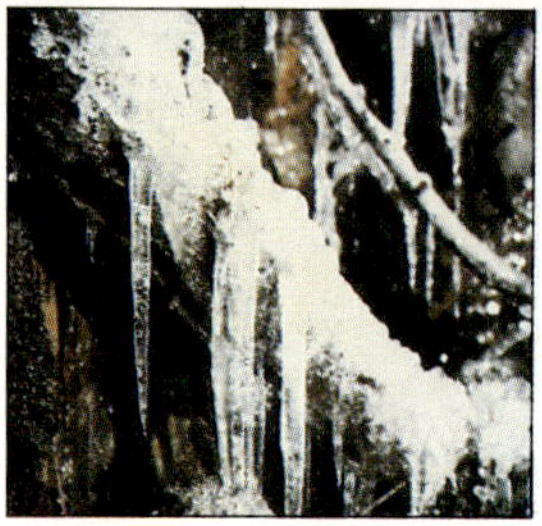

Focus on a detail
Close-ups of frozen water, thick snow on roofs or fences, or sparkling frost on trees or window panes, often evoke the icy feeling of winter better than more distant scenes. Set them against a dark background, far left, and use side-lighting to reveal texture, as in the picture left.

Using the darken setting
Getting the right exposure (pp.20–1) is difficult in snow. With the L/D control at normal, below, the foreground is accurate, but the mountains are indistinct. If the L/D is turned all the way to darken, below right, the shot is too dim. For the improved version, right, the L/D was set one mark toward darken.

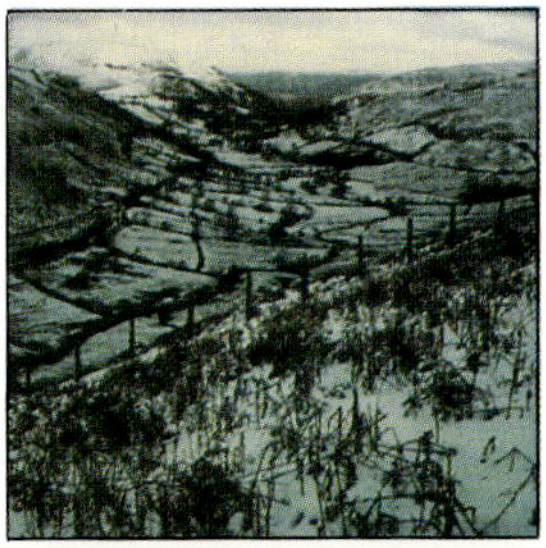

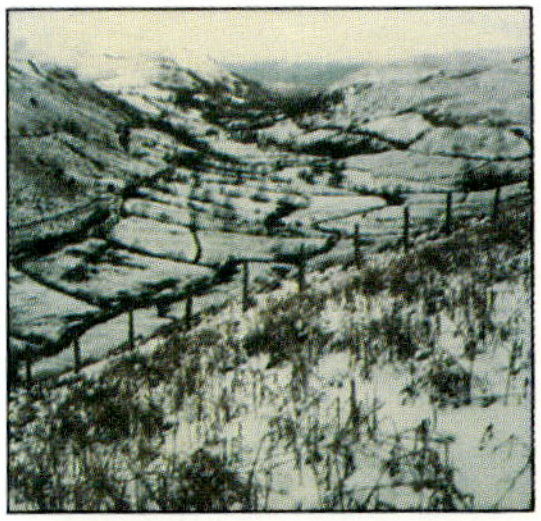

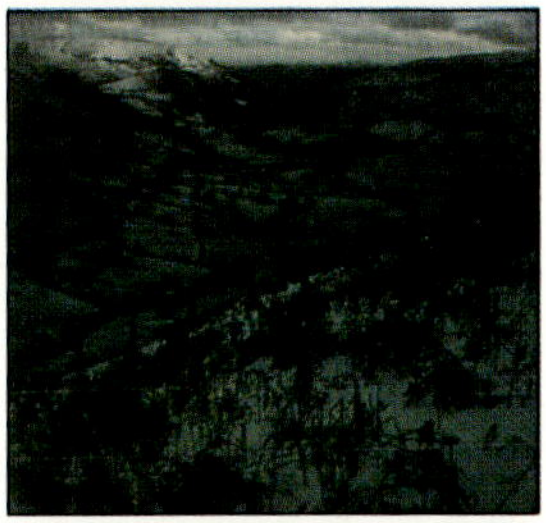

Coping with low temperatures
If instant film is left out in the cold, low temperatures will affect the color of your film as it develops. You will get a blue-toned or a pale, washed-out result. In temperatures below 55°F (13°C) for Polaroid, or 61°F (16°C) for Kodak, you must place developing integral film inside your clothing so that your body heat keeps the picture warm. In temperatures below 65°F (18°C), peel-apart film should be put in the cold clip, shown below, and placed inside your clothing. If you don't follow this procedure, your print will be very blue, as in the picture of the boy and his sled, below.

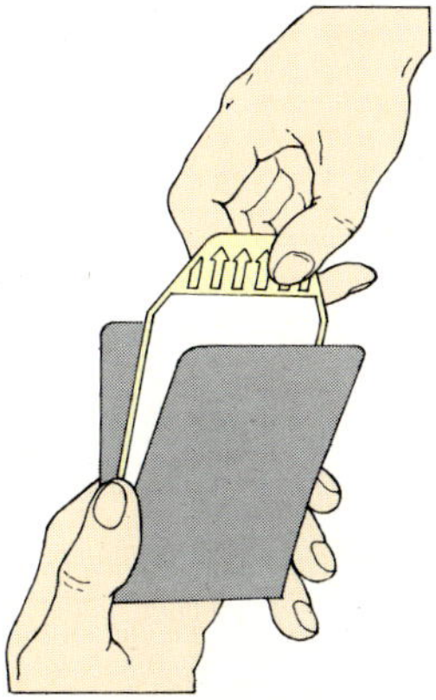

Peel-apart cold clip
For a true result, put film in clip and keep it warm during development (p.26).

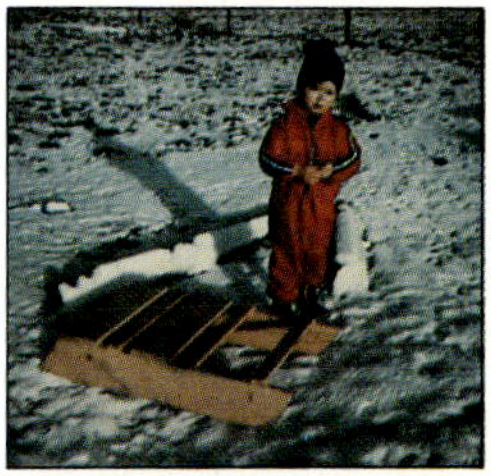

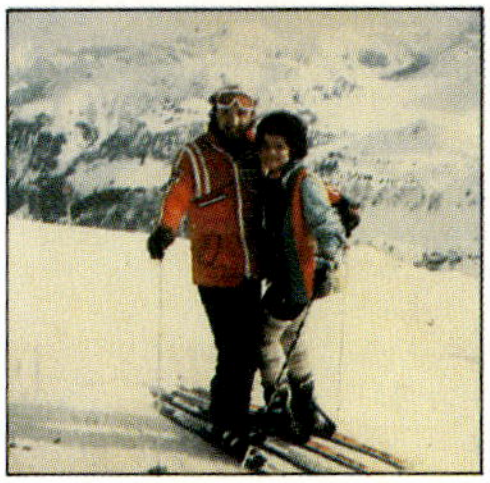

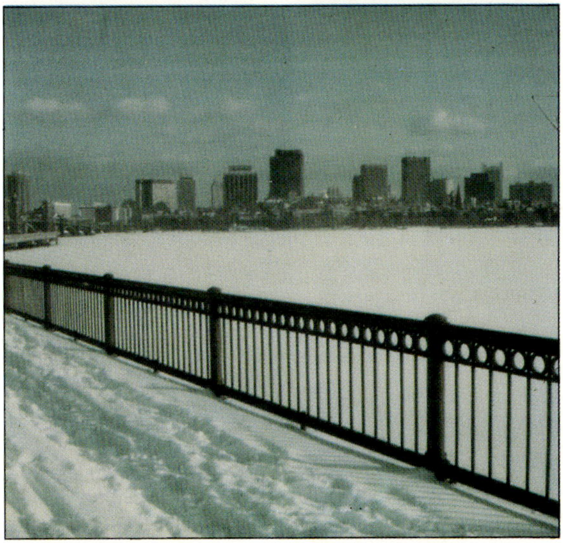

Lighting snow
To bring out the crisp texture and sparkling brilliance of snow, use low back- or side-lighting, as shown above. Snow looks dull and flat when shot with the sun behind the camera. The photographer used the blue cast (due to low temperatures) to convey a cold, crisp atmosphere.

Portraits in the snow
Take portraits of people in snow when they are wearing brightly colored outfits – dull clothes will not stand out enough, right. Whatever the subject, you will enliven snow shots and balance their dominant cold tones by including warm reds and yellows in the picture, as far right.

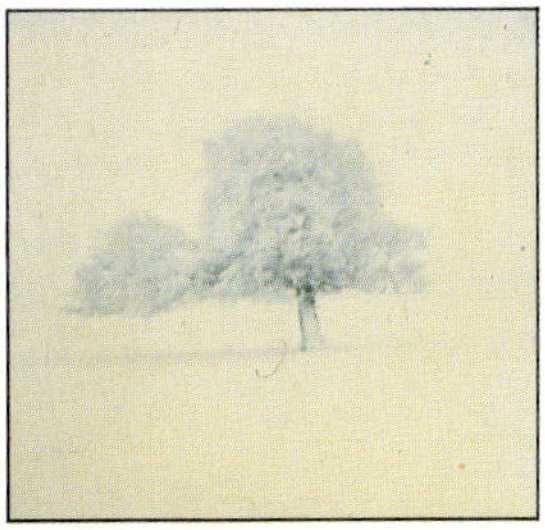

Using the lighten setting
Large areas of snow may affect the electric eye (pp. 20–1), and it will underexpose the picture (the picture will be too dark). When you are shooting a pale subject, such as the snow-laden tree, left, against a lot of snow, move the L/D all the way to lighten.

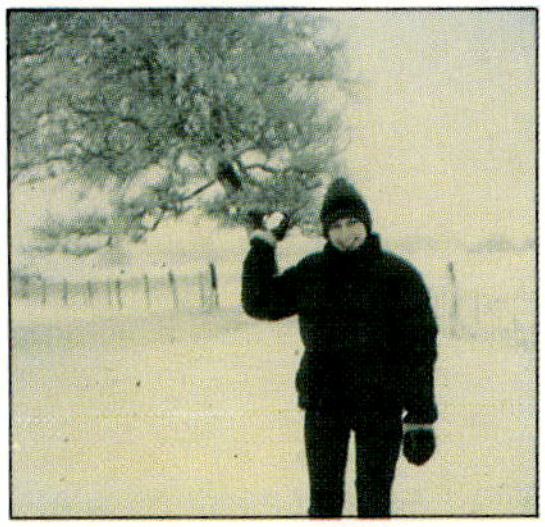

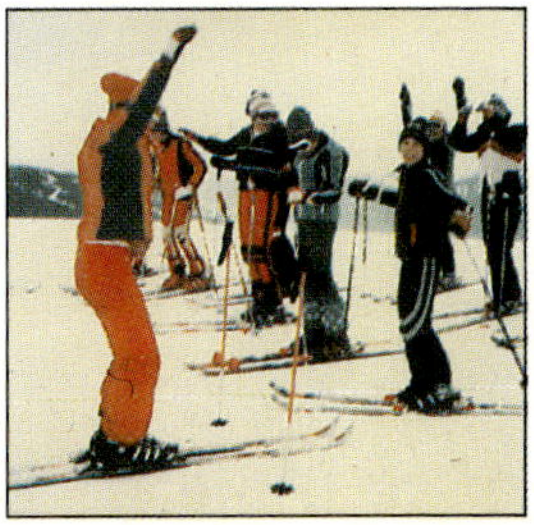

Touring a city

A visit to a strange city gives you an opportunity to photograph interesting buildings. Avoid traditional views of a famous site – a picture postcard is cheaper. Instead try pictures from different viewpoints (p.28), to convey atmosphere. Consider light at various times of day, as well as different weather conditions (p.32). In these shots of Venice, reflections enliven the foreground of a morning scene, far right, while late afternoon sun adds warmth to the color of the rooftops, lower right. A shot from one corner, above right, gives a sense of depth, and the midday light shows sharp detail. An overall view of the square, shot against the light, below, captures the early evening mood of the city.

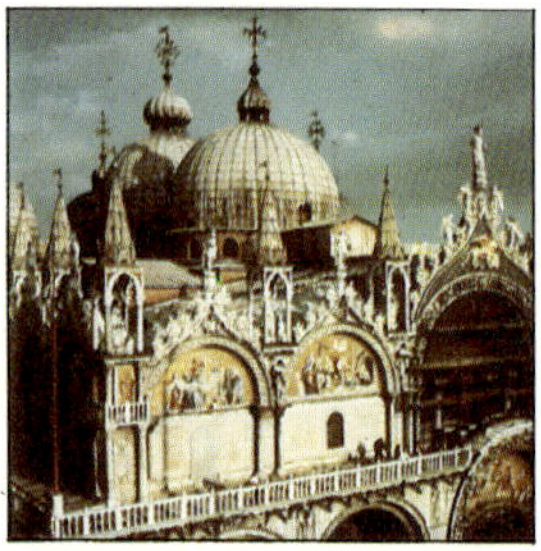

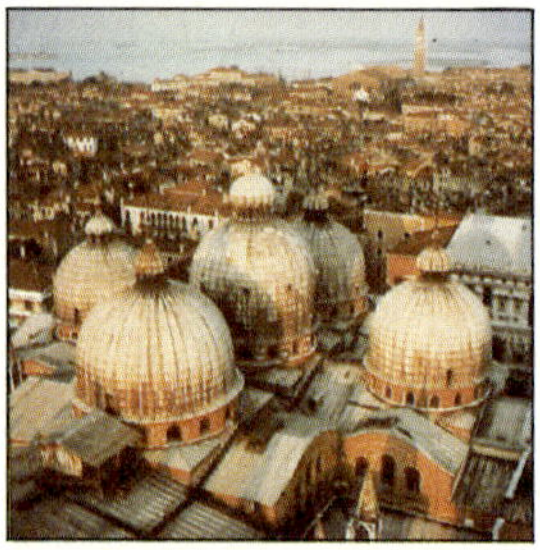

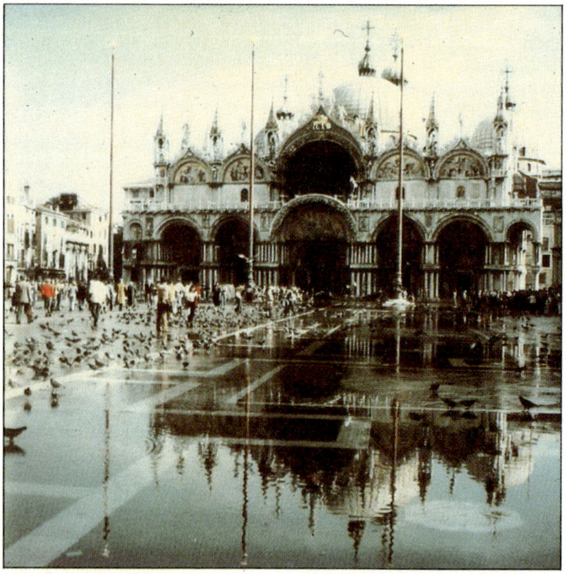

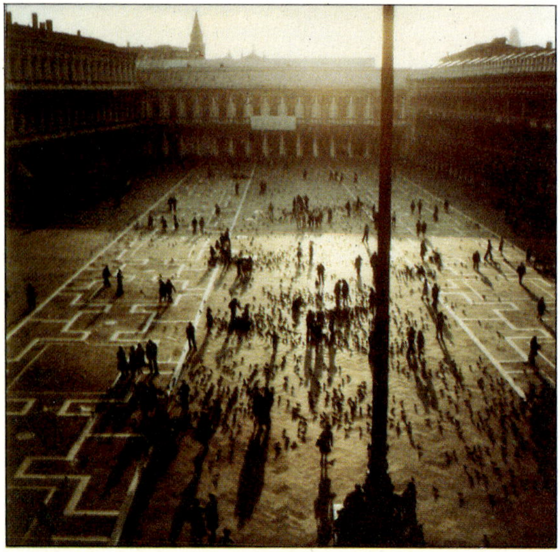

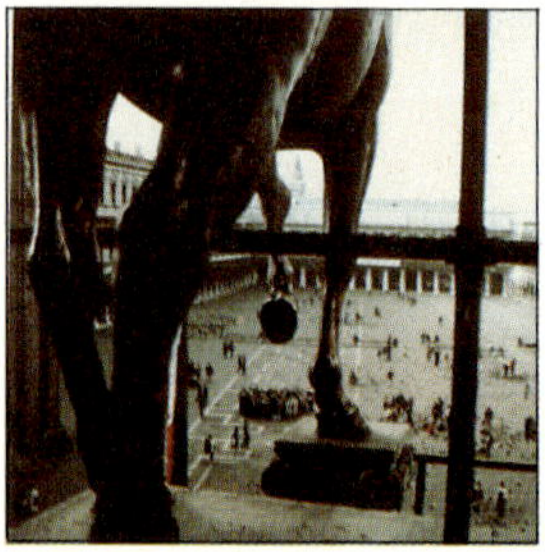

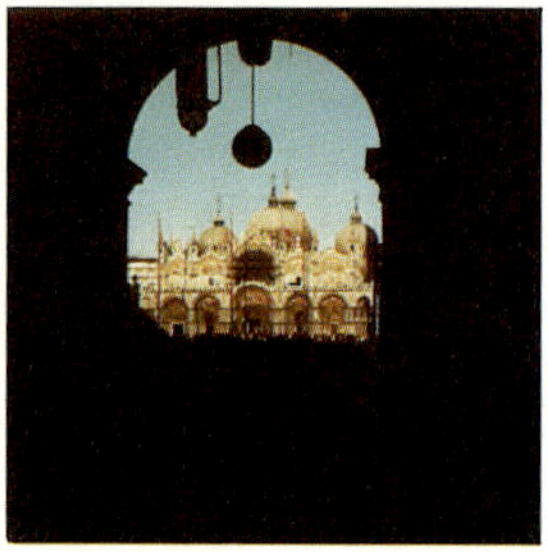

Using foreground frames
To add more interest to an urban subject, find a suitable object to provide a foreground frame for it. The picture, above, uses a sculpture high above St. Mark's to provide a dramatic foreground. You can also use arches, above right, or bridges or doors to frame a scene. Watch out for the exposure – the electric eye may set the exposure for the frame and your subject will be too pale (overexposed). To avoid overexposure, you should move the L/D control toward the darken setting when you are shooting a frame, to ensure that the main subject, and not the frame, is properly exposed.

Exposure problems
A well-exposed shot is hard to get in the extremes of light and shade in narrow city streets. The canal, right, was taken with the L/D control set at normal. It shows good detail on the foreground, but the far end of the canal is overexposed.

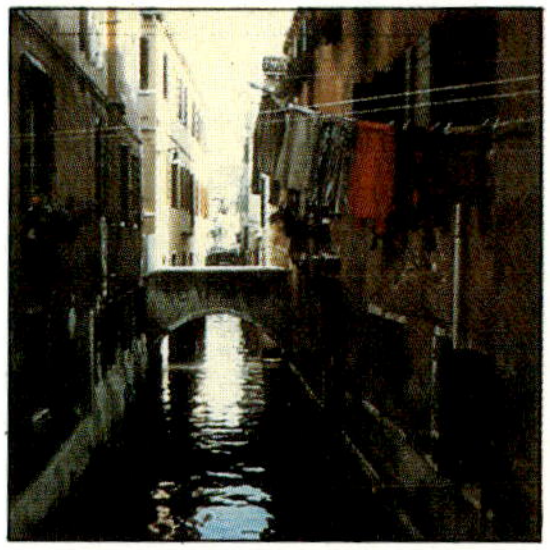

To get detail in this part of the picture, the photographer took another shot with the L/D control set toward darken, above. However the foreground in this second shot is very dark. In this situation you must choose which part of the scene you wish to record in detail.

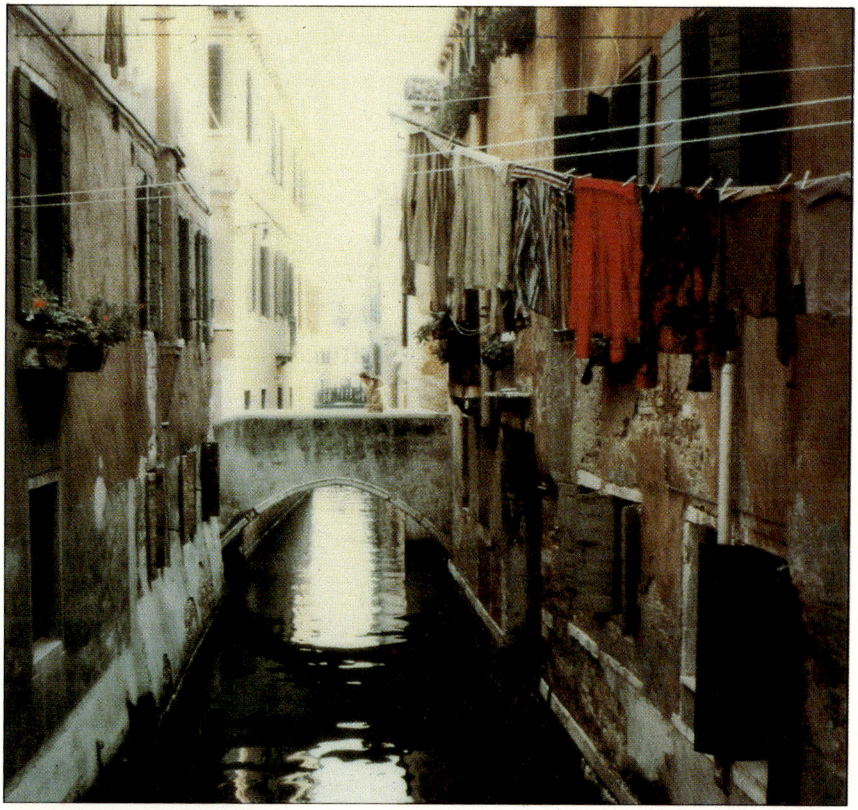

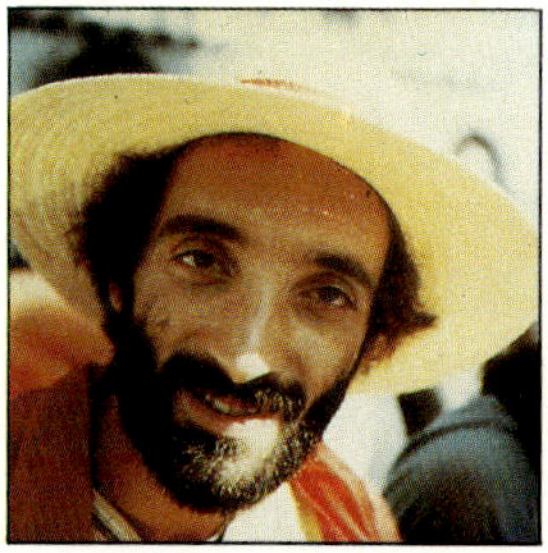

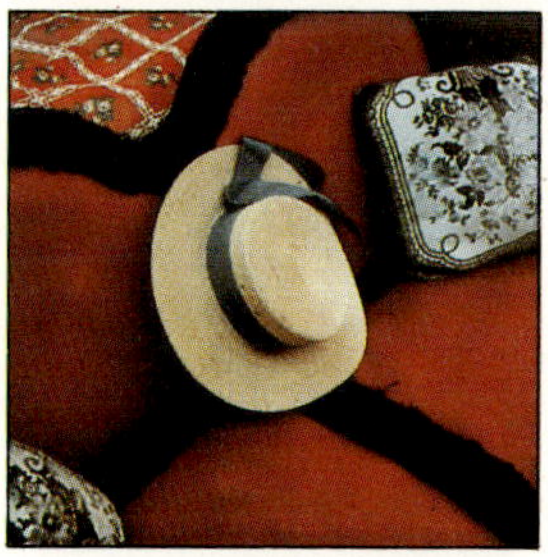

Expressing a theme
Take a series of shots that will convey a theme, making sure you choose images that are rich in color or shape. Rather than taking a single overall view of Venetian gondolas, the photographer took these three close-up shots to capture the romance of a gondola ride.

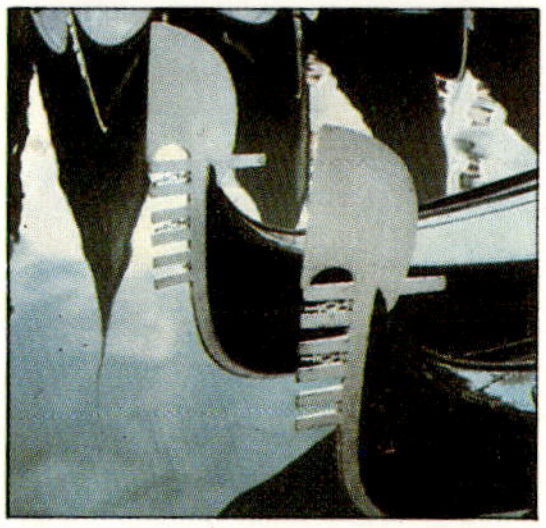

Details for atmosphere
When you are walking around the streets look out for colorful images and strong bold shapes, like the posters, below right, that will evoke memories of the city. Move in as close as you can with your camera (p.79) and fill the frame with color. The small ornament, above right, has been isolated from a confusing background by shooting it close up (pp.78–9). Only a small area of the scene is in sharp focus close up, so focus carefully on your subject. If this picture had been taken at a greater distance, the horse would have been lost among the background images.

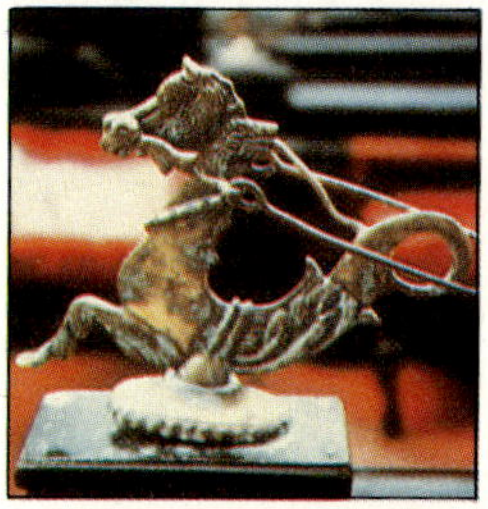

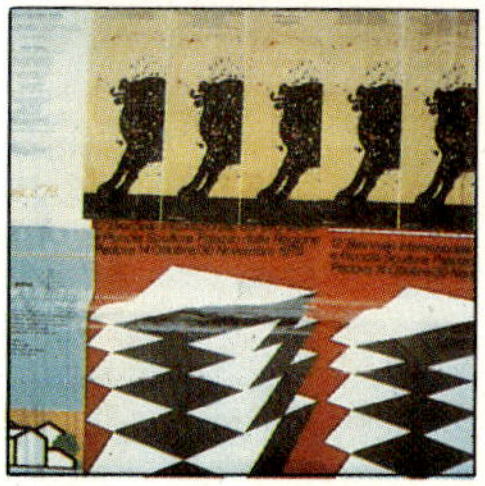

Taking pictures inside buildings

Lighting is crucial to successful instant pictures of interiors – whether your subject is a historic house, as right, or simply a room in your own home. Low natural lighting, artificial lighting, see below, and mixed light sources (artificial and natural light) will all affect your photographs in different ways. Contrast between light and shade is often extreme indoors – you may have to decide between exposing for shadows (L/D at normal) or highlights (L/D at darken). When visiting a historic building, use your instant camera to make a record of the things that particularly impress you. To set an interior in context, take a picture of the exterior, especially when it is floodlit at dusk, as above right.

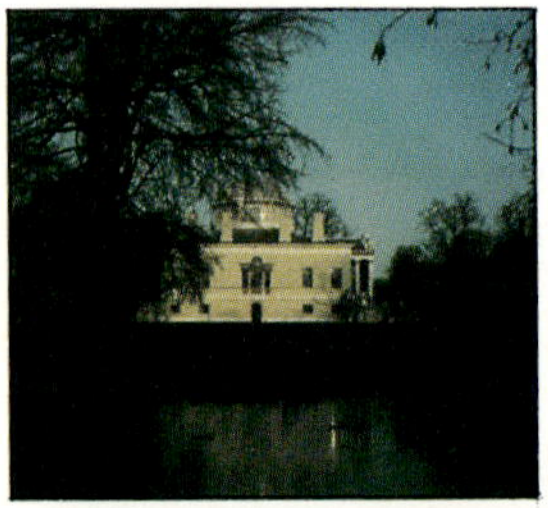

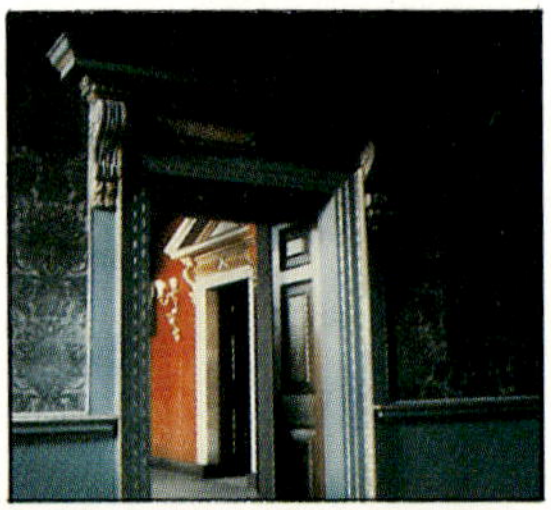

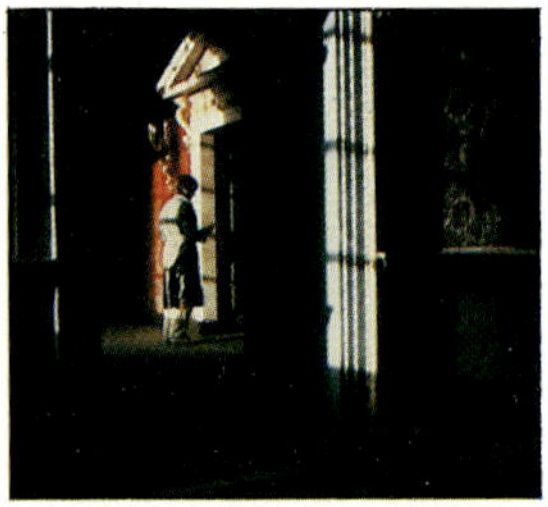

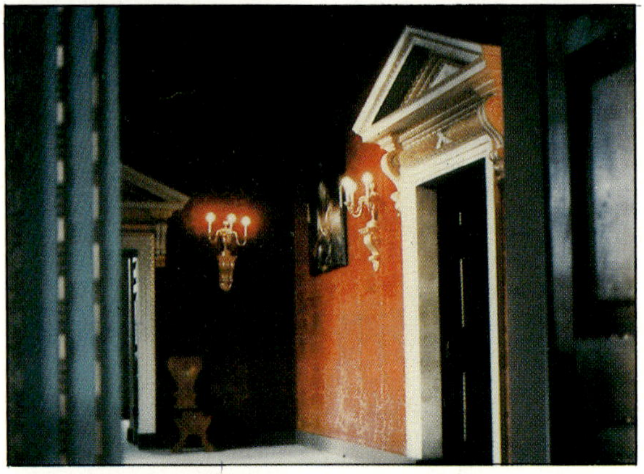

Framing and scale
Walk around the building, looking for unusual ways of conveying the depth and dimensions of the interior. Shooting through an open doorway, above left, leads the eye into the picture, besides framing the corridor beyond. Including a figure in the doorway, above, helps to show the scale of the room.

Using a filter
Artificial light can distort subject colors by adding a warm color cast, right. To record the true colors, below right, make a tungsten-correcting bluish filter out of a gelatin square (see also p.82).

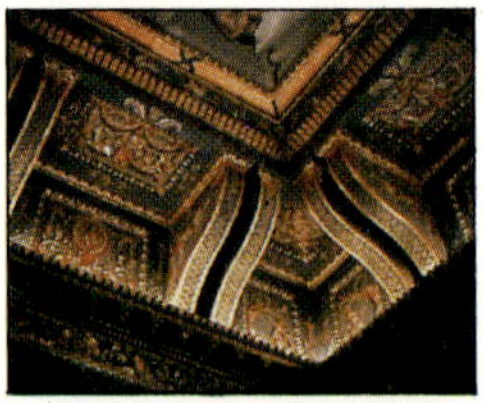

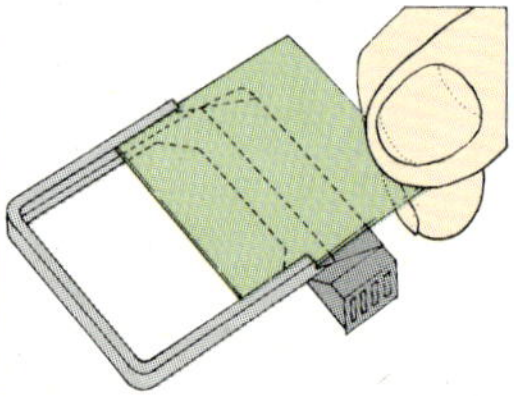

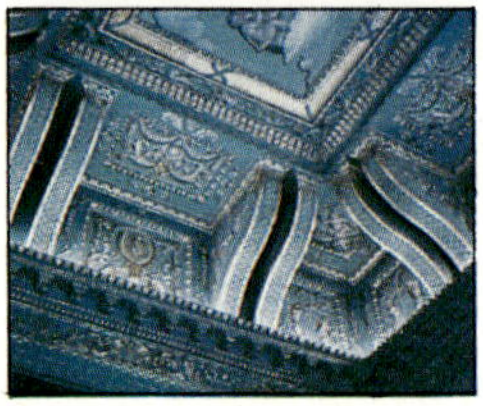

Color and design
Try to record the architectural details that reveal the period and style of a historic building. Always make sure that verticals line up with the sides of your viewfinder frame. Look for colorful features of the design, as in the picture above. The deep, glossy colors of integral film are particularly suited to such richly painted decoration.

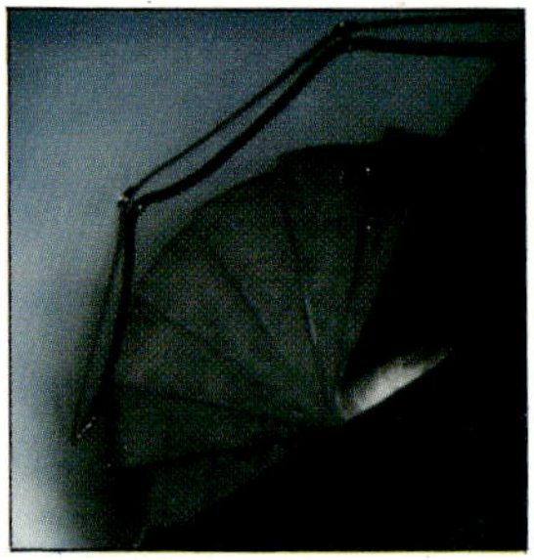

Abstract patterns
Fill the frame with lines and shapes to create an interesting pattern. The picture above was taken looking down a spiral staircase.

Photographing your home
Shooting a room at home gives you the chance to plan lighting and viewpoint carefully. Use daylight or artificial lights unless it is really too dark – the harsh light of flash tends to kill the atmosphere of a room. When you want to soften the lighting, draw curtains or blinds, and switch on extra lamps to lighten dark corners. You may also like to rearrange the furniture if the room looks cluttered. Concentrate on an attractive corner, as above right, or use a high viewpoint to encompass more of the scene, below right. The diagonal beam frames the shot and adds depth. To record the whole room, take several shots and make a panorama (p.87).

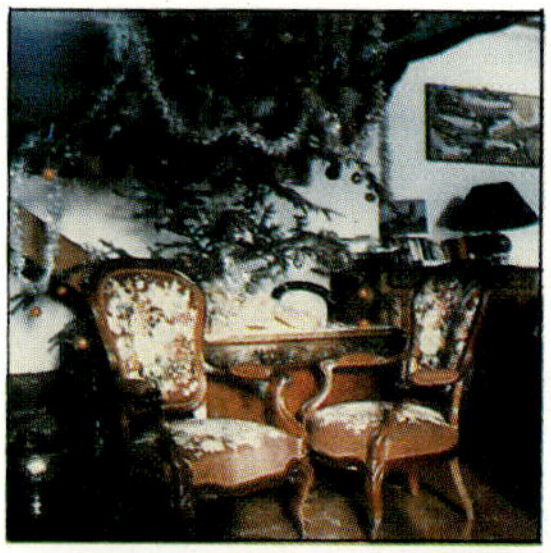

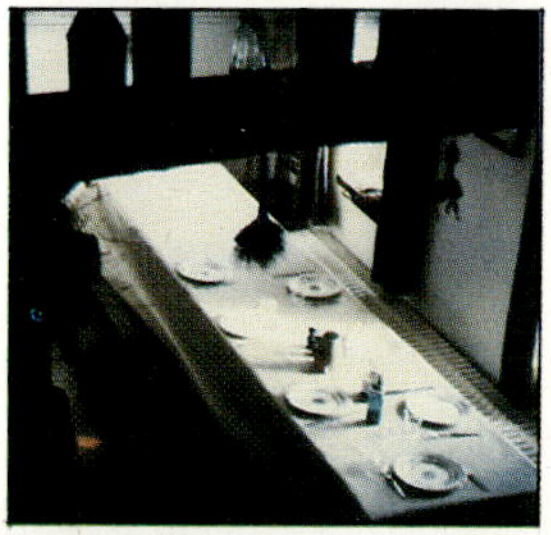

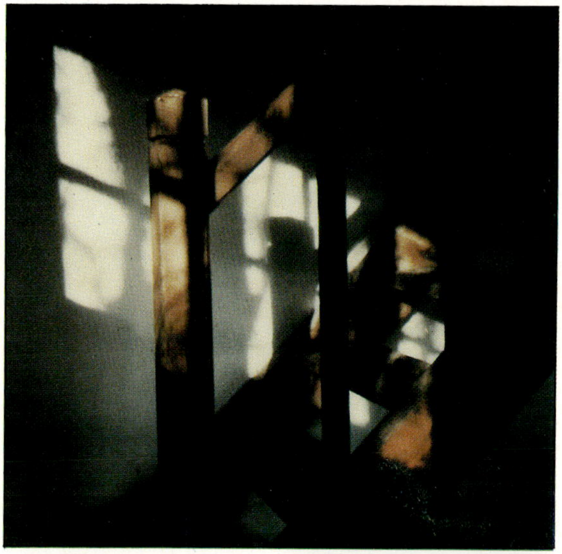

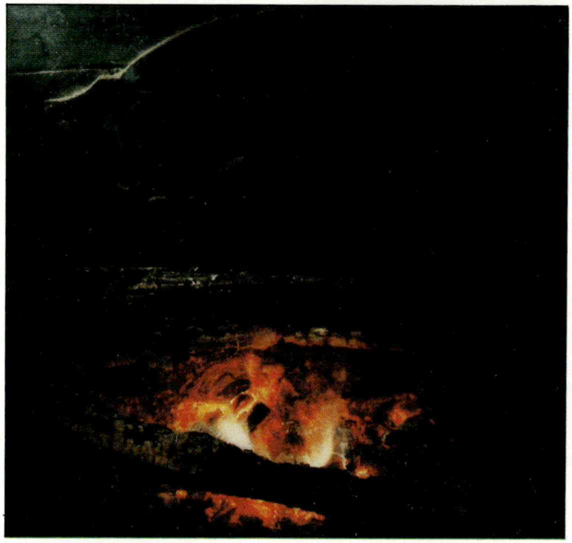

Design details
Photograph striking features of interior design, as above and right. Frame your shots carefully to exclude any distracting details or colors. In the picture above, notice how the shadows and strong lines of the staircase divide up the frame, creating a balanced, abstract design.

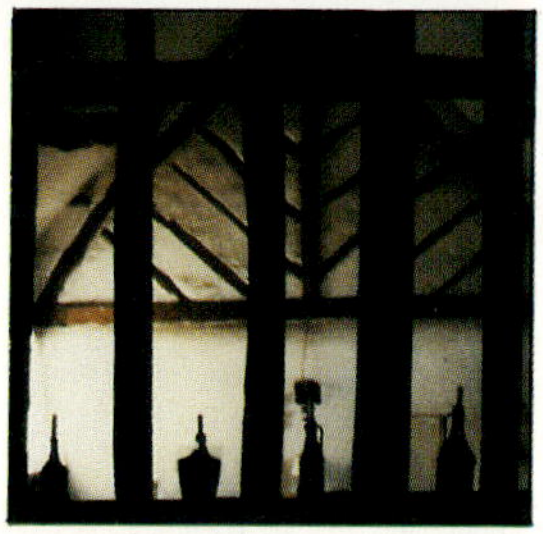

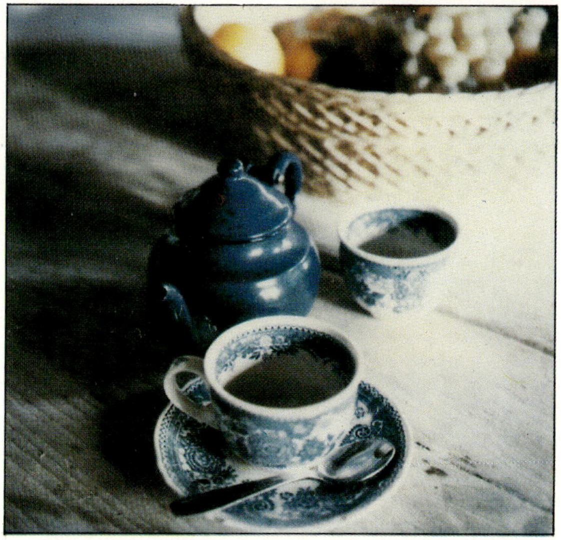

Shooting a log fire
To take a picture of a log fire, turn off all the room lights, move in close and make use of a tripod or support the camera (p.17). Set the L/D to lighten so that you can record details surrounding the flames. For a shot as close as the one above, you must have an SLR instant camera (p.12).

Direction of light
Wait until the direction of light favors those aspects of your subject you are trying to emphasize (p.33). In the picture right, strong, oblique light streaming through a window has thrown dark shadows behind the table setting, giving the picture a sense of form and depth.

Recording hobbies and interests

A friend with an interesting hobby makes a good subject for informal shots. Your main aim should be to link the person closely with his or her activity so that you have an integrated subject. To do this you must choose your viewpoint carefully, studying your subject from many different angles. Move in close and concentrate on hands to emphasize skill and craftsmanship, right. An eye-level viewpoint, below, gives a good overall view of both potter and pot. But you may have to use a low viewpoint to capture expressions, as below center, because people lower their heads when working with their hands. Using a high viewpoint, below right, emphasizes the precision of the hobby. All these shots were taken by daylight, in a brightly lit studio.

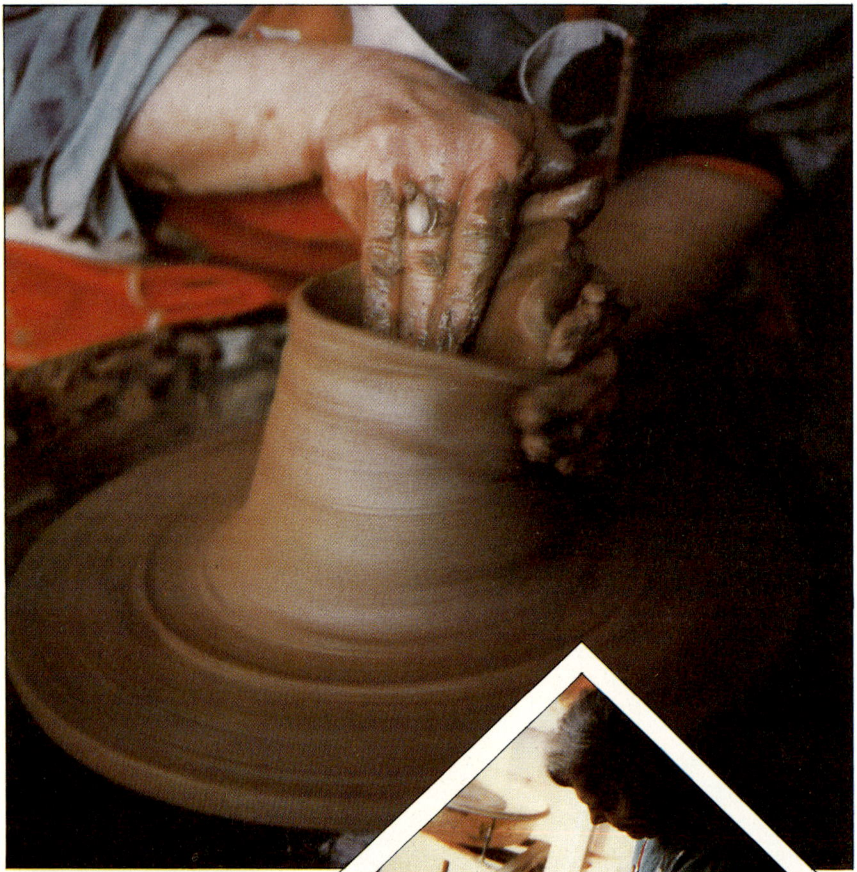

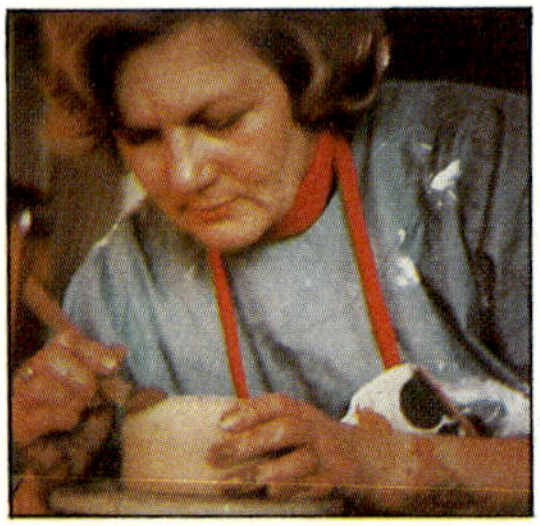

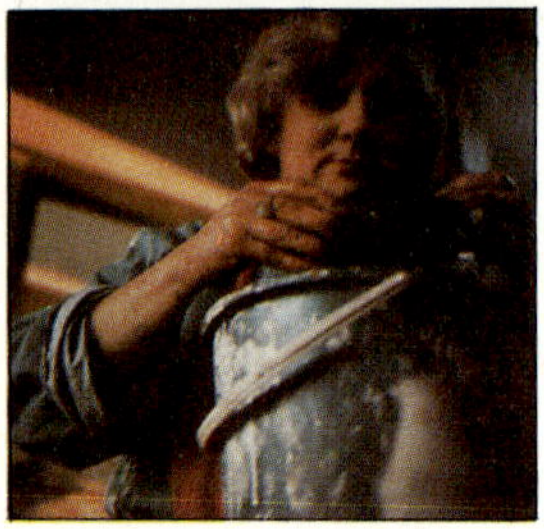

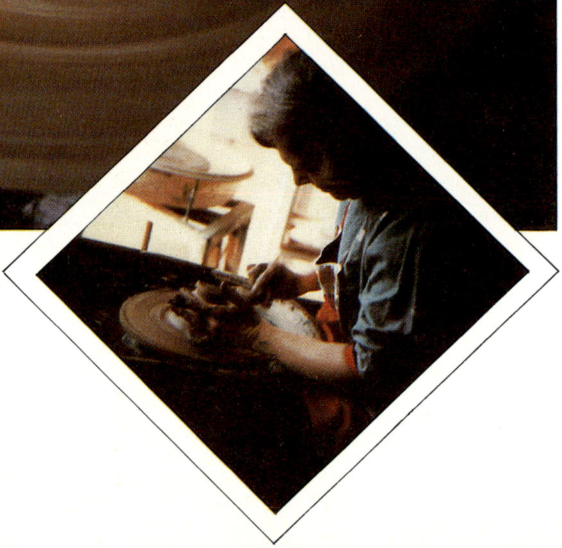

Photographing a scale model layout
If you choose an intricate hobby like model-making, you will want to bring out detail and color, so you may have to use flash to supplement daylight, as below right. It may be best to turn off any room lighting – fluorescent lamps have given the shot above right a cool, greenish cast. For the picture of the model railway and village far right, the photographer moved near to a low window, to use its bright daylight. Take some shots from above, as here, to set the scene for details, as below. Frame your pictures of details tightly, in order to exclude everything but the model itself from the shot.

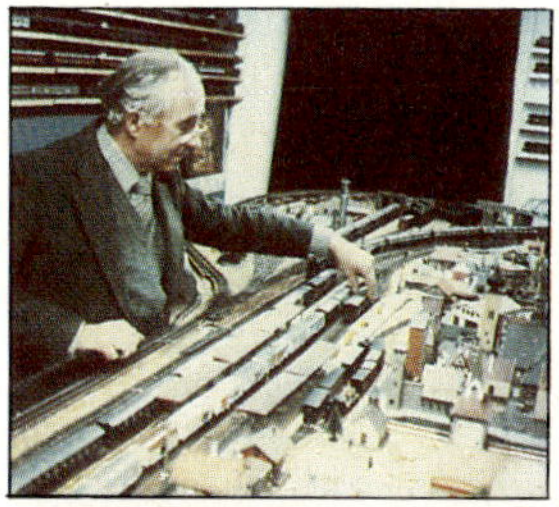

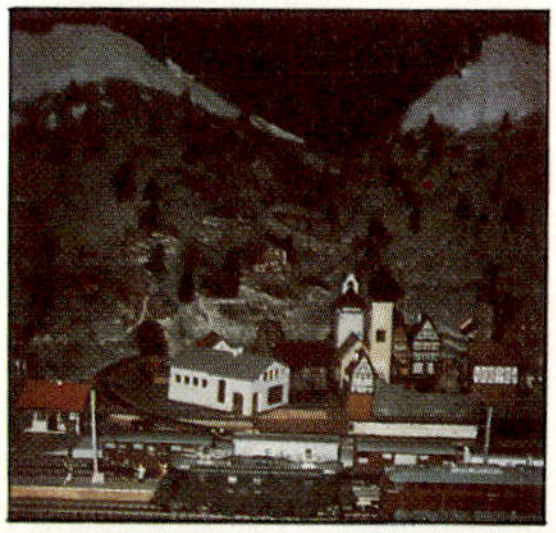

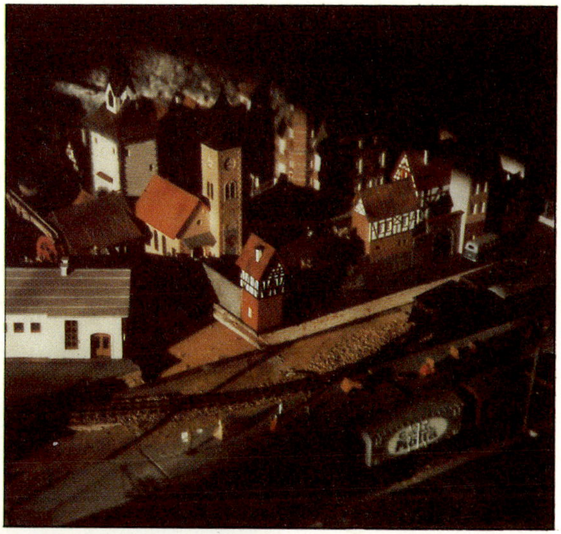

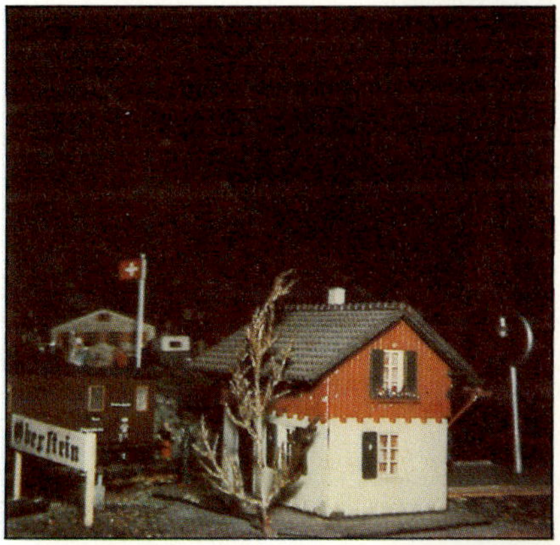

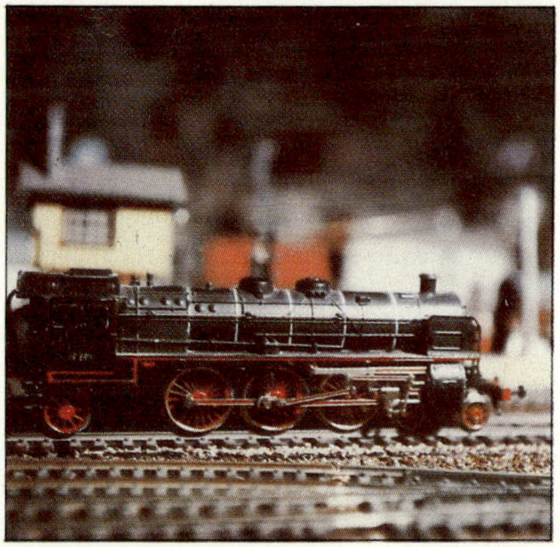

Close-up shots
When photographing models, move in to your closest focusing distance (p. 79), and shoot details. Try to convey an impression of reality by getting down to the level of the layout. When you are shooting very close, particularly by natural light, left, the area of your picture that is sharp will be limited, so make sure that you focus carefully on your subject. Using flash for close-ups, far left, makes more of your pictures sharp and records detail accurately, but you tend to lose realism.

Lighting for atmosphere
When you take indoor pictures of a hobby such as music, make use of the colors of light to enhance mood. Both these shots made use of available light, not flash. Natural light will exaggerate blue tones in your picture, right, particularly in winter weather. You should place your subject by a window and shoot. If you want the warm, orangey-red cast, far right, turn on the room lights and photograph your subject anywhere in the room.

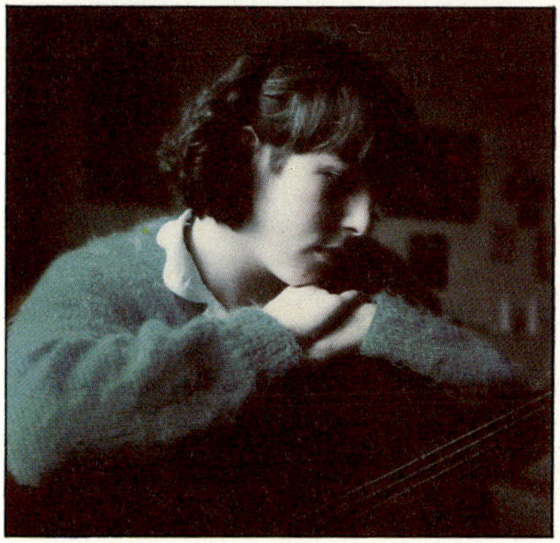

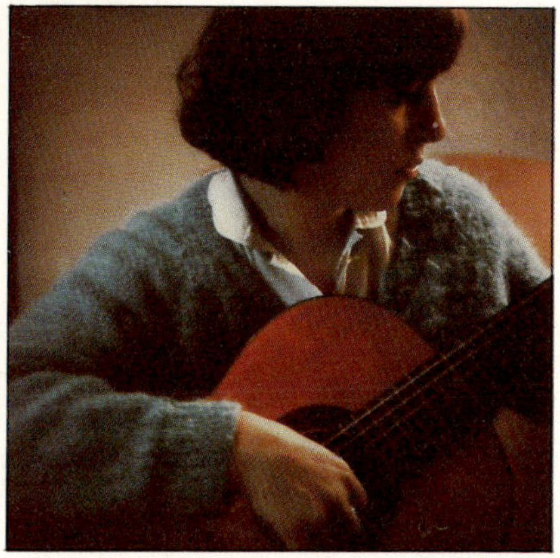

Photographing your possessions

To photograph a treasured possession, take time to light and arrange it properly. With small objects indoors, you can control lighting and background easily. But with large objects outdoors, such as an automobile or boat, you must take care to choose a viewpoint which sets it against an attractive background. Strong light will make the most of bright colors and reflective surfaces – wait for a sunny day. Decide which feature or quality you want to emphasize. Use an oblique, overall view to bring out the sleek lines of a subject, or go in close to frame a detail of the design as tightly as possible.

Design and color
A detail may show the design and style of an object as well as an overall view. The bold colors of a wheel and spare wheel on a vintage automobile form a striking pattern, right.

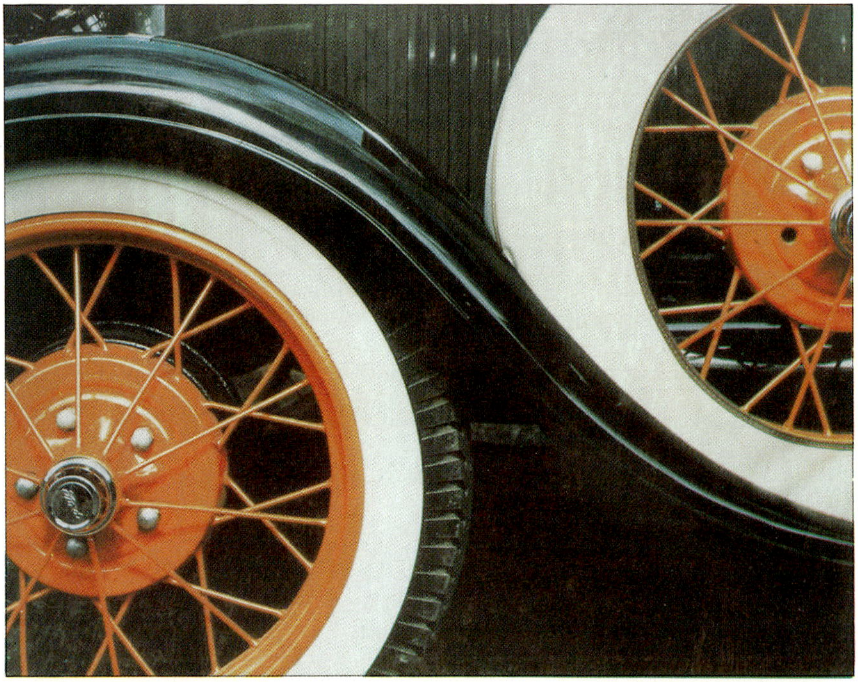

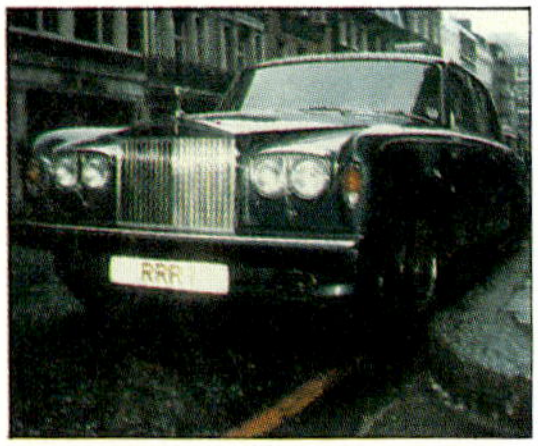

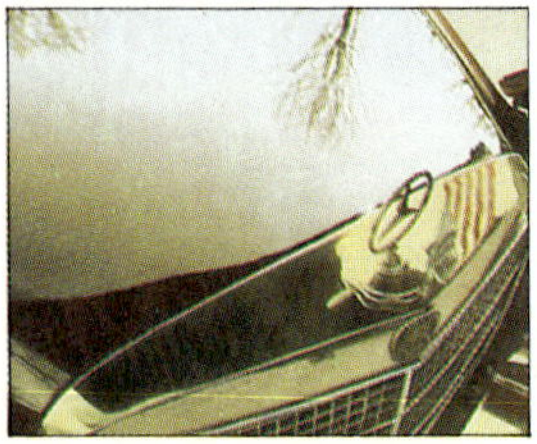

Photographing a car
Choose your viewpoint to highlight your car's best feature: the low, three-quarter view, top left, exaggerates the size of the hood and front wheels, whereas a close, higher viewpoint, bottom left, picks out the gleaming reflections on the polished metal. To emphasize a characteristic detail, such as the insignia on the grill, an accessory close-up lens would be useful (p. 90). Remember to frame your subject so that lines and shapes make an interesting pattern. Photograph your boat in the same way.

Unusual subjects
Don't restrict yourself to obvious subjects or precious items. Keep your eyes open for attractive groupings of everyday objects that suggest atmosphere or remind you of favorite pursuits, as shown right. Look for color, texture and pattern, and be prepared to re-arrange the objects to improve the composition. Try shooting from above as well as from eye level, as shown below right. Remember to frame and focus carefully when taking close-ups (pp.78–9).

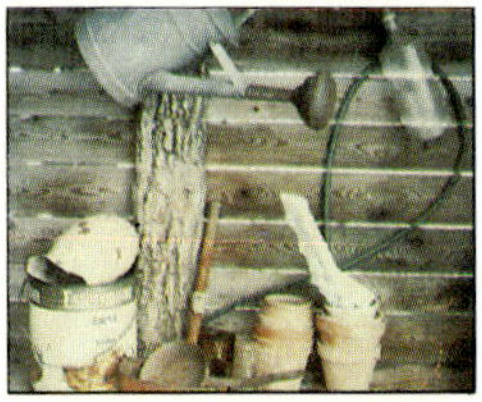

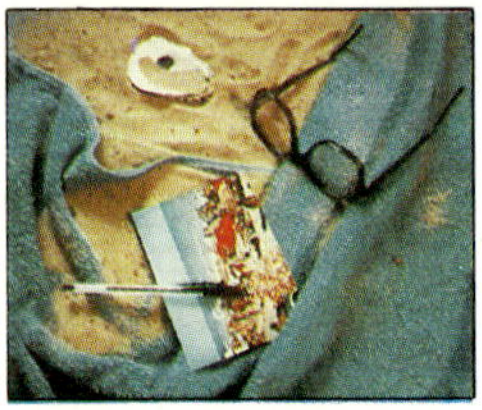

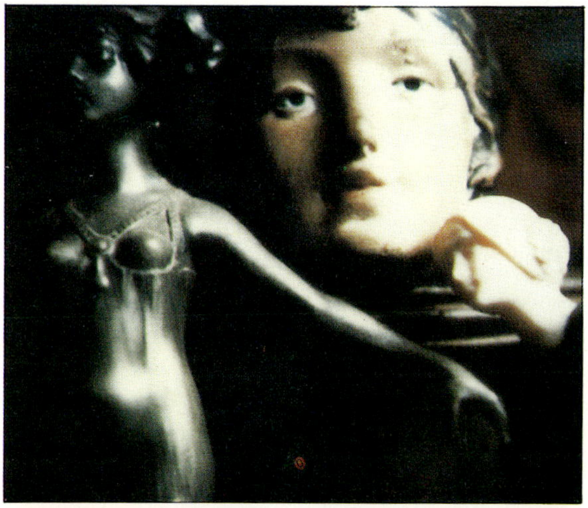

Grouping your subjects

To make a record for insurance purposes, light subjects well and arrange them simply, below. When you want a picture to send to a friend, choose softer lighting and, if you have a self-timer (p. 86), include yourself, right. To capture detail of craftsmanship, move in close, as left.

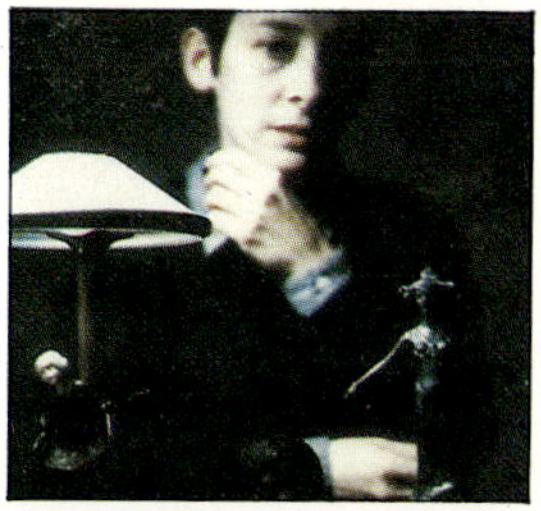

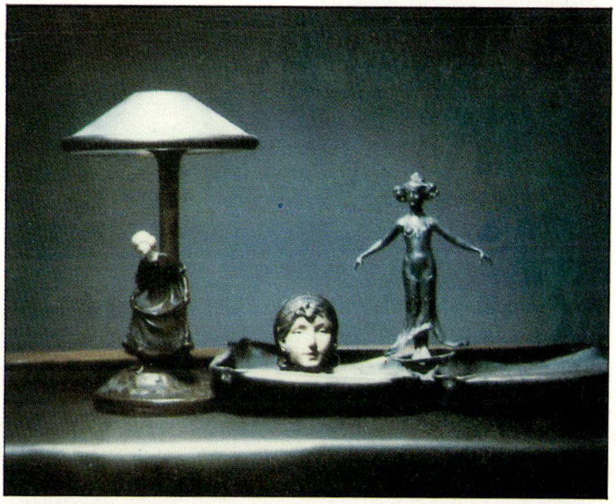

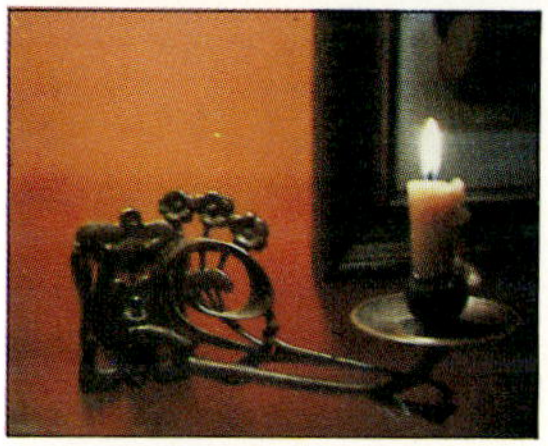

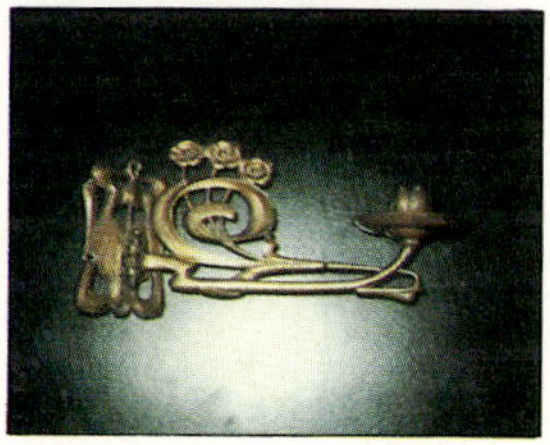

Choosing lighting and background

Flash reflections (p.23) and a dull setting spoil the shot of the candle bracket, above right. For the improved version, above, the object was moved to a more attractive setting, the candle was added, and the shot was taken by artificial light, through a pale blue filter. For the still life, below, unfiltered artificial light gave richness and warmth. The camera set a wide aperture (because the light was dim), softening the colors and shapes of the busy background.

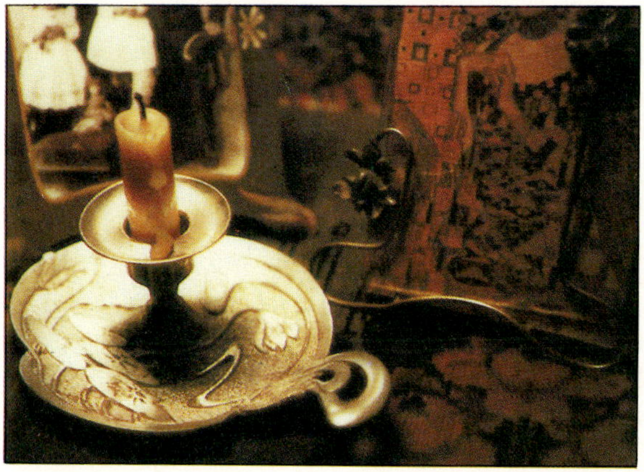

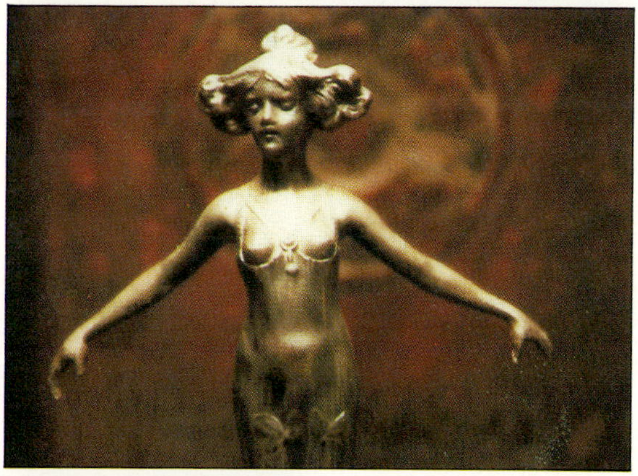

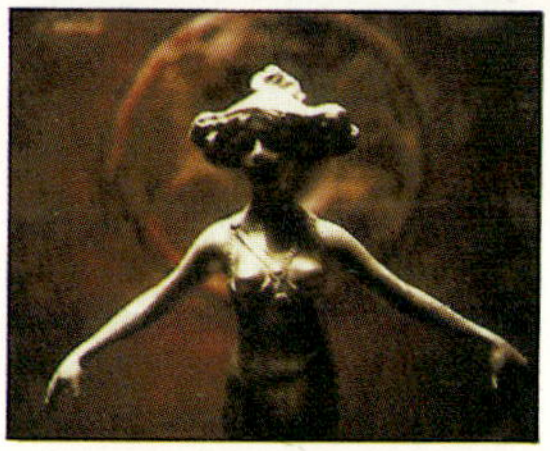

Positioning lights

The statue left was lit by a domestic lamp placed above it, highlighting upper parts but leaving the rest of it dark. The lamp was lowered, above, to the same level as the statue, to achieve a more evenly lit result.

Taking close-up pictures

Most plants and insects are too small to look impressive, even at your camera's closest focusing distance. To make the most of the colors, textures and intricate patterning of the natural world, you must get nearer to your subject. To do this you must have a camera, such as the Alpha, which takes a close-up lens. This attachment acts like a magnifying glass, enabling you to fill the frame with a small subject. When working close-up, accurate focusing is vital. You must also keep the camera, and the subject, quite still (or use flash). Set the camera on a tripod, with a cable release, and use a windshield for outdoor subjects, as below. Bright light will intensify flower color, right.

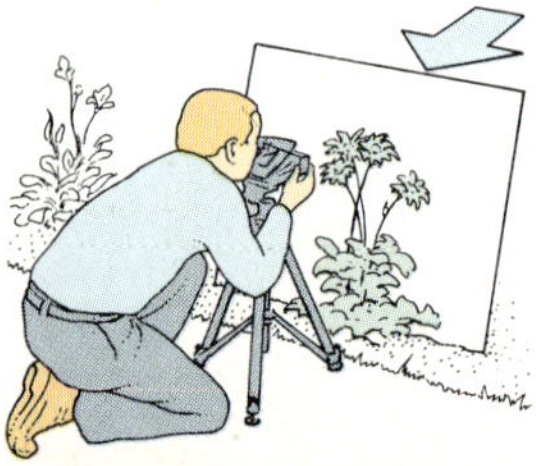

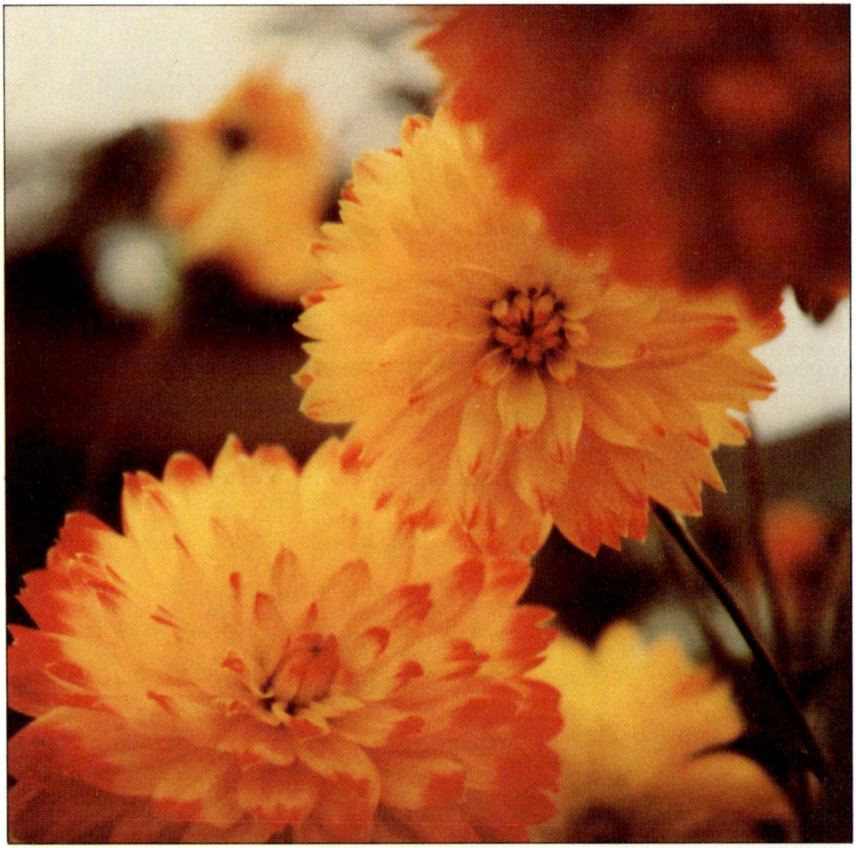

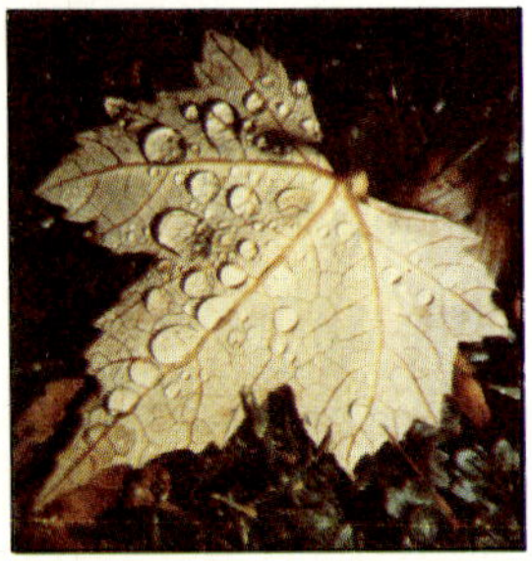

Insects and butterflies
Successful nature close-ups depend on being in the right place at the right time. You must be as quiet as you can and wait for the insect to settle, preferably on a flower or a leaf of a contrasting color, as right. Use diffused flash to ensure sharpness and to bring out the rich wing color and detail.

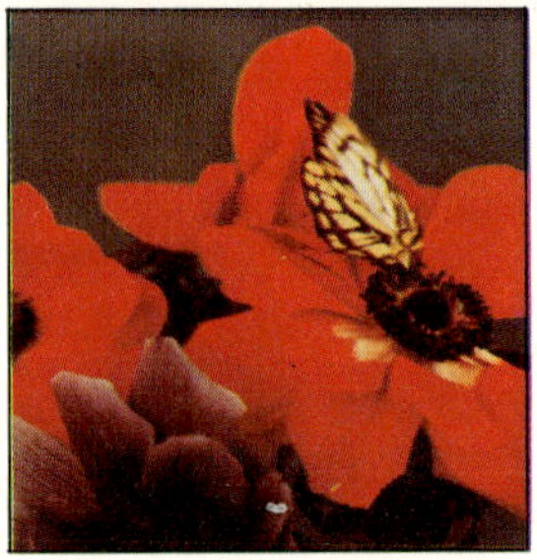

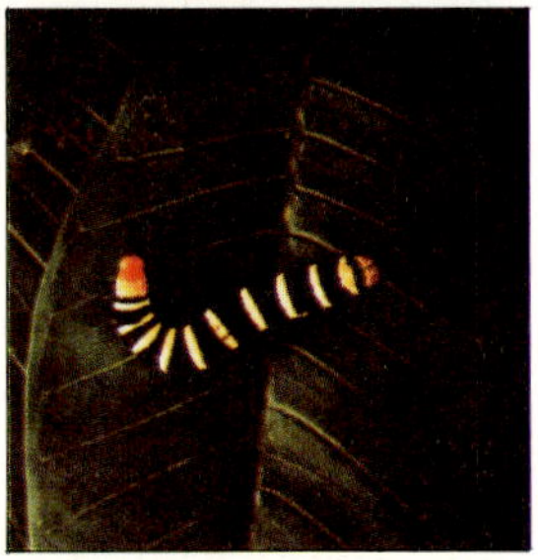

How close can I get?
The picture, below, is taken at 4 ft (1.2 m) – the closest distance possible with most direct vision cameras (pp.8–11). If you have an SLR model (pp.12–13), you can get as close as 11 ins (28 cm), below right, without an attachment. The picture, right, is taken at a distance of 5 ins (12.5 cm) – the closest you can get if you have a close-up attachment for your SLR. Always measure the subject to camera distance exactly, using a rule, when shooting at your camera's minimum focusing distance.

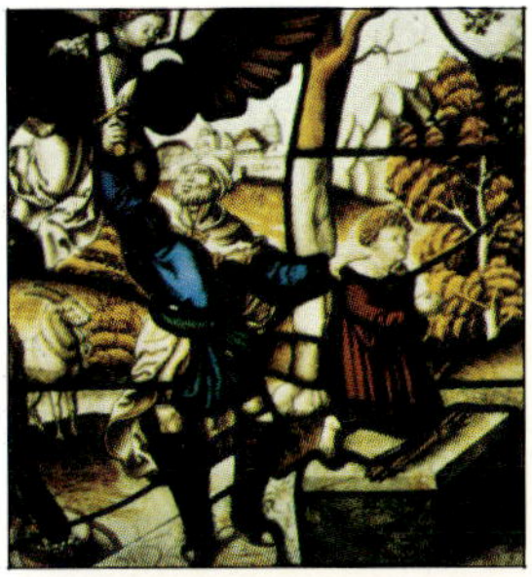

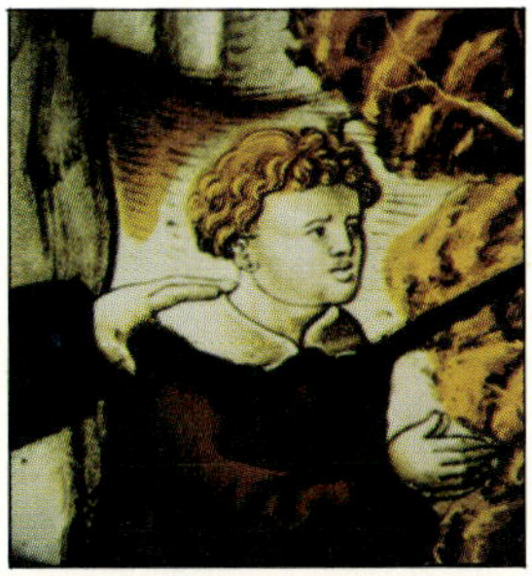

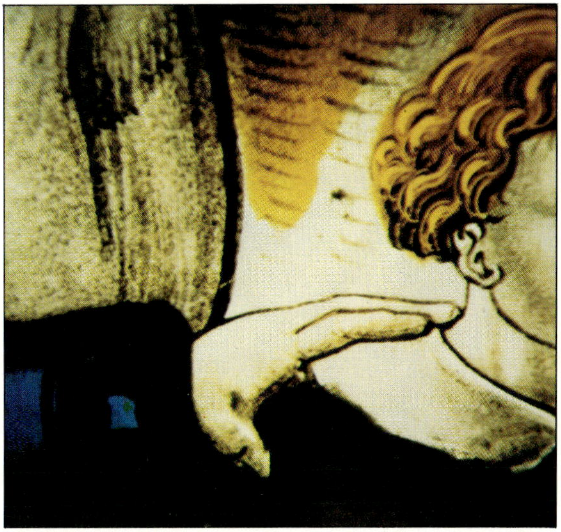

	5 ins	11 ins	3 ft	$3\frac{1}{2}$ ft	4 ft
Polaroid peel-aparts				●	
1000/One-Step					●
2000/Pronto! range			●		
SX70 Alpha		●			
SX70 Alpha + attachment	●				
Kodak cameras					●

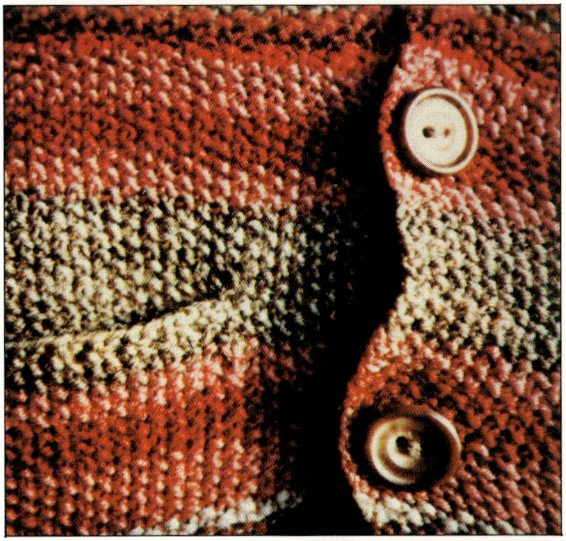

Focusing on detail
Take close-up pictures to show off your craft skills: get in close to pick up an interesting texture, above, or detail, right. Include relevant items, such as the scissors and thread, right, and make sure that there is plenty of color in the subject. Frame your picture so that lines and shapes make an interesting pattern.

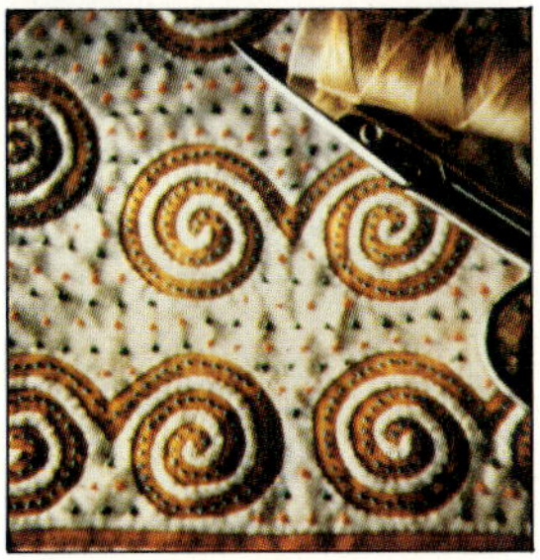

Using the L/D control
With small reflective subjects you may get a richer result if you move the L/D control toward darken. For the top picture, the L/D control was set at normal; for the second shot, below, it was moved one mark toward darken.
Also use the L/D control in a close-up picture with:
- A pale subject with a dark or shadowed background – darken.
- A dark subject with a bright, reflective or pale background – lighten.

Only follow these instructions, if the background is a large part of the picture area (40% or more).

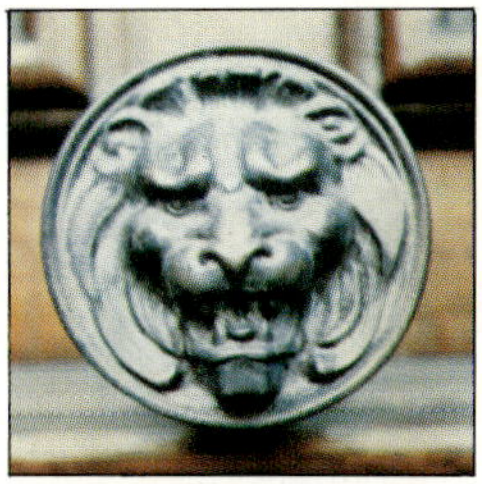

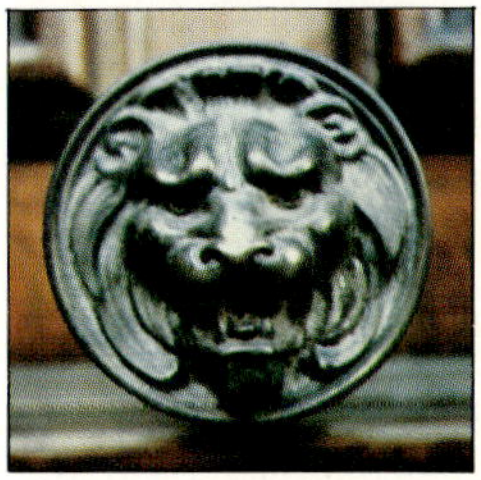

Fun with film

The emulsion of a Polaroid SX70 picture is still fluid during the first few minutes of its life. Using a blunt tool, see below, you can move the emulsion inside the photograph for effect. Sharp pictures with light and dark areas and some texture are the best shots for this technique. Experiment with photo failures at first. Start gently with a small area; use a light, even stroke and follow the lines of the picture. You can press harder for a more powerful effect, but be careful as you may reveal the white and black underlayers. Once the emulsion is broken, it can be worked with for several hours. Have your manipulated picture enlarged (p.89) – this enhances its painted look.

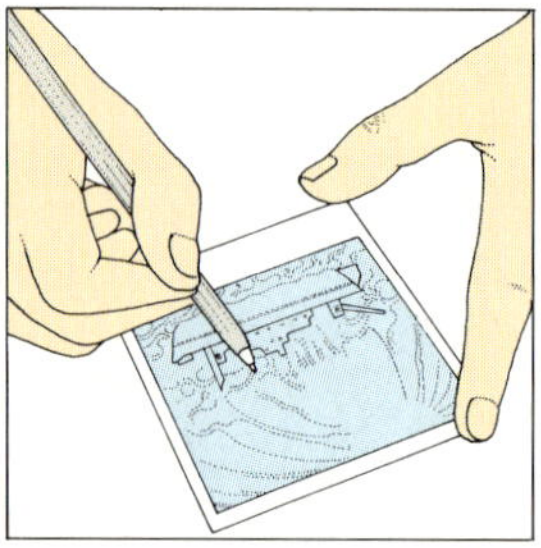

The palette knife effect
Take a blunt-ended implement and, pressing on a hard, flat surface, smear large areas of the picture. This method is best used on plain background areas. In the picture, right, it is used to suggest a stormy sea behind a toy boat. Areas that are left photographic will stand out against the manipulation.

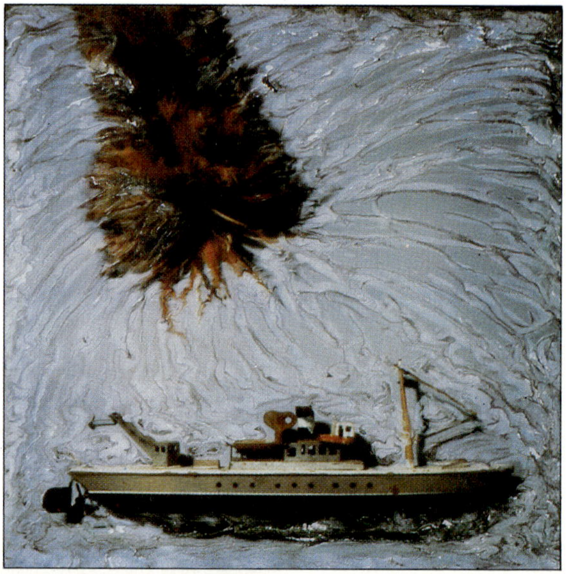

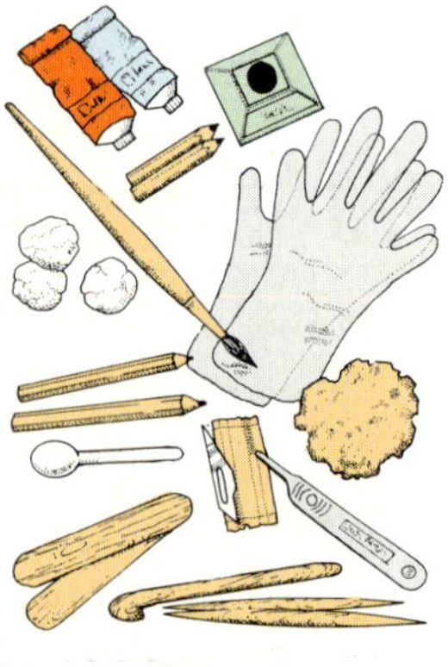

Fun with film equipment
You should have metal or wooden tools; plastic gloves; cotton balls; a craft knife; paints and brushes.

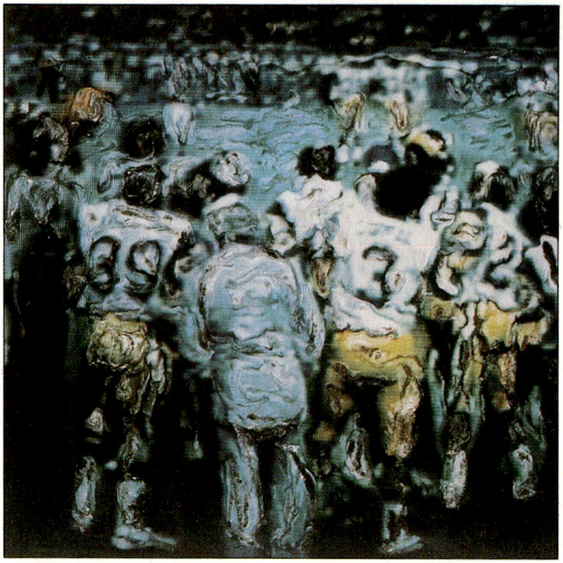

Complex manipulations
You can stretch the outlines of an image for effect – they can be bent slightly or completely distorted, according to the degree of manipulation. Decide how much is best for your subject. In the picture, left, the degree of distortion increases as your eye moves along the line of baseball players, slipping from form into blur and giving an impression of movement. Faces are hard to manipulate effectively – you are unlikely to get good results. If you want to include people in a manipulation choose a shot of their backs, as in the picture left, or concentrate on distorting hair and eyes. Leave the remainder of the face undisturbed.

Painting instant pictures
You can transform SX70 shots with paint or ink after removing the back of the picture, right. But *you must wear protective gloves* or the caustic fluid inside the picture will burn your hands. Don't allow children to try this technique unsupervised.

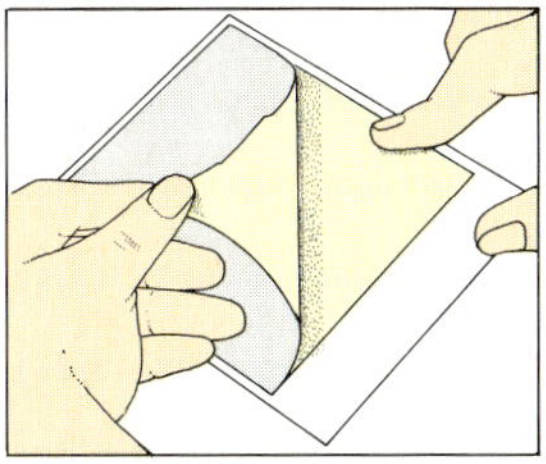

Removing the back
Using a sharp craft knife, cut the black plastic next to the white margin on three sides so that you can peel away the black picture back.

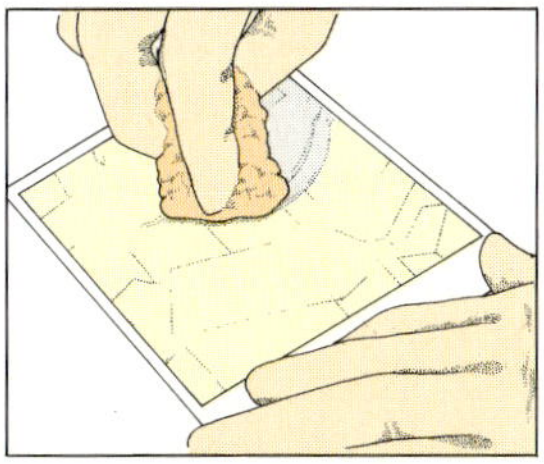

Removing the chemicals
Carefully wash the white emulsion with absorbent cotton. If you want to remove part of the image completely, rub hard to wash off the emulsion.

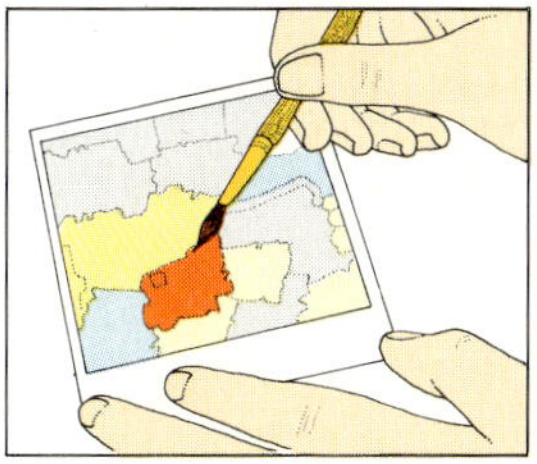

Painting
Paint on top of the emulsion for subtle color, or on to the transparent plastic in areas where you have removed the emulsion for a stronger painted effect.

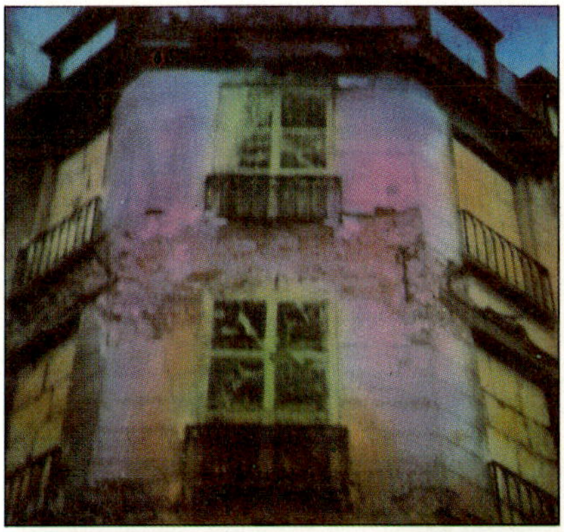

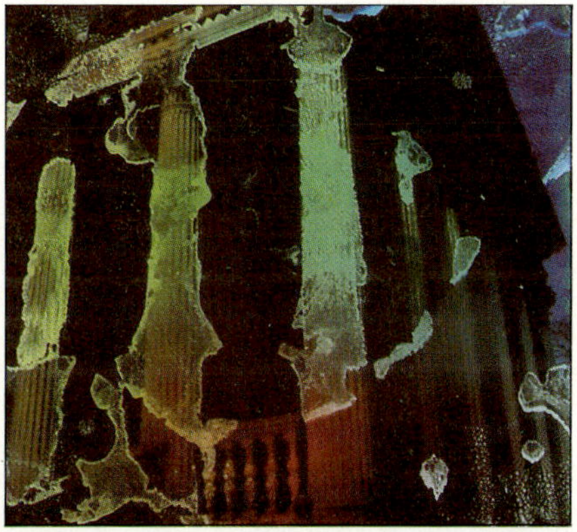

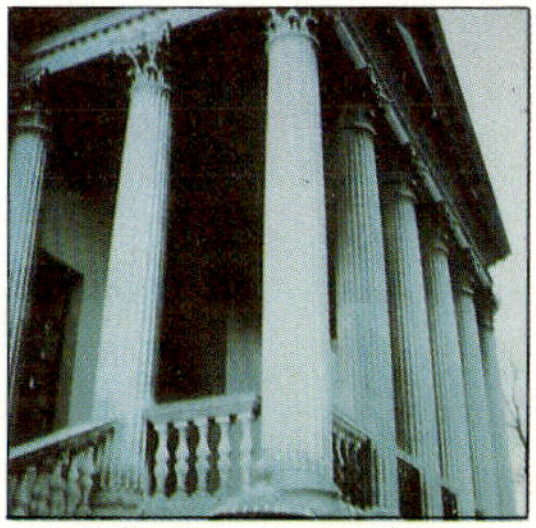

Effects with colored ink
The portico above was transformed with inks, left. Inks can be used without changing an outline, far left.

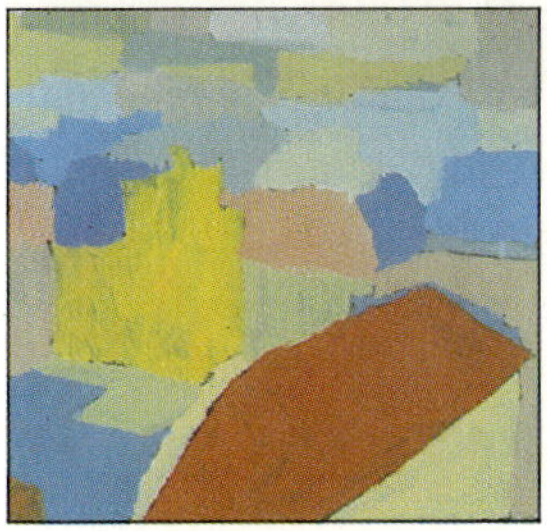

Using paints
The picture above shows the back of the finished image, right. It indicates what areas of color were painted to create the effect. The soft colors of the paint enhance the photographic outlines of the picture. You should still follow the advice on using color (pp.36–9) when you are working in paint or ink.

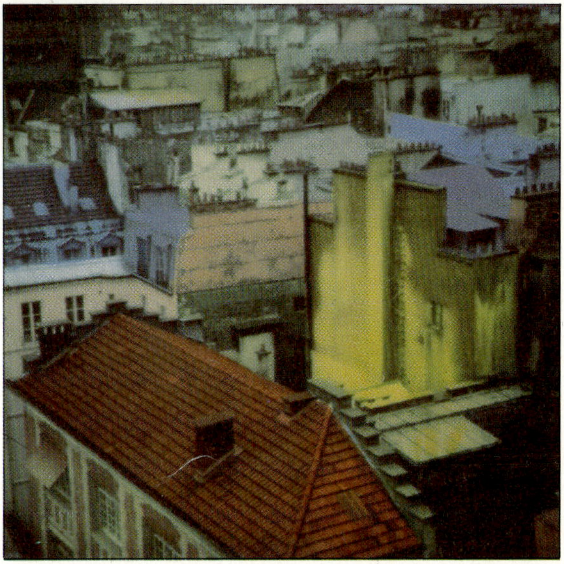

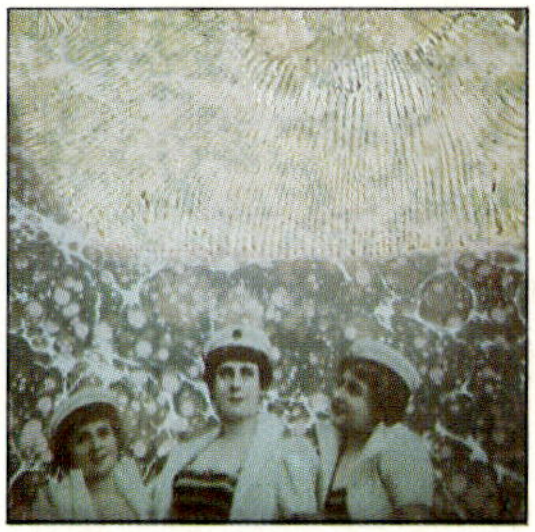

Crackling the picture
To achieve a crackled background, above, the picture was held about 4 ins (10 cm) from a lighter. Any source of heat will have the same effect. Use this technique to distort emulsion before painting.

Don't allow children to try the techniques on this page unsupervised.

Fun with filters and screens

You can create interesting effects with filters over your lens, or screens inserted in your film pack. Filters can change the color or quality of light, as shown here, mask part of the picture, or even produce multiple images. Generally, clear filters will not affect exposure, but colored ones will. You can buy gelatin filter squares and tape them to your camera, right, or cut them to fit the accessory holder, top right. You can also hold mounted filters designed for other cameras over your lens. With clear filters, cover the lens only. With colored ones, cover the eye too. If you cannot cover the eye, or your picture is still dark, set the L/D to lighten.

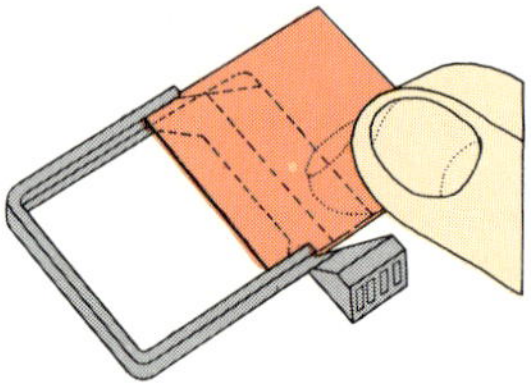

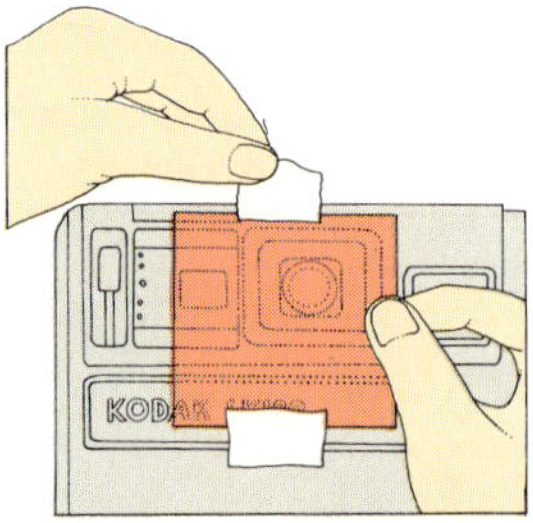

Colored filters

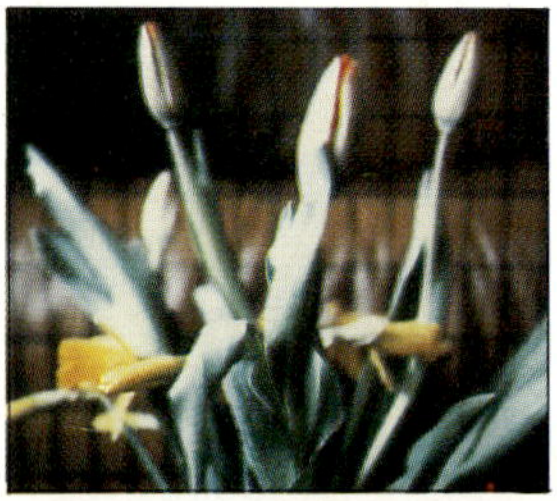

The vase of flowers, left, was shot unfiltered, and with various colored filters, below. Pale filters "warm up" or "cool down" the image; strong colors change it dramatically. The picture below was taken with a yellow filter for a powerful, golden effect.

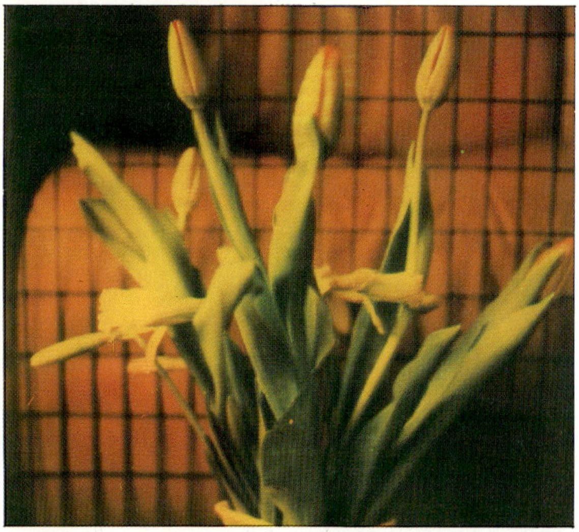

Frosted and dual filters
A colorless, frosted filter softens the image, right. You can achieve similar romantic effects with greased glass, netting or gauze – or try ribbed glass for a more abstract effect.

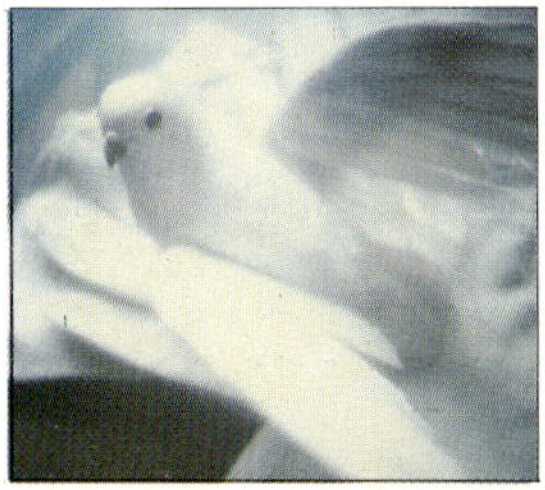

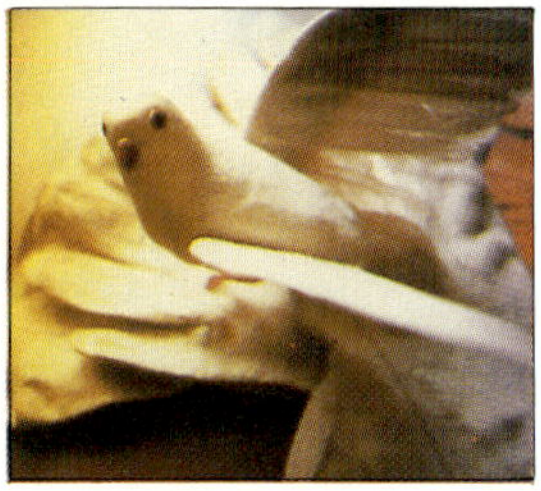

Two-color filter
A half-yellow, half-red filter gives a warm glow to the shot above.

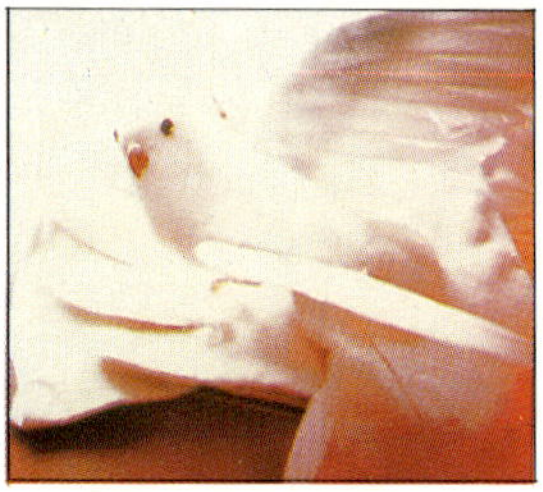

Part-colored filter
A red filter with a clear area was used off-center for this shot.

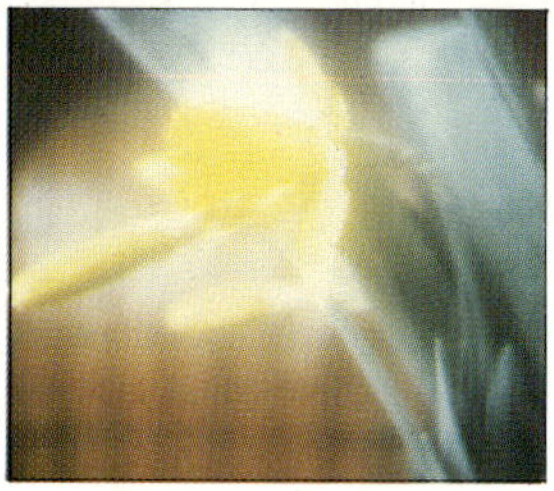

Pale yellow, frosted filter
This filter creates a soft, sunny effect, well suited to the spring daffodil, above.

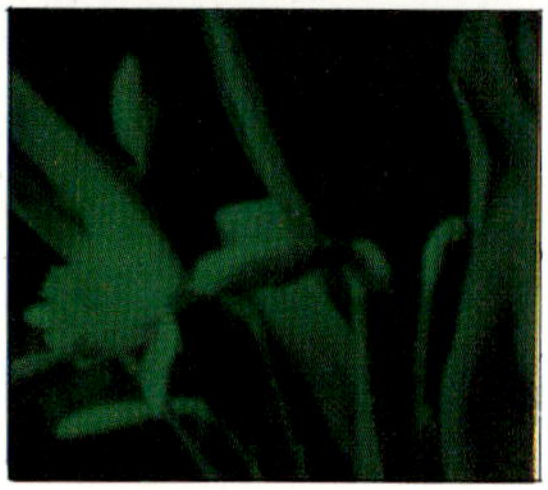

Strong green filter
This filter gives a surreal effect. Strong filters suit simple, bold shapes.

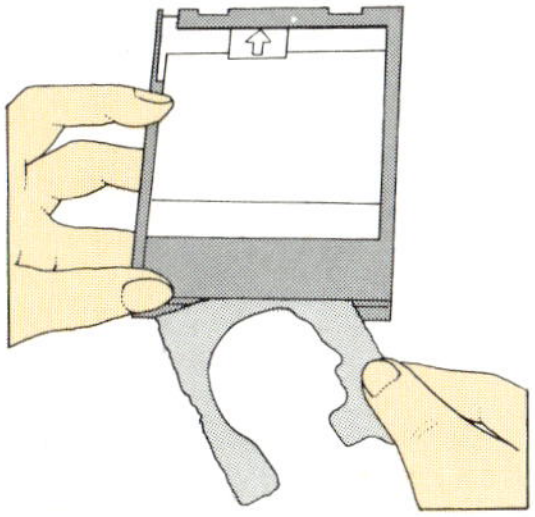

Screens in the pack

A thin screen placed in the pack will mask part of the film from light, and trace dark patterns on the image. Cut your screen to fit tightly inside the pack, and slide it gently under the film cover, as above. Be very careful not to damage your camera.

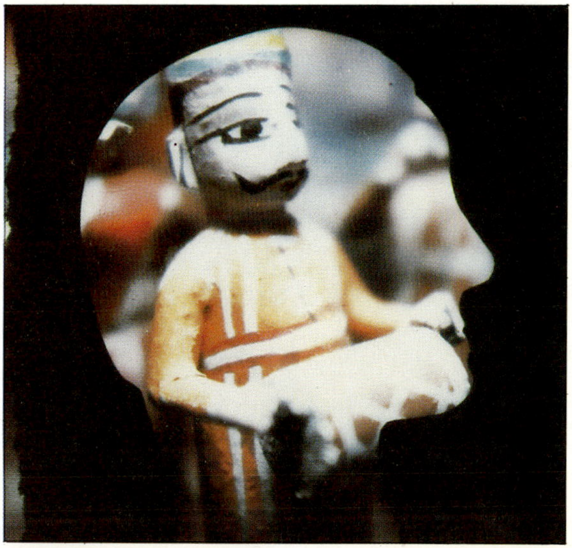

Materials for screens
Screens should be very thin, strong enough not to tear or crumple, and rigid enough to lie flat – plastic is best. You can decorate clear plastic with various patterns. If you use adhesive dots, your picture will emerge with spots, below. Cut out shapes from opaque material to produce a frame, left.

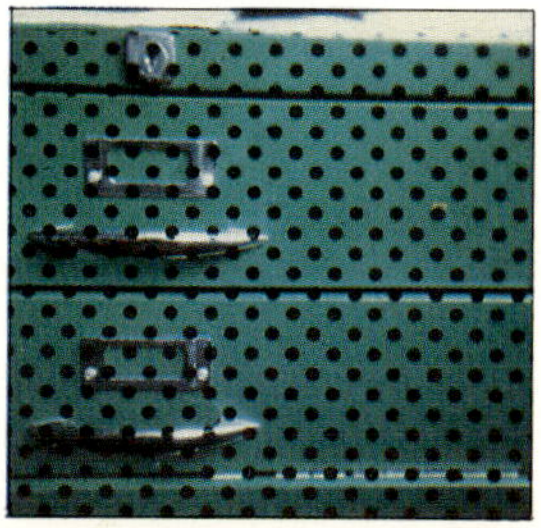

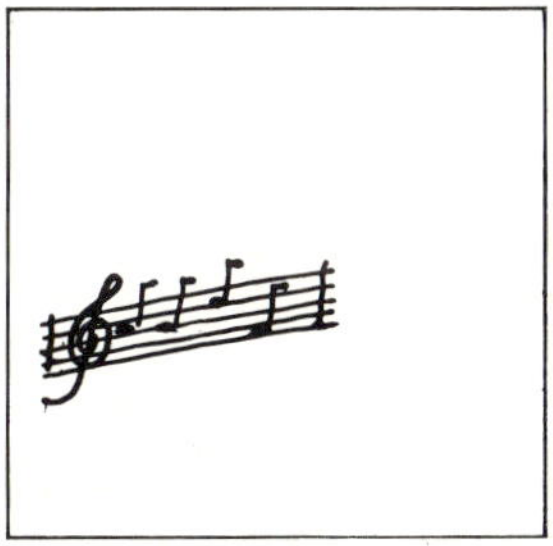

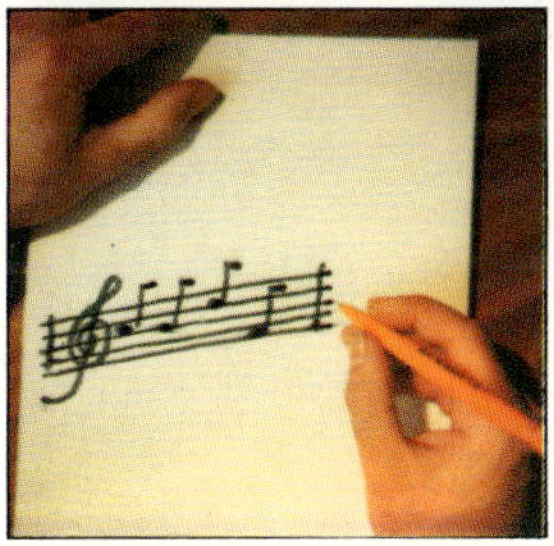

A written screen
You can write a message on a clear plastic screen and add it to your picture. Judging how to align message and subject is difficult. So keep to simple images, such as a signature in one corner. If the music above had been written on the paper and then photographed, the image would not have been so clear. With a written screen, however, you can see every note.

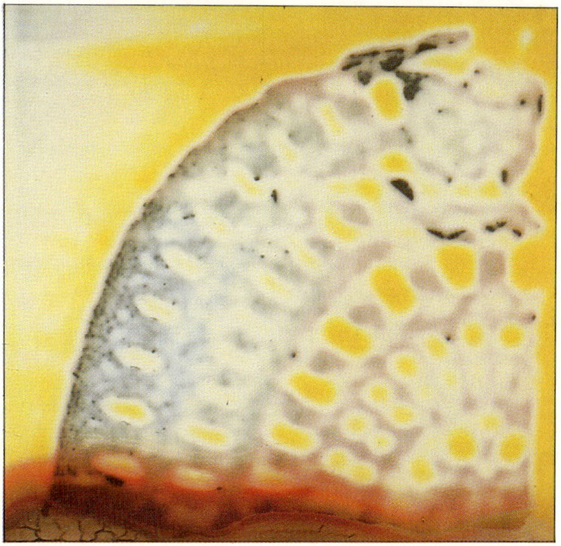

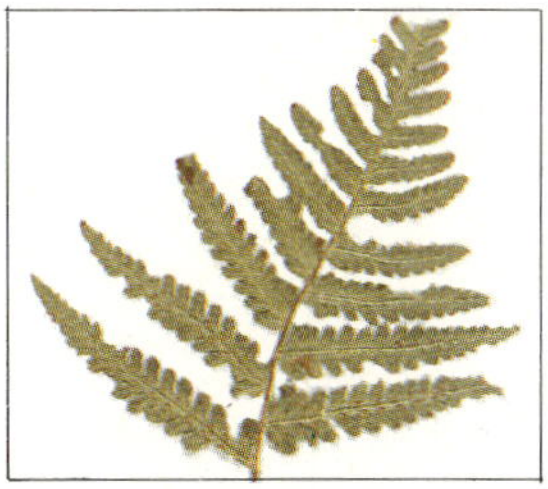

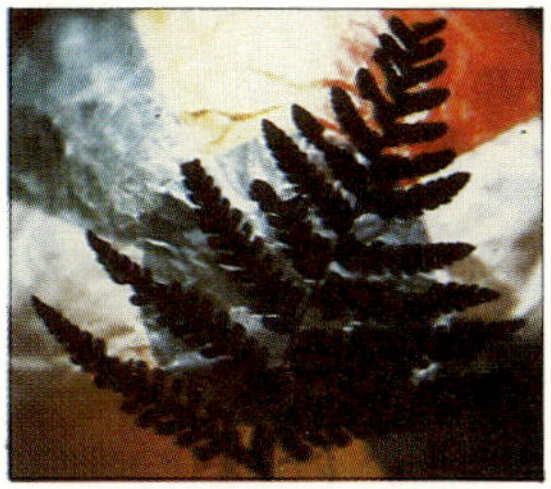

Making photograms
Sandwich any small, flat object between two thin pieces of plastic, above, and place this in the pack. Shoot a colorful object, putting the lens out of focus for a bright background.

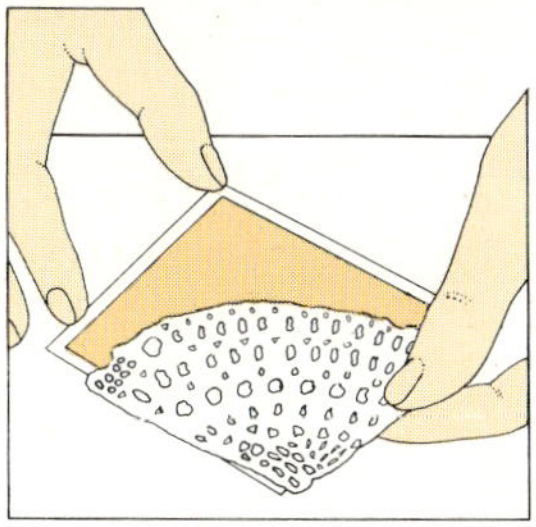

Instant photogram
In dim light, carefully remove one piece of integral film from the pack, and place on it a small, flat object with an interesting outline. Now put them on a brightly lit windowsill, left. You will get an attractive pattern, as in the picture above. Colors will be unpredictable.

Mounting and storing prints

If you are pleased with the instant pictures you have taken, it is worth spending a little time and money on displaying them well. You can easily ruin prints if you mount or store them incorrectly. Follow these simple rules:

- Don't write on prints. Pen marks show through peel-aparts, and a pen will break the dyes on an integral picture
- Don't use glue, rubber cement or cellophane tape – they may cause a chemical reaction which will ruin your print
- Don't dry mount an instant print – pressure will distort the image
- Don't cut an integral print – you will release dangerous caustic fluid

Some rules do not apply to manipulations, pp.80–1.

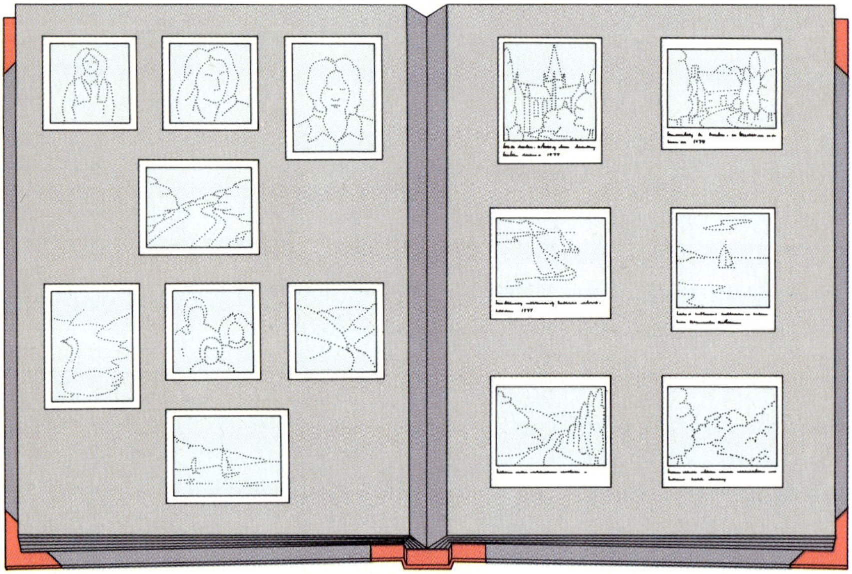

Why has it faded?
Never display pictures in direct sunlight or they will fade, even if they are covered with glass. And never leave exposed prints on the back shelf of an automobile.

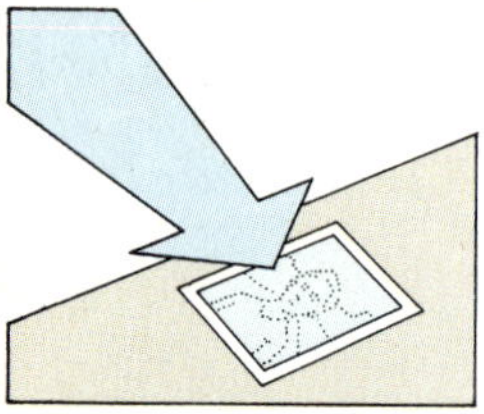

The action of the sun will affect the dyes in your print and it will lose its rich coloring.

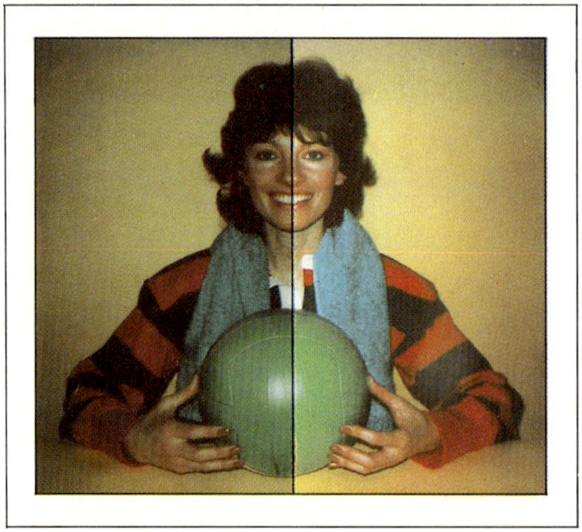

Labeling your prints
The best way to record information – such as subject, place and date – on your pictures is to use self-adhesive labels. Write or type on these labels, then apply them to the wide margin of integral pictures or to the back of peel-apart prints.

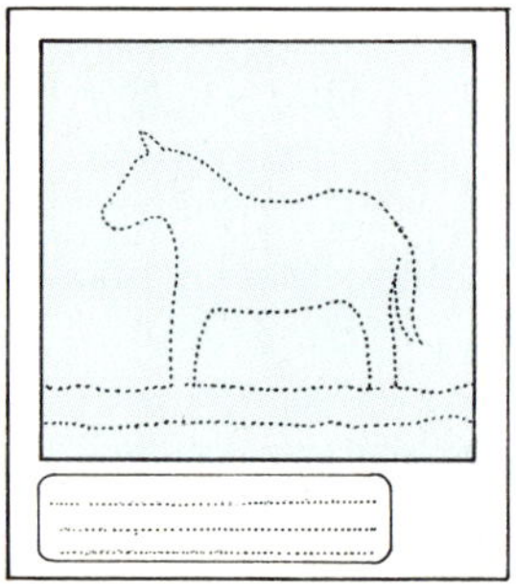

Albums and frames
You can choose from a range of albums and frames that have been especially designed for instant pictures. Albums may have card or plastic pockets, or self-adhesive pages with a cling-film overlay. As well as special instant picture frames, any frame of the right size can be used as long as you cut a card overmat, see below. Cubes should only be used for peel-apart prints, and you should allow prints to dry for several days before you put them in the cube. Albums and frames that allow the air to circulate are the best choice for your instant pictures. Instant prints can form a bond with glass, making them impossible to remove – an overmat placed between the print and the glass is essential.

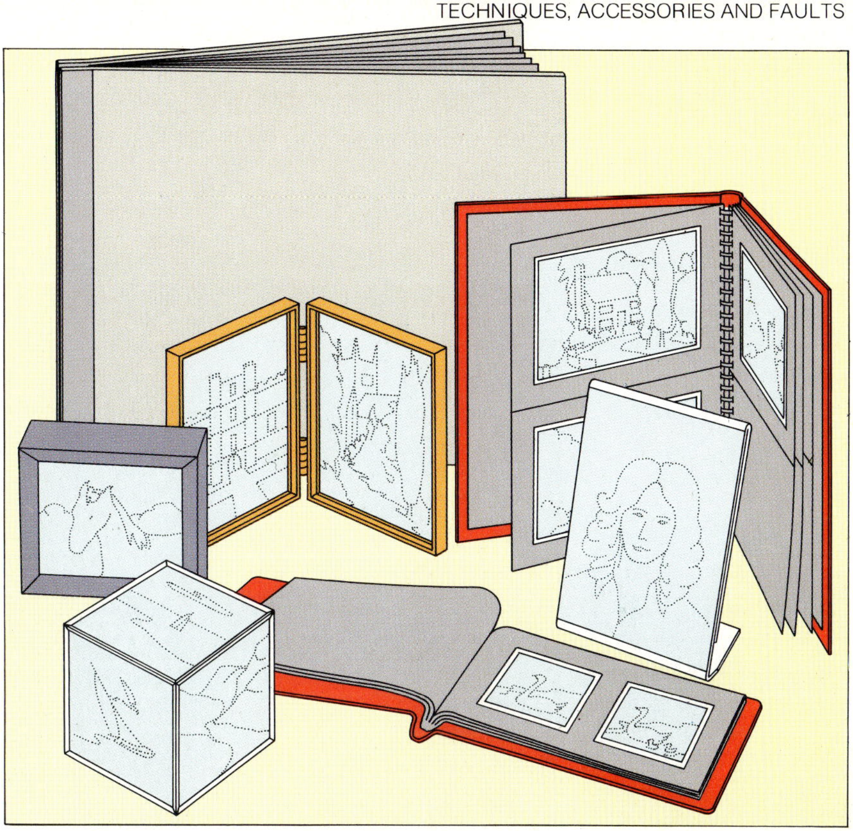

Making a mount

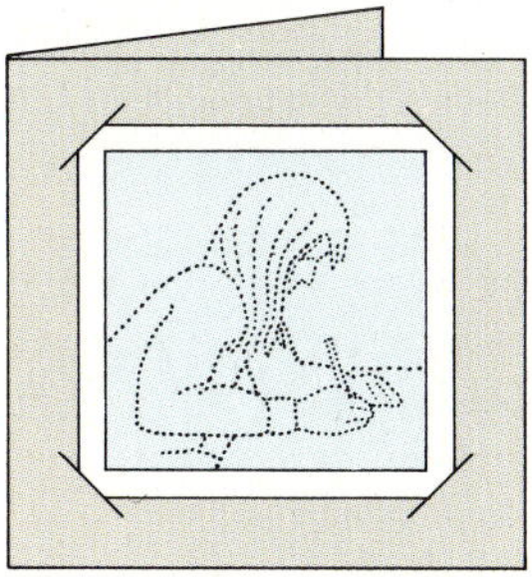

To avoid using glue on your instant photographs, use a paper mount with cut-outs. Cut two pieces of card to fit your chosen frame. Then cut out the picture area in the top piece of card (the overmat). Stick the paper mount to the card, placing glue on the edges of the mount only.

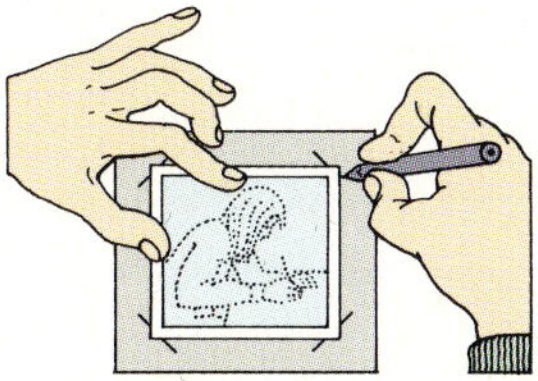

Mark four diagonal lines on the mount at the print corners.

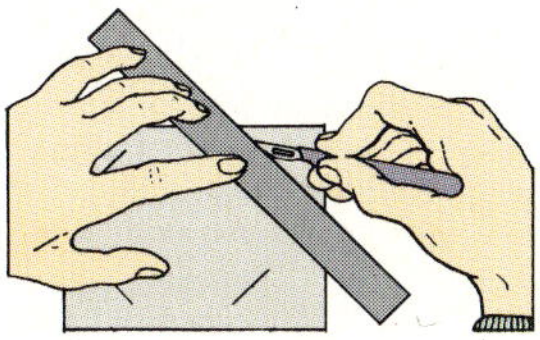

Using a ruler to guide you, cut open the four slots for the picture corners.

Masking a print

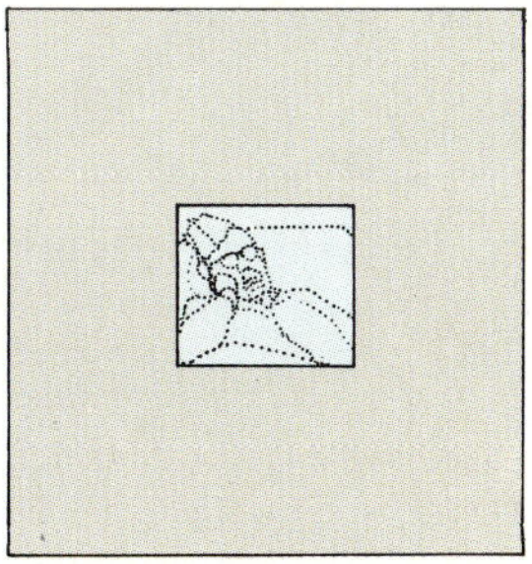

You can also use mats to mask ugly picture areas – you can hide framing errors or faults such as marks on the picture edge (p.91). When you trace out the picture area on an SX70 print use a soft pencil and don't press hard or you will break the emulsion and spoil the image.

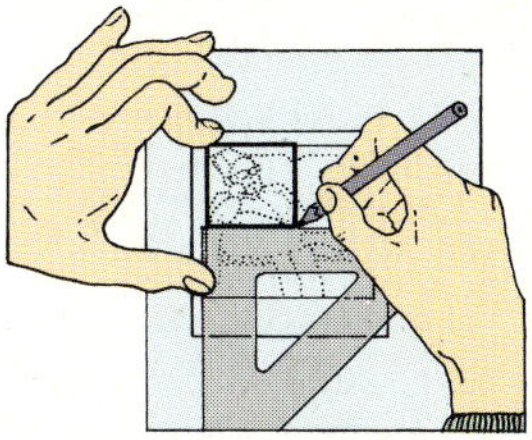

Trace the picture area you want to show using a soft pencil.

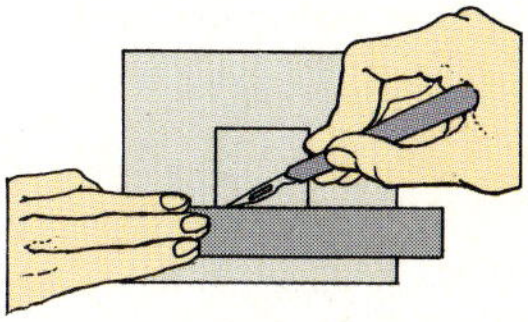

Cut out an overmat to cover the unwanted areas in your picture.

Special uses for pictures

You can take advantage of instant pictures for many purposes. Self-portraits, family pictures, or holiday shots make interesting greetings cards to send to friends and relatives. Or you can mount groups of pictures together for special presentations, see facing page.

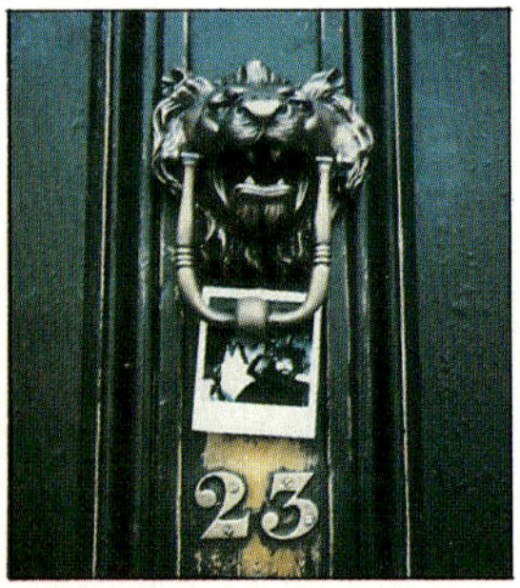

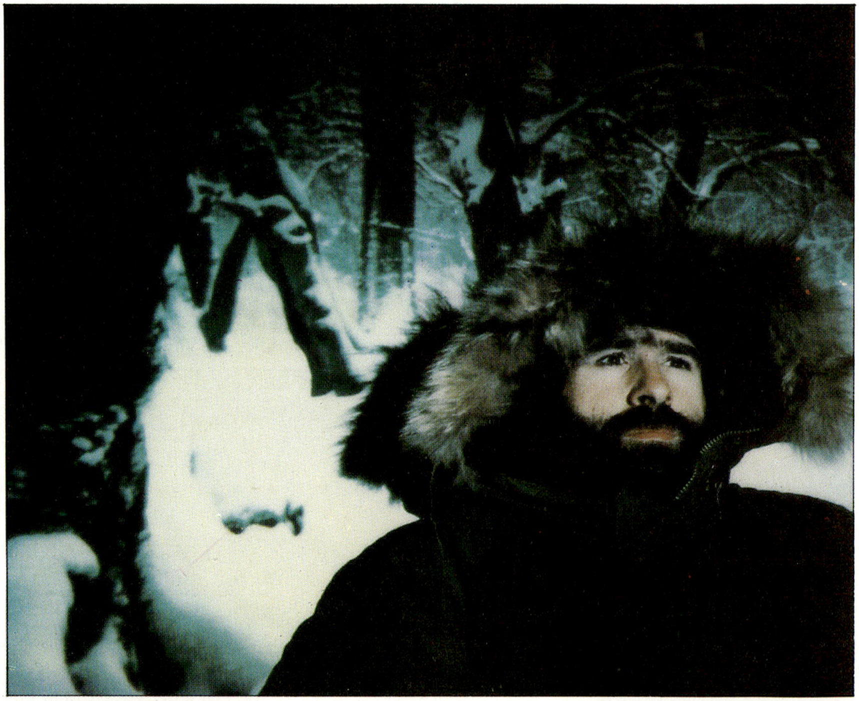

Party invitation cards
The self-portrait, right, was rephotographed attached to the subject's front door, above. Copies of the shot made unusual invitations.

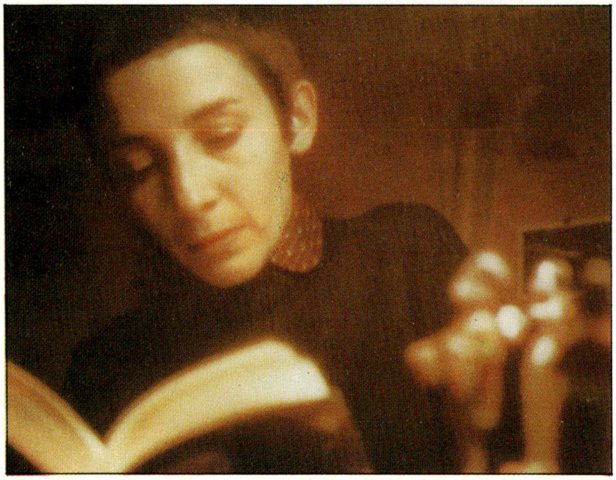

Taking self-portraits
A self-timer enables you to take your own portraits. Before you shoot, consider lighting and background as you would for any other subject. When you are ready, put the timer on the camera and press the button. You have 12 seconds to get into position. You can also take self-portraits in a mirror, or photograph your own shadow. You can use the timer to include yourself in a group. Arrange the group, top right, leaving a space for yourself. Set the timer, and take your place, right.

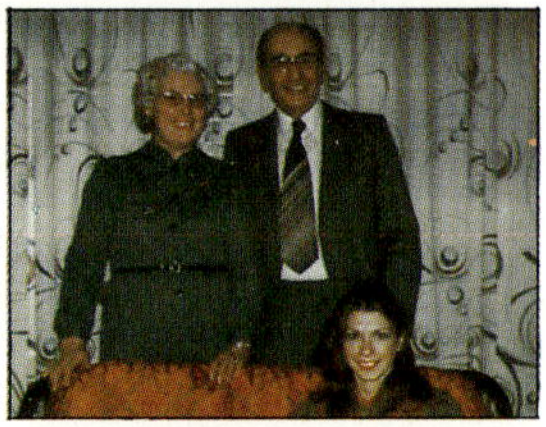

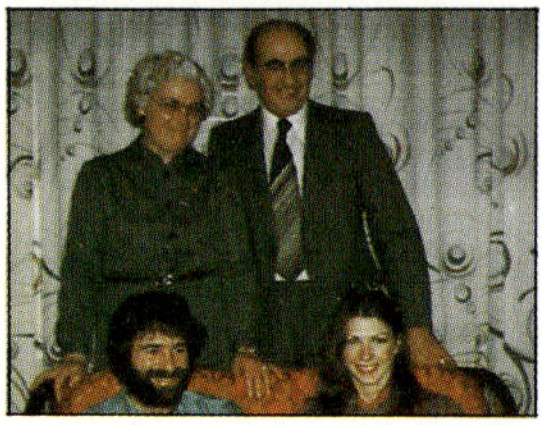

Storyboards and picture montage

Instant pictures are well suited to making storyboards and montages. You can design a presentation in advance, and shoot extra pictures to fill in gaps as you go along. Never glue prints directly – for methods of mounting, see pp.84–5. With montage (mounting pictures together to form one image), you can re-create panoramas too wide for a single shot, or build composite portraits, below. Storyboards have many uses – planning a home movie, for instance. You can also record favorite sequences from TV or video. To photograph screen images, turn on all the room lights, and place a board on top of the set to shield the screen from reflections. Moving TV images will blur. With video, you can freeze a frame to shoot it.

Alphabet storyboard
When a child is learning the alphabet, shoot instant pictures of colorful, familiar objects to represent each letter, and mount them up in sequence, as right. You can do the same for numbers (one train, two cats, three apples, and so on) or to illustrate a favorite story.

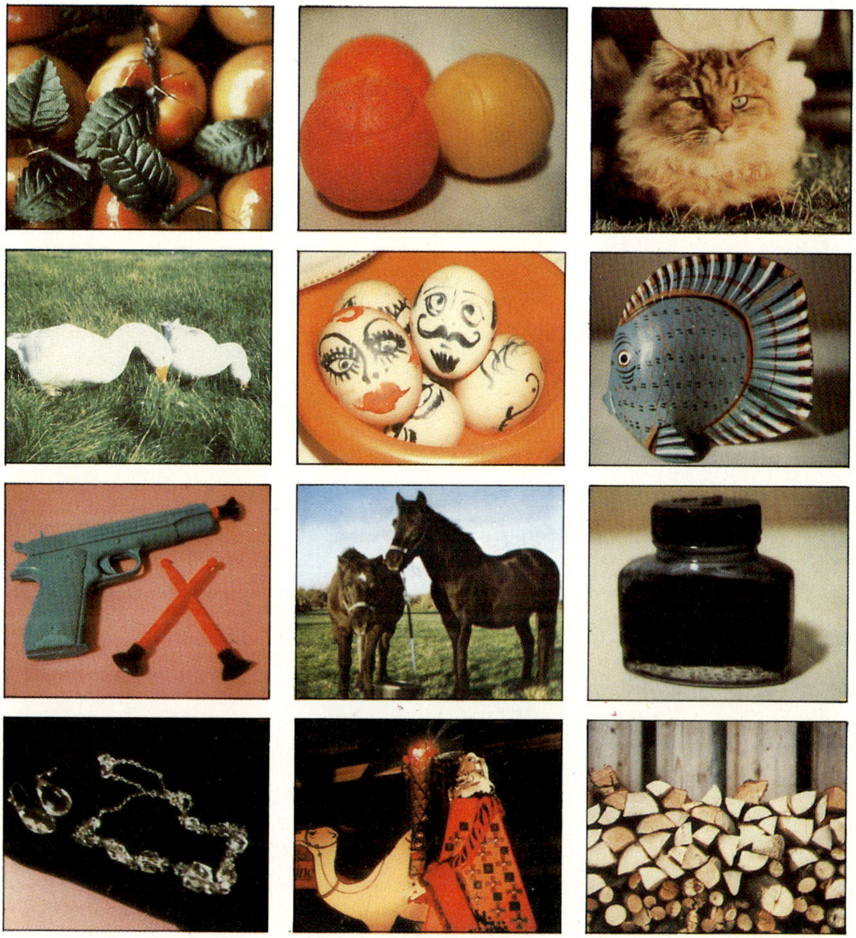

Montage portrait
For an unconventional portrait of someone you know well, collect a series of detail shots of your subject and mount them in one frame, right. Choose bright colors and look for characteristic detail – favorite clothes, typical expressions. Study your subject's features – eyes, profile, mouth, and hands – and concentrate on those which are most striking or photogenic, and which show character.

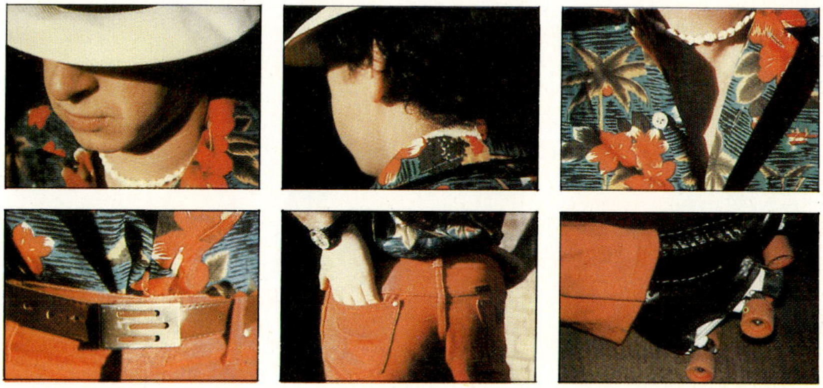

Professional instant photography

When you have your portrait taken by a professional on instant film, the photographer will generally use equipment that is very different to your own. Polaroid make a range of instant film backs for non-instant professional cameras, below. These quality cameras have the advantage of interchangeable lenses, and control over aperture and shutter speed (p.6). A 5 × 4 ins (12.7 × 10 cm) back for Kodak film is also available. Peel-apart film is made for large format cameras – 5 × 4 ins (12.7 × 10 cm) and 8 × 10 ins (20 × 25.4 cm). These are used for portraiture and commercial work. The picture, right, was taken on an 8 × 10 ins film with a studio camera, and the studio lighting was arranged to create a soft, evenly lit result. 8 × 10 ins instant film is very resistant to fading.

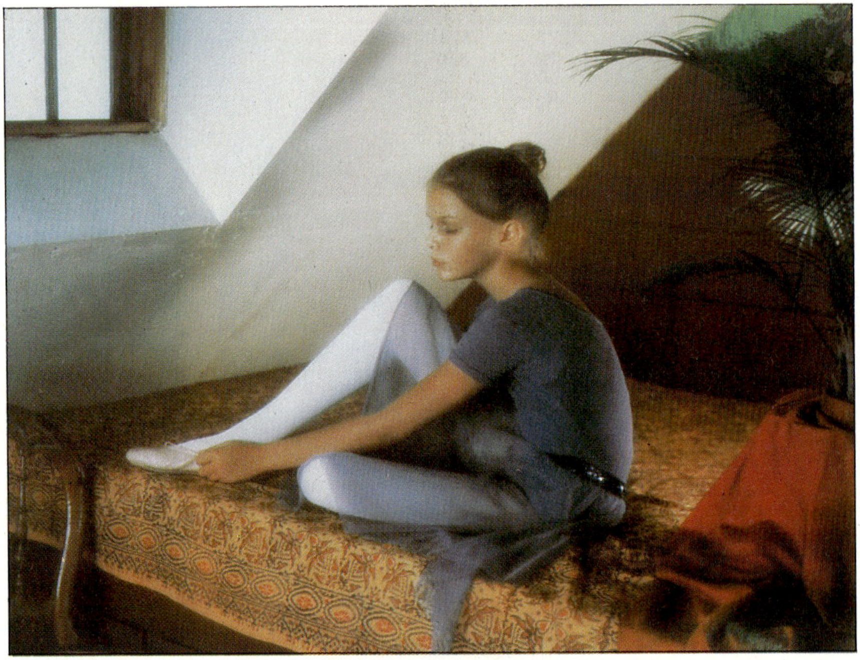

Professional equipment for instant photography
1 A $2\frac{1}{4} \times 2\frac{1}{4}$ ins format SLR for location work
2 Polaroid back for **1**
3 View camera: a large SLR for studio work
4 5 × 4 ins back: Polaroid or Kodak backs are available for view cameras
5 8 × 10 plate camera: precision SLR for studio work
6 8 × 10 ins film holder: fits most 8 × 10 plate cameras
7 8 × 10 ins film processor: accepts holder, **6**, and develops film automatically

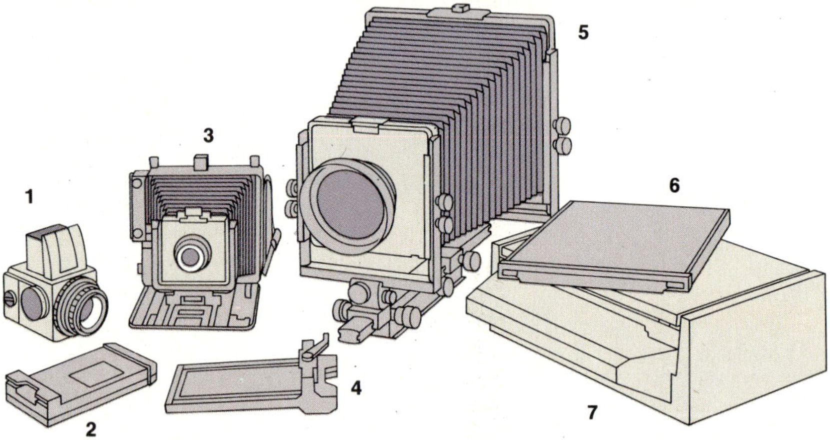

Using a copy service

You can obtain accurate copies of your instant pictures at a reasonable cost. If your friends want copies of a picture do not try to take another shot of the subject with your instant camera – it is cheaper to get copies made of the original.

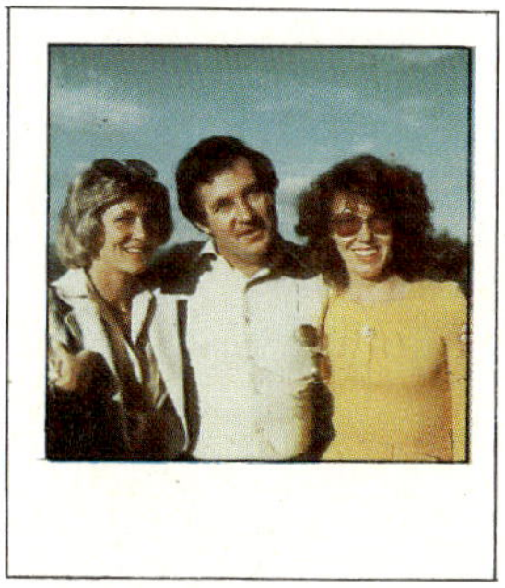

Polaroid original

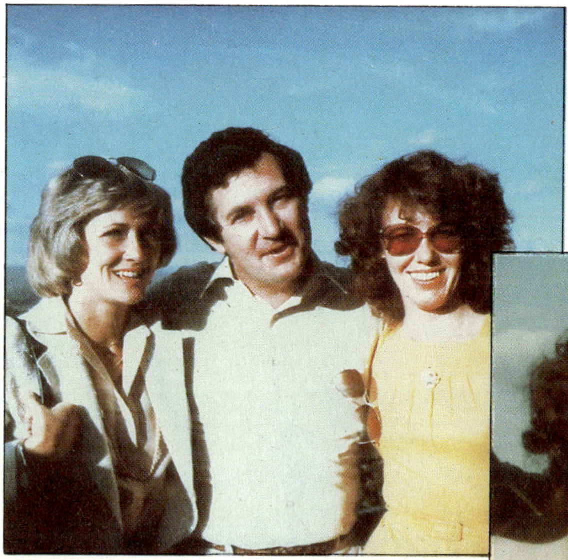

Polaroid copy

Polaroid copies
Polaroid provides a copy service, via any Polaroid dealer. It offers same-size copies of any Polaroid print, and enlargements up to 8 × 10 ins (20 × 25.4 cm). If there is a detail in one of your prints that you like, an enlargement of that detail can be made.

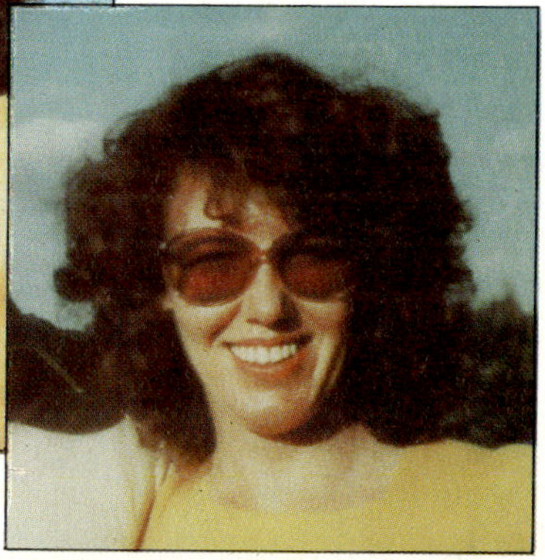

Polaroid detail copy

Kodak copies
Kodak processing houses will copy pictures taken on their instant film in the same way that they copy a conventional print when the negative is lost. In addition, many commercial firms offer a copy service for all types of instant picture. When you send your instant print to be copied, pack it between two pieces of card in a padded envelope or it may be badly damaged in the mail.

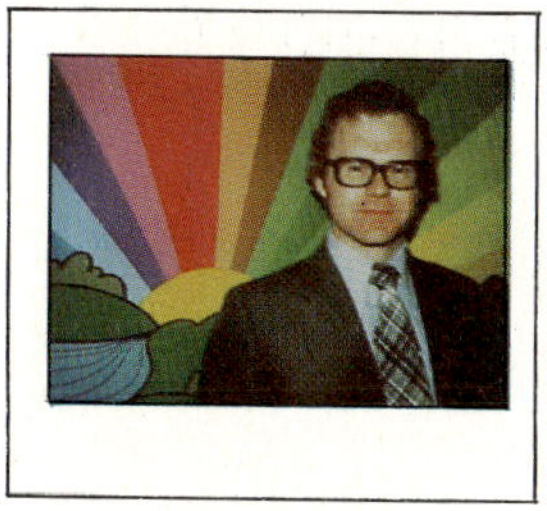

Kodak original

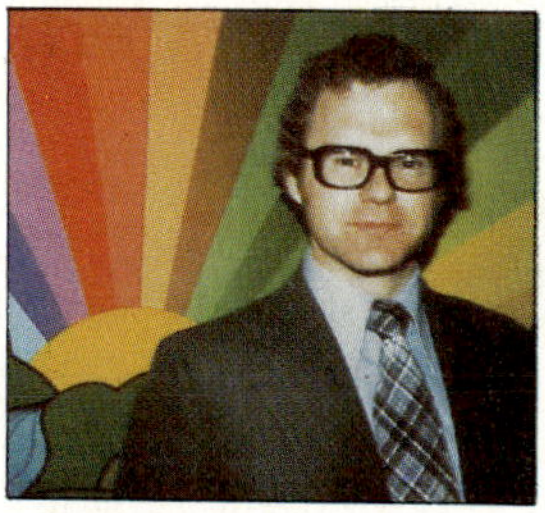

Kodak copy

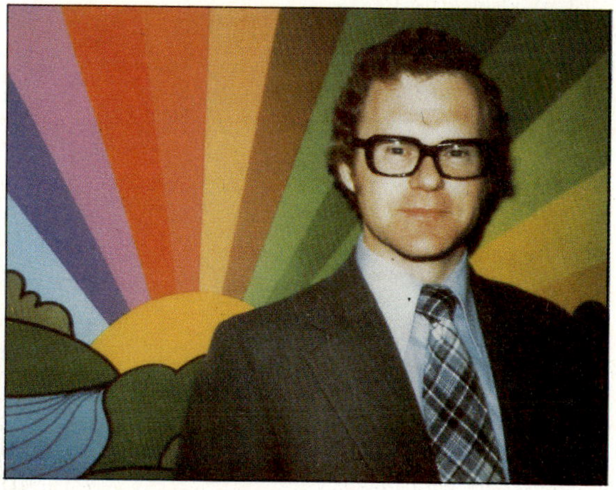

Kodak enlargement

Accessories for your camera

The illustration, right, shows a range of useful accessories:
1 Carrying cases.
2 Close-up and tele lenses, see below.
3 Tripod and mount Standard tripods fit most cameras, but some models require a mount.
4 Lens shade for some models. Shields the lens in bright sun, to prevent flare.
5 Cable release for some models. Use with tripod for low light shots (pp. 45 & 60).
6 Self-timer for some models. Delays shutter action for 12 seconds (p.86).
7 Remote shutter button for some models. Enables you to fire the shutter without disturbing the camera – use for time exposures (p.45).
8 Accessory holder – clips on SLR camera, for some accessories.
9 Neck straps (all models).

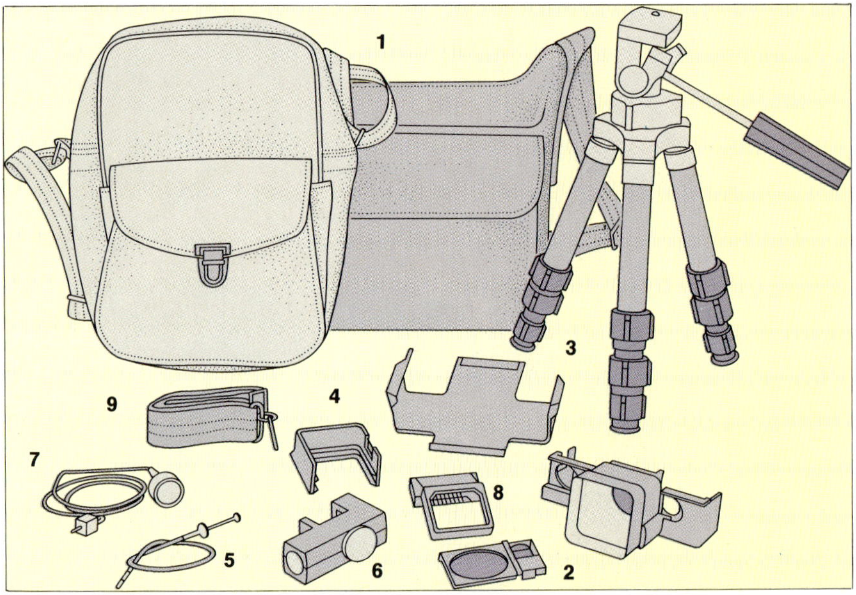

Tele and close-up lenses
The SLR tele attachment enlarges the image and so enables you to shoot details from a distance and fill the frame. Use your tele lens for natural looking portraits and candids, or to enlarge your subject when you cannot get close in, or to make the background seem nearer to your subject. For flash shots with the tele lens use bars *not* a gun, move the L/D $2\frac{1}{2}$ marks toward lighten, and keep within a range of 3–12 ft (1–3.7 m). The close-up lens, on the other hand, reduces the minimum distance for a sharp image with an SLR to 5 ins. Use it for still life and nature shots (pp.78–9).

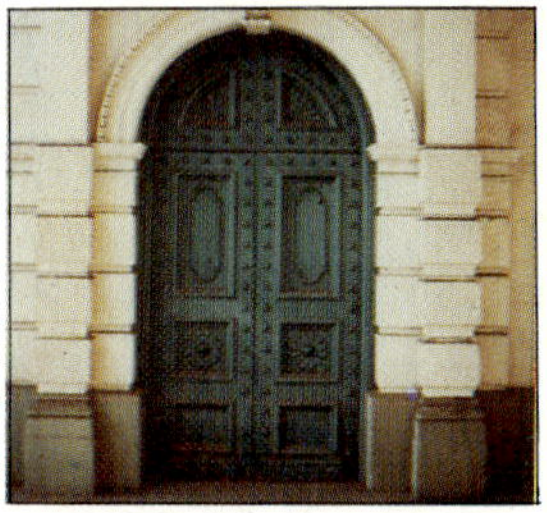

1 Normal lens

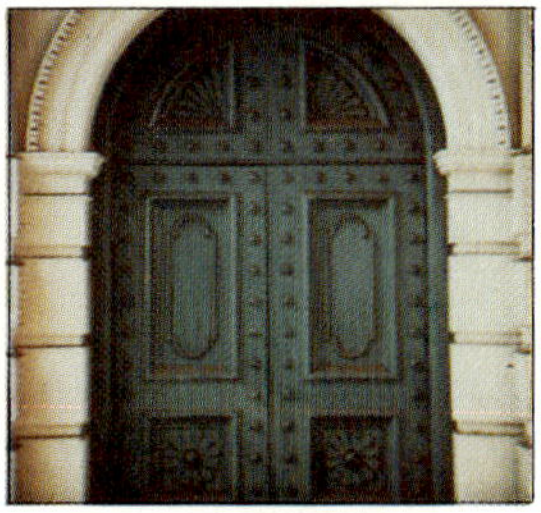

2 Tele attachment

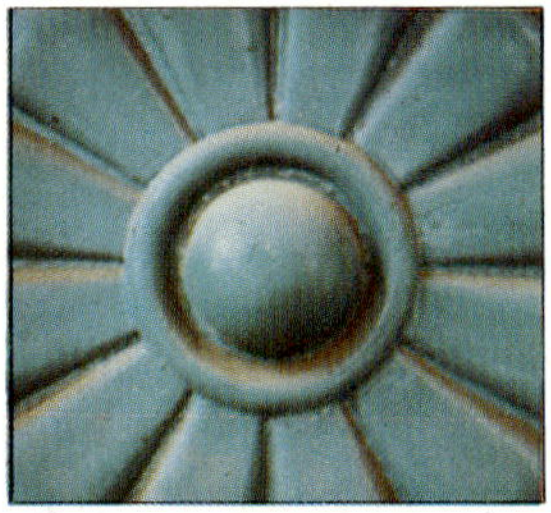

3 Close-up attachment

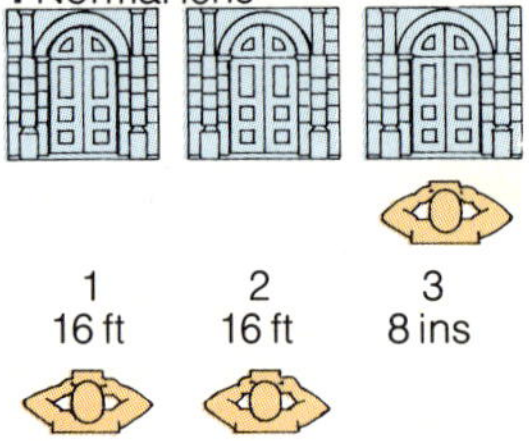

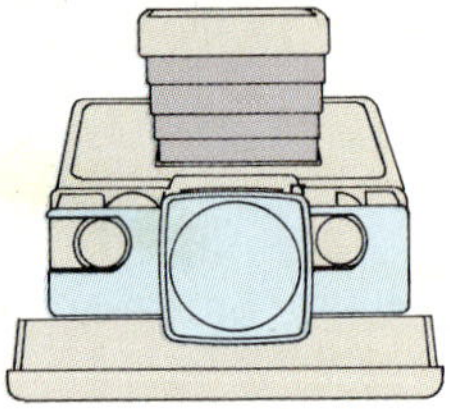

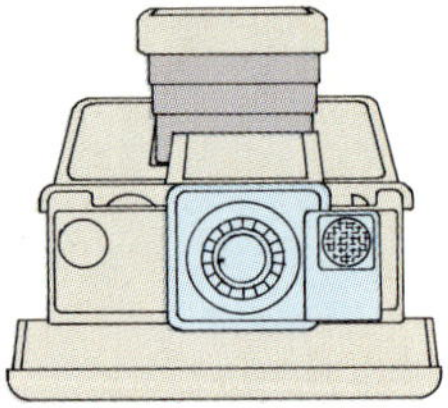

Faults and solutions

Exposure faults
Too much light causes overexposure, center right. Too little causes underexposure, right – perhaps the flash failed, or you were out of flash range (p.23). Check the L/D control (p.20) and batteries (pp.9, 11 and 22). With peel-apart, you may have pulled the wrong tab (p.26) or set the wrong ASA (p.8). You will get a fogged picture, far right, if you open the film door or handle the film pack roughly (p.14).

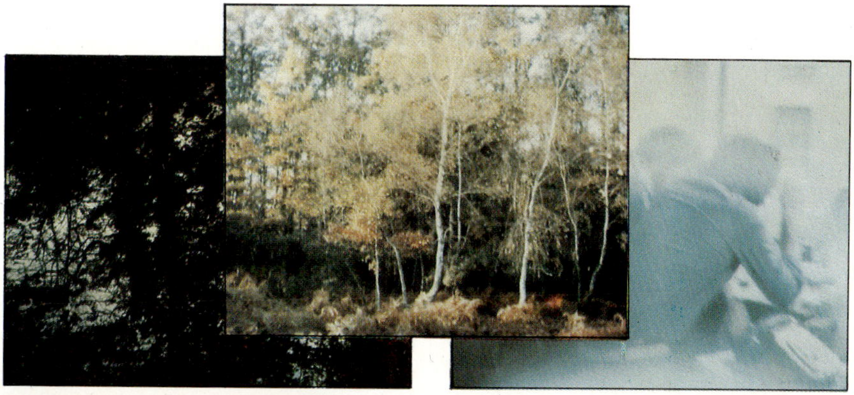

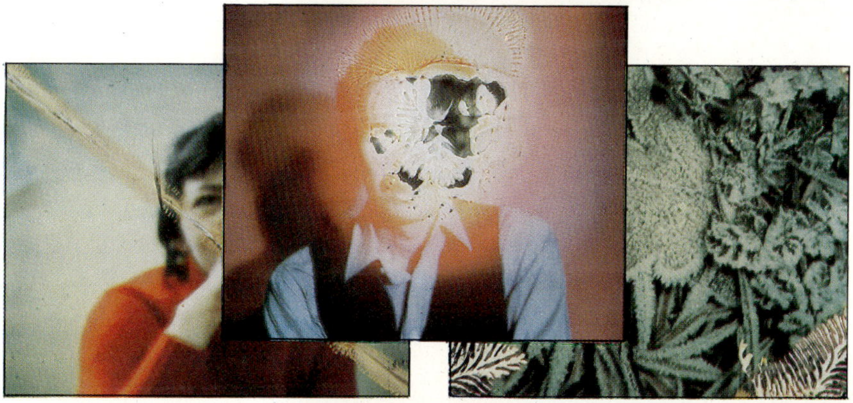

Marks on the picture
Feathery marks on your print, left, or creases across your picture, far left, are caused when an integral print is bent during development. Crackling, center left, is a result of direct heat during development. Always keep your developing prints completely flat, and well away from hot surfaces, such as radiators or automobile hoods, and hot objects, such as lamps. Sometimes this defect can be used intentionally for a creative effect, see p.81.

Camera handling faults
When the motor on an integral camera is obstructed, by a finger in the bellows (p.25) for example, two pictures may emerge at once and they will be only partly exposed, far right. When you use your camera indoors, and you don't use flash to shoot movement, you will get a dark, blurred subject, right. In dim daylight if you don't support your camera, or your subject moves, you will get blur, center right.

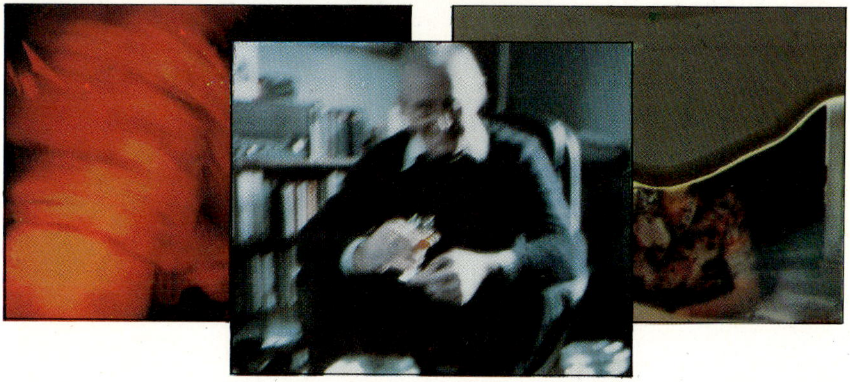

Index

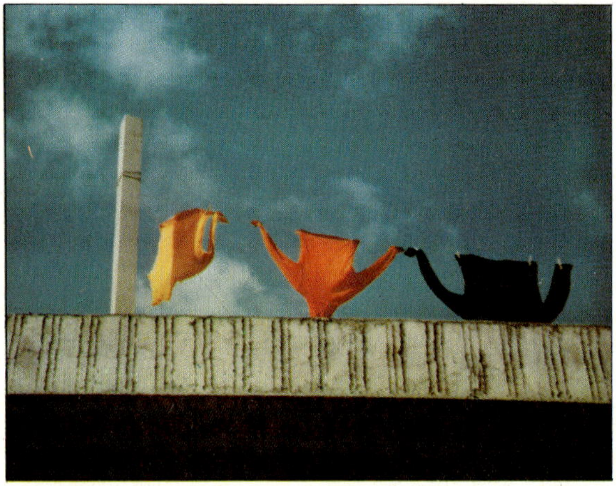

Acknowledgments

Photographs by: N.Alexanian 43tr **R.Belcher** 30bl **W.Berger** 30bc **S.Bicknall** 50t,bc;59cl,br **J.Bones** 66t **C.Boursnell** 31t,br **D.Bradfield** 15;21c;36b **D.Bradley** 89t **W.Buckley** 30tl **A.Davenport** 43bl **F.Dustin** 49t **E.Erwell** 31bl **W.Field** 30cr; 54bl,bc;55bl,br **H.Foley** 30br **J.Gill** 67bl **J.Haveman** 39br **B.P.Hitchcock** 9r;42r;63t,br; 64tl,bl;69cl **P.Huf** 7bl **C.James** 76bl **E.Judice** 88 **S.King** 63br; 87 3rd row c **L.Kraft** 47tl,r **P.Laytin** 39tr **M.Mahr** 2;5;11l; 34–5 except box; 49bl;50bl,br; 51;52–3;56–7;72–5;77;79;80t; 81;82–3;86br;87tl **U.Mack** 36t **H.Munzig** 39bl;78t **J.Nemec** 87 1st row r **M.Peiree** 33tr;78br **J.Pearson** 3;7tl;48l **T.Pearson** 59cr **R.Perry** 55tr **J. van der Plaas** 54t;66br **B.Ravanesi** 67tl **Ravenna** 44r;62t **I.Reethot** 67tr;78bc **A.Ross** 43cl **S.Ross** 91 **J.Sanders** 43cr;69tr; **G.Schnitzer** 80b **C.Sieburth** 38t **J.-L.Sieff** 30c **J.Sims** 7cl;28–9; 32–3 except tr,bl;37c;38br;39cr; 40 except tr;41t;44bl;45;46;47 except t;54br;60 except bc;64tr, cr,br;65;68b;69tl,bc;86 except br;87 box, 4th row c;92 **M.Smith** 62br **R.Twaroy** 55tl **T.Walker** 38bl;76tr **K.Williams** 62bl;68t **A.Windig** 43br **R.Wolf** 13;67br **D.Zipes** 60bc
Remainder by A. de Lory
Dorling Kindersley and the author thank all the people who have helped to produce this book including Ken Oberg, David Atkinson, and the staff of Kodak U.K.; Andrew Parkhouse, Barbara Hitchcock, Sherry Lassiter, Ellen in der Rieden and the staff of Polaroid U.K., U.S.A., and Holland;Kodak-Pathe Library, Paris; Charles Elliott; Lucy Liddell; Ian Carr and Tony Wallace; Harry Pepper; John Marshall of Smeets
Illustrations by:
Norman Lacey, Venner Artists
Diagrams by:
Gary Marsh, Sean MacGarry
Typesetting services by:
Contact Graphics
Origination services by:
City Engraving